The Crock Pot Connoisseur:

Delicious Slow Cooker Recipes For (Very) Busy People

by Peggy Paulson

with a Foreword by Rachael Ray

NMD Books
Simi Valley, CA

Copyright 2011 – Peggy Paulson

Visit our Web site at http://www.NMDbooks.com.

The Crock Pot Connoisseur:
Delicious Slow Cooker Recipes For Busy People
by Peggy Paulson

ISBN: 978-1-936828-20-3 (Softcover)

First Edition April 2011

Introduction by Racheal Ray

When I was a girl, my mother used to slow cook many of our weekend meals. She'd assemble the ingredients in the morning, place them in a huge kettle, and let the meat and vegetables simmer all day long. This was her way of using up aging vegetables and making those budget cuts of meat edible.

Ever since man first tamed fire, slow cooking was discovered as a way to soften up and tenderize those tough slabs of meat and fibrous rooty vegetables. In prehistoric times, indigenous peoples often cooked wild root plants in a slow burning fire pit for a full 24 hours.

This released the nutrition locked into the bulbs and made them much more tender and tastier to eat. Tough meat cuts especially benefit from slow cooking. Slow cooking these chewy cuts broke down the collagen in the meat and turned it into a gelatinous broth.

As the fibers of the meat separated and shrunk during slow cooking, the juices would moisten the meat and turn even the toughest cuts into a mouth watering meal.

As food preparation became more refined, family chefs looked for quicker ways to prepare their meals. Modern appliances and easy fixing meals meant that all day cooking was a thing of the past. Slow cooking was considered an archaic pastime and primarily used to for stewing old hens, preparing kettles of soup and baking beans.

With canned bean selections pretty limited in the early 1960s, it's no wonder that the West Bend developed an electric bean cooker called the Bean Pot. This early electric slow cooker resembled a tradition crockery bean pot which rested on a warming tray.

The Naxon Utilities Corp of Chicago developed their own version of a bean cooker, called the Beanery. This primitive slow cooker was a self contained unit and the precursor of the modern slow cooker. In 1970, the Rival company acquired the assets of the Naxon Utilities Corp and the rights to the Beanery. Rival refined the looks of the Beanery, and in 1971, introduced the Rival Crock-pot slow cooker.

The Crock Pot was an instant success and soon housewives across America included Crock Pots in their lineup of must have appliances. In 1974, Rival redesigned the Crock Pot once again to include a removable stoneware liner. This removable liner made it much easier to store the food in the refrigerator and made cleanup a snap.

After only 10 years, Crock Pot sales reached $30 million dollar in 1981.

These days, Crock Pots and slow cookers aren't quite as popular as they once were, and are often the butt of Wedding Gift jokes. I myself received six of them back in the late 1970s! All six of the Crock Pots were returned since I already had one of my own ~ Mom's old Rival's 1971 debut Crock Pot in Brady Bunch orange. 35 years later, her old crock pot is still being used twice a week to prepare family dinners. I think of it as my little secret for cooking mouthwatering meals on a shoe-string budget.

How Crock Pot cooking can save time & money in the kitchen. The idea behind the slow cooker is still a sound one. That long, slow simmering does tenderize tough cuts of roasts and chicken, and bring a fullness of flavor to home made soups. It's also ideal for cooking dried beans and legumes which require hours of slow simmering to soften. Stews and soups aren't all that Crock Pots can do ~ in our household, we slow cook everything from casseroles to rice & pasta dishes, steamed puddings and even breads.

The greatest advantage of all, is something that our mothers discovered back in 1971. Fifteen minutes of prep time in the morning meant that a steaming hot dinner greeted our families at the door after a long day at school and work. For a family watching pennies, even after 35 years, Crock Pot cooking continues to be an easy and affordable way to prepare evening meals.

Crock Pot Recipes

7   Crock Pot Appetizers

From casual football games in the family room to sparkling holiday parties, the appetizer recipes for the crock pot are sure to please!

17   Crock Pot Beef

Beef in the crock pot comes out moist and juicy from slow cooking. Try out one of hundreds of recipes, for an easy home cooked meal.

59   Crock Pot Chicken

From whole chicken in the crock pot to Tex-Mex favorites, the variety of recipes in our collection can't be beat.

102   Crock Pot Chili

Tasty chili is super easy in a crock pot. Throw everything into the crockpot and let the spicy, mouth-watering aroma fill the air while you relax.

111   Crock Pot Fish and Seafood

Versatile, tasty, and low fat are attractive enough; but adding the ease of crock pot cooking makes fish and seafood recipes an even better choice.

114   Crock Pot Pasta

With tasty comfort food like homemade macaroni and cheese and stuffed shells, a home cooked family meal is easy with pasta and a crock pot.

121   Crock Pot Pork

Pork is a winner for variety and taste in recipes. Our huge collection of pork crock pot recipes is sure to have a few favorites you'll love.

142   Crock Pot Soup

Easy to make, infused with flavor, and filling enough to make a meal; our crock pot soup recipes are the best prescription for warming your soul.

163   Crock Pot Turkey

The crock pot turkey recipes we've put together include spicy barbecue and elegant Turkey Madeira. Turkey in the crock pot is far from ordinary!

167 Crock Pot Vegetables and Side Dishes

Try side dishes in the crock pot, an easy way to free up time when cooking a meal. The side dish is already cooking while you focus on the main dish.

172 Crock Pot Dessert

For a comforting dessert after a long day, we have delicious dessert recipes for the crock pot. All are easy to make and the perfect end to a meal.

Crock Pot Appetizers

CROCK POT ARTICHOKE & CHEESE DIP

Ingredients:
1 lb. shredded Mozzarella
1 cup grated Parmesan
1 cup (8 oz. jar) mayonnaise
1 cup (8 1/2 oz.) artichoke hearts, drained and chopped
Minced onions

Directions:
1. Mix ingredients together.
2. Cook in in lightly buttered 3 1/2 quart Crock Pot on high for about 1 hour.
3. Serve with broken up French bread or wheat crackers

CROCK POT BEST DIP EVER

Ingredients:
1 (1 pound) package Velveeta
1 can Chili - no beans
1 pound medium or spicy sausage, browned and crumbled

Directions:
1. Put all ingredients into the Crock Pot on low until blended and then keep it there to serve.

CROCK POT BOILED PEANUTS

Ingredients:
1 1/2 quarts green uncooked peanuts
1/2 cup salt
2 1/2 quarts water

Directions:
1. Wash Peanuts until water runs clear. Put clean peanuts in crock pot, add salt and water; stir.
2. Cook, covered, on high for 5 to 7 hours. Add additional water during cooking, if necessary, to keep peanuts covered.

BROCCOLI CHEESE DIP

Ingredients:
2 (10 oz.) boxes of frozen chopped broccoli
2 cans cream of mushroom soup
1/4 cup sour cream
1/2 lb. Mexican Velveeta cheese
1/2 lb. reg. Velveeta cheese
1 Tablespoon garlic salt

Directions:
1. Cook and drain broccoli. Melt cheese in slow cooker/Crock Pot.
2. Mix soups, sour cream, broccoli and garlic salt. Mix into melted cheese.
3. Serve as dip with tortilla chips.

CROCK POT BROCCOLI DIP

Ingredients:
1 pkg.(10oz) frozen chopped broccoli
2 ribs celery, chopped
1 medium white onion, chopped
3/4 stick margarine
2 rolls garlic cheese
1 can cream of mushroom soup
1 medium can mushroom pieces
1 can sliced water chestnuts
2 teaspoons Worcestershire sauce

Directions:
1. Cook broccoli until tender. Saute celery and onion in margarine until tender.
2. Place broccoli and sauteed vegetables in slow cooker/Crock Pot; add mushrooms, cheese, cream of mushroom soup.
3. Stir well and heat on low until cheese is melted. Add water chestnuts and Worcestershire sauce. Serve warm in the slow cooker/Crock Pot, with chips or crackers.

CROCK POT CAJUN PECANS

Ingredients:

1 pound pecan halves
4 Tablespoons butter, melted
1 Tablespoon chili powder
1 teaspoon salt
1 teaspoon dried basil
1 teaspoon dried oregano
1 teaspoon dried thyme
1/2 teaspoon onion powder
1/4 teaspoon garlic powder
1/4 teaspoon cayenne pepper

Directions:

1. Combine all ingredients in Crock Pot. Cover and cook on high for 15 minutes.
2. Turn on low, uncovered, stirring occasionally for 2 hours. Transfer nuts to a baking sheet and cool completely.

CROCK POT CHEESE & ARTICHOKE DIP

Ingredients:

8 ounces process American cheese (Velveeta)
1 can (10oz) 98% fat-free cream of mushroom soup
2 teaspoons Worcestershire sauce
1/4 cup evaporated milk
1 teaspoon dry mustard
1 1/2 cups shredded cheddar cheese
1/3 cup chopped roasted red pepper
1 can artichoke hearts, drained and coarsely chopped

Directions:

1. Combine all ingredients in the slow cooker/Crock Pot. Cover and cook on low for 2 to 3 hours, until melted.
2. Stir well and serve with assorted crackers, bread cubes, or chips.

CROCK POT CHILI BEEF DIP

Ingredients:

1 (11 oz.) can condensed chili beef soup
3 oz. pkg. cream cheese, softened
1/2 cup sour cream
1 Tablespoon water
1 teaspoon prepared mustard
1 teaspoon Worcestershire sauce
1/2 teaspoon chili sauce
1/4 teaspoon hot pepper sauce, optional

Directions:

1. In slow cooker/Crock Pot, combine all ingredients; mix well.
2. Cover and cook on low for 1 1/2 to 2 hours, stirring occasionally, or until cheese is melted and dip is hot.
3. Serve warm with tortilla or corn chips.

CROCK POT CHILI CHEESE TACO DIP

Ingredients:

1 lb. hamburger
1 can chili (no beans)
1 lb. mild Mexican Velveeta cheese, cubed or shredded

Directions:

1. Brown hamburger; drain and place in slow cooker.
2. Add chili and cheese; cover and cook on low until cheese is melted, about 1 to 1 1/2 hours, stirring occasionally to blend ingredients.
3. Serve warm with taco or tortilla chips.

CROCK POT CLASSIC SWISS FONDUE

Ingredients:

1 clove garlic
2 1/2 cups dry white Rhine, Chablis or Riesling wine
1 Tablespoon lemon juice
1 lb. Swiss cheese, grated
1/2 lb. Cheddar cheese, grated
3 Tablespoons flour
3 Tablespoons kirsch
Freshly ground nutmeg
Pepper
Paprika
1 loaf Italian or French bread, cut into 1-inch cubes

Directions:

1. Rub an enameled or stainless steel pan with garlic clove. Heat wine to a slow simmer (just under boiling). Add lemon juice.
2. Combine cheeses and flour and gradually stir in. Using a figure-8 motion, stir constantly until cheese is melted.
3. Pour into lightly greased Crock-Pot. Add kirsch; stir well. Sprinkle with nutmeg, pepper and paprika.
4. Cover and cook on High setting for 30 minutes, then turn to Low setting for 2 to 5 hours. Keep on Low setting while serving.
5. Using fondue forks, dip bread cubes into fondue.

CROCK POT COCKTAIL KIELBASA

Ingredients:

2 rings of Kielbasa (about 2 lbs)
1 (18 oz) jar apple jelly
1 (9 oz) jar prepared mustard

Directions:

1. Slice Kielbasa 1/4 to 1/2 inch thick. Mix jelly and mustard in slow cooker/Crock Pot. Add sliced Kielbasa and mix until meat is covered.
2. Set slow cooker/Crock Pot on low to cook for 2 hours and keep on low while serving. Stir periodically.

CROCK POT CRAB DIP

Ingredients:

1 lb. Velveeta cheese
1 lb. butter or margarine
2 cans crab meat

Directions:

1. Heat together. Keep warm in fondue or slow cooker/Crock Pot. Serve with bread sticks.

CROCK POT CREAMY SPINACH DIP

Ingredients:

8 ounces Cream cheese, cubed
5 ounces Frozen chopped spinach
2 Tablespoons Pimento, diced
1 teaspoon Worcestershire sauce
1/4 teaspoon Garlic salt
1/4 cup Whipping ceram
2 Tablespoons Parmesan cheese, grated
2 teaspoons Onion, finely chopped
1/2 teaspoon Thyme

Directions:

1. Combine cream cheese and cream in Crock Pot. Cover and heat until cheese is melted, 30 to 60 minutes.
2. Add remaining ingredients. Cover and heat 30 minutes.
3. Serve with raw vegetables, crackers, or bread pieces.

CROCK POT CHEESE DIP

Ingredients:
2 lb. Velveeta cheese
2 cans Rotel tomatoes and chilies
1 can cream of mushroom soup
1 small jar picante sauce
1 teaspoon garlic powder
Dash of Worcestershire
1 lb. premium ground beef
1 medium onion, chopped
1 lb. sausage

Directions:
1. Mix all of the liquids and cheese together in a Crock Pot set on low until the cheese melts.
2. While this is cooking, brown meats and chopped onion. Drain grease off of meats and add spices, then add to Crock Pot and stir.
3. Cook on low 2 to 4 hours, keep on low to serve with chips and crackers.

CROCK POT CHEESE FONDUE

Ingredients:
10-oz. can cheddar cheese soup
1 lb. block process cheese spread cut in 8 pieces
1 lb. swiss cheese, grated
12-oz. can beer (or apple cider)
1/2 teaspoon hot pepper sauce
2 drops liquid smoke flavoring

Directions:
1. Place all ingredients in slow cooker/Crock Pot. Stir to mix. Cover and cook on low for 2 hours.
2. After 1 hour of cooking time, stir. Before serving, whisk to blend.
3. Serve with bread sticks or veggies for dipping.

CROCK POT CHEESY BACON DIP

Ingredients:
2 pkgs. (8 oz) cream cheese, softened, cut into cubes
4 cups shredded Colby-Jack Cheese
1 cup half-and-half
2 Tablespoons mustard
1 Tablespoon chopped onion
2 teaspoons Worcestershire sauce
1/2 teaspoon salt
1/4 teaspoon hot pepper sauce
1 lb. bacon, cooked and crumbled

Directions:
1. Place cream cheese, Colby-Jack cheese, half-and-half, mustard, onion, Worcestershire sauce, salt and pepper sauce in crock pot.
2. Cover and cook, stirring occasionally, on low 1 hour or until cheese melts. Stir in bacon; adjust seasonings.
3. Serve with crusty bread or crackers.

CROCK POT HAMBURGER-SAUSAGE DIP

Ingredients:
1 pound ground chuck
1 cup picante sauce
1 can cream of mushroom soup
2 pounds Velveeta cheese, cut into pieces
1 pound pork sausage
1 teaspoon garlic powder
1 can Rotel tomatoes
3/4 teaspoon oregano

Directions:
1. Combine picante sauce, garlic powder, soup, tomatoes, oregano and cheese in Crock Pot.
2. Brown ground chuck and sausage until it is done. Drain very well and place in slow cooker/Crock Pot.
3. Cook on low until cheese is melted. Serve with your favorite chips.

CROCK POT HOT DIP

Ingredients:

1 pound Italian Sausage - hot
1 pounds Velveeta - Mexican type - hot
1 can rotel tomatoes (drained)
1 jar pace picante sauce - hot
1 jalapeno pepper - finely diced

Directions:

1. Brown sausage and drain along with jalapeno pepper.
2. Add to slow cooker/Crock Pot with other ingredients and simmer on low for 1 hour or more until melted and blended.
3. Serve with tortilla strips or chips, large Fritos corn chips, or even lightly toasted and cubed sourdough bread.

CROCK POT LITTLE SMOKIES

Ingredients:

2 packages Cocktail wieners
1 Medium bottle chili sauce
1 Medium jar grape jelly

Directions:

1. Combine in Crock Pot and cook on low 6 to 8 hours

CROCK POT SCRABBLE

Ingredients:

2 cups wheat chex
2 cups corn chex
2 cups rice chex
3 cups thin pretzel sticks
1 (13 ounce) can or jar of salted peanuts or assorted mixed nuts
1 teaspoon garlic salt
1 teaspoon celery salt
1/2 teaspoon seasoned salt
2 Tablespoons grated parmesan cheese
1/3 cup melted butter
1/3 cup worcestershire sauce

Directions:

1. In large (double) paper bag, mix together pretzels, cereals, and nuts along with the garlic salt, celery salt, seasoned salt, and grated cheese.
2. Empty bag into large mixing bowl and sprinkle the melted butter and worcestershire sauce over all mixing gently with your hands.
3. Empty bowl into slow cooker/Crock Pot and cook on low for 3 or 4 hours.
4. Tear open paper bags you used to originally mix the scrabble and spread them out onto a counter.
5. Spread heated slow cooker/Crock Pot scrabble onto torn open bags and let dry for a minimum of one hour letting the paper absorb any excess moisture.
6. Store in Rubbermaid or Tupperware type airtight containers. Keeps for several weeks without going stale.

CROCK POT SPICY DIP

Ingredients:

2 lb. Velveeta cheese
2 lb. hamburger, cooked and drained
1 large jar Old El Paso taco sauce (or Rotel tomatoes)
1 large onion, chopped fine

Directions:

1. Mix all together in Crock Pot where cheese will melt and all will remaining warm.

CROCK POT HAMBURGER DIP

Ingredients:

2 pounds lean ground beef
1 cup chopped onion
2 cloves garlic, minced or 1/4 teaspoon garlic powder
salt to taste
2 cans (8-ounces each) tomato sauce
1/2 cup ketchup
1 1/2 teaspoons oregano
2 teaspoons white granulated sugar
2 packages (8-ounces each) cream cheese, softened and cut in cubes
2/3 cup grated Parmesan cheese
1 teaspoon mild chili powder

Directions:

1. In skillet, brown ground beef with onion, discard fat.
2. Pour browned meat and onion into Slow Cooker. Add garlic, salt, tomato sauce, ketchup, oregano, sugar, cream cheese, Parmesan cheese and chili powder.
3. Set slow cooker/Crock Pot on LOW until cream cheese has melted and is thoroughly blended, 1 1/2 to 2 hours.
4. Stir, taste and adjust seasoning if desired.
5. Serve with cubed French bread or tortilla chips. If spicier dip is desired, use hot chili powder in place of mild chili powder. Finely chopped jalapenos may be added, if desired.

CROCK POT HEARTY BEEF DIP

Ingredients:

8 ounces Cream cheese, cubed
1 1/4 ounces Sliced dried beef, diced
2 Tablespoons Green onion, chopped
1/4 cup Milk
1/4 cup Pecans, chopped
1 Garlic clove

Directions:

1. Combine cream cheese and milk in greased Crock Pot. Cover and heat until cheese is melted, 30 to 60 minutes.
2. Add remaining ingredients; stir thoroughly. Cover and heat 30 minutes.
3. Serve with crackers or bread pieces.

CROCK POT HOT ARTICHOKE DIP

Ingredients:

6 ounces Artichoke hearts, marinated
1/3 cup Mayonnaise
1 Tablespoon Pimento, diced (optional)
1/2 cup Parmesan cheese, grated
1/3 cup Sour cream
1/8 teaspoon Garlic powder

Directions:

1. Drain and chop artichoke hearts. Combine all ingredients and place in Crock Pot. Cover and heat 30 to 60 minutes until hot.
2. Serve with tortilla chips or assorted crackers.

CROCK POT HOT BROCCOLI DIP

Ingredients:

1 (10 oz.) chopped frozen broccoli, thawed
1 stick margarine
1 medium onion, chopped
1 (10 3/4 oz.) cans of cream of mushroom soup
14 oz. Velveeta cheese, cut up
1 to 2 1/2 oz. can mushroom stems and pieces

Directions:

1. Combine first 3 ingredients in a saute pan and cook until onions are clear. Transfer to the slow cooker/Crock Pot.
2. Add soup, cheese, and mushrooms, heat on low for about 1 1/2 to 2 hours, or until cheese is melted and mixture is hot.
3. Dip with large corn chips or can be poured over baked potatoes. Freezes well.

CROCK POT HOT DOG HORS D'OEUVRES

Ingredients:

2 (1 lb.) pkgs all beef hot dogs, sliced in half
1 lb. bacon, sliced in half
Brown sugar

Directions:

1. Wrap each hot dog half with bacon strip. Fasten with toothpick.
2. Layer in slow cooker/Crock Pot, sprinkling each layer with a thin layer of brown sugar. Repeat layers until hot dogs run out.
3. Cook on low for 2-3 hours, stirring gently with wooden spoon every 30 minutes.

CROCK POT
HOT 'N' SPICY PECANS

Ingredients:

1/4 cup butter, cut in pieces (4 oz)
6 cups pecans
2 teaspoons chili powder
1/2 teaspoon onion salt
1/2 teaspoon garlic powder

Directions:

1. Place cut up butter in Crock Pot and heat, uncovered, on high until melted (15 to 20 minutes). Add pecans; stir to coat.
2. Cover and cook on high 30 minutes. Uncover and cook on high 2 1/2 hours longer, stirring occasionally.
3. Sprinkle with the seasonings and toss to coat; Spread on a baking sheet to cool.
4. Store in an airtight container in the refrigerator for up to 6 weeks, or freeze for up to 3 months. Serve at room temperature or warm.

CROCK POT HOT SPINACH DIP

Ingredients:

2 (10 oz.) pkgs. frozen chopped spinach
1 large jar jalapeno Cheez Whiz
1 can cream of mushroom soup
1 (3 oz.) pkg. cream cheese
2 Tablespoons dried minced onion

Directions:

1. Thaw spinach completely. Drain, and squeeze as much moisture as possible from spinach.
2. Combine all ingredients in the slow cooker/Crock Pot and cook on low about 2 hours, until hot (stir a few times to blend well).
3. Keep warm in Crock Pot or chafing dish. Serve with corn chips or crackers.

CROCK POT
APPETIZER MEATBALLS

Ingredients:

Half a bag frozen meatballs from a warehouse-club sized bag
2 packages of brown gravy

Directions:

1. Place meatballs into the slow cooker/Crock Pot.
2. Take the 2 packages of brown gravy, mix them up according to the directions and then pour over the meatballs.
3. Heat on low for 4 hours.

CROCK POT MARINER FONDUE

Ingredients:
2 cans (10 3/4 oz each) condensed cream of celery soup
2 cups grated sharp process cheese
1 cup chunked cooked lobster
1/2 cup chopped cooked shrimp
1/2 cup chopped cooked crabmeat
1/4 cup finely chopped, cooked scallops
dash paprika
dash cayenne peppe
1 loaf of French bread, cut into 1 inch cubes

Directions:
1. Combine all ingredients except bread cubes in lightly greased Crock-Pot; stir thoroughly.
2. Cover and cook on High for 1 hour or until cheese is melted. Turn to Low for serving.
3. Using fondue forks, dip bread cubes into fondue.
Makes about 1 1/2 qts.

CROCK POT MEXICAN CHEESE DIP

Ingredients:
1/2 pound Velveeta
1 teaspoon Taco seasoning (optional)
1/2 can Ro-Tel Tomatoes with chilies

Directions:
1. Cube cheese and place in Crock Pot. Cover and heat 30 to 60 minutes, until melted, stirring occasionally.
2. Stir in tomatoes and seasoning. Cover and continue heating 30 minutes.
3. Serve with tortilla chips or corn chips.

CROCK POT PARTY HAMBURGER DIP

Ingredients:
1 pound Hamburger
1 1/2 pounds Velveeta
1 can Ro-Tel tomatoes and chiles
1/2 Onion, diced
1 8 - 12 oz fresh mushrooms, sliced

Directions:
1. Brown hamburger, mushrooms & onion; drain.
2. Melt Velveeta in slow cooker. Add remaining ingredients and simmer (high) for about 30 minutes.
3. Serve with corn chips or crackers. Turn pot to low while serving.

CROCK POT PARTY MIX

Ingredients:
7 cups assorted cereal (oat, rice, wheat in various shapes)
1 cup peanuts, pecans, cashews, or mixed nuts
1 cup mini pretzel sticks
1/2 cup butter, melted
4 Tablespoons Worcestershire sauce
dash hot pepper sauce
1/2 teaspoon seasoned salt
1/2 teaspoon garlic salt
1/2 teaspoon onion salt

Directions:
1. Combine cereals, nuts and pretzels in Crock Pot.
2. Mix melted butter with remaining ingredients and pour over the cereal mixture, tossing to coat.
3. Cook uncovered on high for 2 hours, stirring about every 30 minutes. Turn to low and cook another 2 to 6 hours.
4. Store in an airtight container. Makes about 10 cups.

CROCK POT PICANTE CHEESE DIP

Ingredients:
1 1/2 pounds ground beef (browned)
1 can (11 oz.) cream of mushroom soup
2 pounds processed cheese (Velveeta)
1 stick margarine
1 onion, chopped
2 Tablespoons chili powder
1 cup picante sauce

Directions:
1. Brown meat and onion. Drain. Add all ingredients to slow cooker/Crock Pot and cook on low heat until cheese melts, about 1 1/2 hours.
2. Serve in slow cooker/Crock Pot with tortilla chips.

CROCK POT PIZZA DIP

Ingredients:
1 large cream cheese softened
1 jar pizza sauce
1 small can chopped olives
1 medium onion chopped
1 pkg. sliced pepperoni
1 pkg. grated cheese for pizza

Directions:
1. Spread cream cheese in bottom of slow cooker/Crock Pot. Then mix up the pizza sauce, onion, olives and pepperoni and spread on top of the cream cheese.
2. Sprinkle with the pizza cheese and cook on low until the cheese on top melts. Serve with tortilla chips.

CROCK POT PIZZA FONDUE

Ingredients:
1 lb. ground beef
2 cans Chef Boy-ardee pizza sauce with cheese
8 oz. grated cheddar cheese
8 oz. grated Mozzarella
1 teaspoon oregano
1/2 teaspoon fennel seed
1 Tablespoon cornstarch

Directions:
1. Brown ground beef and drain. Add all other ingredients place in slow cooker/Crock Pot and heat through.
2. Serve with tortilla chips.

CROCK POT REFRIED BEAN DIP

Ingredients:
1 (20 oz can) refried beans
1/4 teaspoon salt
1 cup shredded cheddar cheese
1 (4 oz can) chopped green chiles
2 Tablespoons bottled taco sauce
1/2 cup chopped green onions
tortilla chips

Directions:
1. In Crock Pot combine beans with cheese, chiles, onions, salt, and taco sauce.
2. Cover and cook on low for 2 to 2-1/2 hours. Serve hot from the pot.

CROCK POT REUBEN DIP

Ingredients:
1 small can sauerkraut
1 (8 oz.) cream cheese
1 (6 oz.) shredded Swiss cheese
6 ounces diced corned beef
2 Tablespoons Thousand Island Dressing

Directions:
1. Drain and rinse sauerkraut, mix with cream cheese and Swiss cheese. Add diced corned beef and Thousand Island dressing.
2. Cover and heat on low until cheeses are melted, stirring occasionally to blend all ingredients.
3. Serve warm with crackers or cocktail rye bread.

CROCK POT REUBEN PARTY SPREAD

Ingredients:
1 lb. corned beef, chopped
2 cups shredded Swiss cheese
1 8oz can sauerkraut, drained
1/2 cup mayo
1/2 cup Thousand Island dressing

Directions:
1. Mix, put in crock pot. Heat until cheese is melted. Serve on rye bread.

CROCK POT SPICY REFRIED BEAN DIP

Ingredients:
2 cans refried beans, (16ounce each)
1 package taco seasoning mix, about 1 1/4 oz
1/2 cup chopped onion
2 cups Monterey jack cheese, shredded
a few drops Tabasco sauce, to taste
chopped jalapeno or mild chiles, to taste

Directions:
1. Place refried beans, taco seasoning, onion, cheese, and Tabasco sauce in the slow cooker/Crock Pot; stir well.
2. Stir in chopped chiles. Cover and cook on low until cheese is melted, about 1 hour; add a little water if mixture seems too thick.
3. Serve from the slow cooker/Crock Pot with French bread, crackers, or chips.

CROCK POT VELVEETA SALSA DIP

Ingredients:
1 pound Velveeta Cheese spread, cubed (can use light
1 package Picante sauce or salsa
2 Tablespoons Cilantro (optional)

Directions:
1. Place brick of Velveeta and jar of picante sauce in a slow cooker or Crock Pot, and turn on high stirring occasionally until melted and blended.
2. Stir in cilantro when melted. Serve with tortilla chips.

CROCK POT RECIPE - BACON CHEESE DIP

Ingredients:
16 slices bacon, diced, fried and drained
2 8-ounce packages cream cheese, softened and cubed
4 cups shredded cheddar cheese
1 cup half-and-half
2 teaspoons Worcestershire sauce
1 teaspoon dried minced onion
1/2 teaspoon dry mustard
1/2 teaspoon salt
dash hot sauce

Directions:
1. Put all ingredients in the Crock Pot and cook on low, stirring occasionally until cheese melts, about 1 hour.
2. Taste and adjust seasonings, add bacon, and keep on low to serve. Serve with cubed or sliced French bread.

CROCK POT RECIPE - EASY CHILI CHEESE DIP

Ingredients:
1 (1 pound) package Velveeta
1 can Chili - no beans
1 pound medium or spicy sausage, browned and crumbled

Directions:
1. Put all ingredients into the Crock Pot on low until blended and then keep it there to serve.

Crock Pot Beef

CROCK POT APPLE CIDER STEW

Ingredients:
1-2 lbs. beef or venison stew meat
8 carrots, sliced thin
6 potatoes, sliced thin
2 apples, chopped
2 teaspoons salt
1/2 teaspoon thyme
2 Tablespoons minced onion
2 cups apple cider

Directions:
1. Place carrots, potatoes, and apples in crock pot.
2. Add meat and sprinkle with salt, thyme, and onion. Pour cider over meat and cover.
3. Cook on low heat 10-12 hours. Thicken gravy.

CROCK POT SMOTHERED STEAK

Ingredients:
1 1/2 lb. round steak, cut in strips
1/4 teaspoon pepper
1 green pepper, sliced
1 (1 lb.) can tomatoes
3 Tablespoons soy sauce
1/3 cups flour
1 teaspoon salt
1 lg. onion, sliced
1 (4 oz.) can mushrooms, drained
1 (10 oz.) pkg. frozen green beans (French style)

Directions:
1. Put steak strips, flour, salt and pepper in crock pot. Stir well to coat steak.
2. Add remaining ingredients. Cover and cook on low 8 hours (high for 4 hours). Serve with rice.

CROCK POT BEEF POOR BOY

Ingredients:
4 to 5 lb. roast
1 pkg. dry onion soup mix
1 cup water
1 Tablespoon Italian seasoning

Directions:
1. Put all in crock pot in the morning. Cook on "low" all day.
2. Before making sandwiches, use forks to pull meat apart.

CROCK POT CABBAGE ROLLS

Ingredients:
8 or more lg. cabbage leaves
1 lb. ground beef
1 egg, beaten
1 can tomato soup
1/4 teaspoon pepper
4 Tablespoons onion, chopped
1 cup rice, cooked

Directions:
1. Pour boiling water over cabbage leaves and let stand for 5 minutes.
2. Season meat, add onion, rice and beaten egg. Roll a portion of the filling into each leaf. Fasten ends with toothpicks.
3. Place in crock pot and cook on low for 10 to 12 hours.

CROCK POT CASSEROLE

Ingredients:

2 large potatoes, sliced
2 to 3 medium carrots, sliced
1 (#2) can peas, well drained
3 medium onions, sliced
1 1/2 lbs. ground beef, browned
2 stalks celery, sliced
10 oz. can tomato soup
10 oz. can water

Directions:

1. Place layers of the vegetables in the order given in crock pot. Season each layer with salt and pepper.
2. Put the lightly browned ground beef on top of the celery. Mix the tomato soup with the water and pour over the layers.
3. Cover and set on low for 6 to 8 hours, stirring occasionally.

CROCK POT NO PEEK STEW

Ingredients:

2 lbs. chuck or stew meat, cubed
2 cups potatoes, cut up
2 cups carrots, cut up
2 cups celery, cut up
1 large onion
1 cup each frozen green beans, peas, corn
1 can Campbell's tomato soup
1 can water
2 Tablespoons Minute Tapioca
1 1/2 Tablespoons cornstarch
1/4 teaspoon pepper
1 teaspoon parsley flakes
1 teaspoon salt and salt substitute
1 teaspoon Lawry's seasoned salt

Directions:

1. Mix all ingredients together in crockpot. Cover and cook on low for 10 to 12 hours.

CROCK POT SOUPER ROAST

Ingredients:

2-3 lb. blade or arm roast
1 envelope onion dry soup mix
1 can cream of mushroom soup
1/2 cup red wine
1/2 cup water

Directions:

1. Mix onion soup (dry) and mushroom soup to make a thick paste. Spread both sides of roast with onion, mushroom mixture.
2. Put in crock pot. Mix wine and water together and gently pour over roast, turn crock pot on high for 2 hours.
3. Turn crock pot to low and cook 3 to 5 hours longer. This makes its own gravy.

CROCK POT GRANDMA'S SUPPER

Ingredients:

1 lb. ground chuck
2 large onions, diced
3 or 4 medium potatoes
1 quart milk

Directions:

1. In crock pot, put layer of ground chuck; layer onion, layer potatoes; add milk.
2. Cook on high until potatoes are tender, 3 to 4 hours on High

CROCK POT COMPLETE DINNER

Ingredients:

2 to 3 lbs. cube steak, browned
6 medium potatoes, peeled & sliced
2 (12 oz.) jars Heinz brown gravy

Directions:

1. Layer meat and potatoes, adding gravy to each layer. Top with gravy.
2. Cover and cook on low 6 to 8 hours or high 3 to 4 hours. Season as desired. Serve with side dish vegetables.

CROCK POT STEAK FOR TWO

Ingredients:
Thin round steaks
1 small onion
Cream of mushroom soup
Mushrooms

Directions:
1. In crock pot put 1 can cream of mushroom soup, 1/2 can of water. Mix together.
2. Cut one small onion, add to soup. Cut mushrooms in half and add to soup.
3. Brown meat in skillet. Put meat in soup in crock pot for 8 hours on low.

CROCK POT ENCHILADAS

Ingredients:
1 lb. hamburger
1 onion, chopped
1 small can chilies
1 small can mild enchilada sauce
1 can golden mushroom soup, undiluted
1 can cheddar cheese soup, undiluted
1 can cream of mushroom soup, undiluted
1 can cream of celery soup, undiluted
1 large pkg. Dorito chips

Directions:
1. Brown hamburger and chopped onion, pour off grease.
2. Put all ingredients in crock pot except Dorito chips. Mix and cook low 4 to 6 hours.
3. Last 15 minutes before you are ready to eat, add Dorito chips and stir.

CROCK POT REUBEN CASSEROLE

Ingredients:
1 (8 oz.) pkg. noodles, cooked
1 can corned beef
3 1/2 cups sauerkraut
6 slices American cheese
16 oz. sour cream
1 (10 1/4 oz.) can cream of chicken soup
6 slices Swiss cheese

Directions:
1. In a buttered quart crock pot, layer half the noodles, half the meat, all the sauerkraut, all the American cheese.
2. Mix the sour cream and the chicken soup together and layer half of the soup mixture. Then layer the rest of the noodles, meat, soup mixture and then lastly the Swiss cheese.
3. Cook on high for 2 hours, so that it bubbles well.
4. Turn down to low for 1 or 2 hours. It helps to stir before serving, to mix the layers together some.

CROCK POT ROAST

Ingredients:
3 to 4 lb. boneless pot roast
1 cup of 7-Up soda
Celery salt
2 bay leaves
2 garlic sections, chopped or sliced

Directions:
1. Wash roast and pat dry with paper towels, place in crock pot, pierce top of roast with fork and sprinkle top with celery salt.
2. Add bay leaves and garlic, pour 7-Up over all and set crock pot on high for 4 hours, then low 2 hours or put on low for 8 hours.
3. Remove roast to platter to cool. Discard liquid. Serve with your favorite vegetables, rolls and salad.

CROCK POT CHINESE BEEF & PEA PODS

Ingredients:

1 to 1 1/2 lb. family steak, thinly sliced, sm. chunks (works well to freeze it & then cut while partially thawed)
1 can beef consomme soup
1/4 cups soy sauce
1/4 teaspoon ground ginger
1 bunch green onions (about 8)
2 Tablespoons cornstarch
2 Tablespoons water
1 can sliced water chestnuts, drained
1 small can bamboo shoots, drained
1 small can bean sprouts, drained
1 (7 oz.) pkg. frozen Chinese pea pods, partially thawed

Directions:

1. Combine steak in crock pot with consomme, soy sauce, ginger and onion. Cover and cook on low for 5 to 7 hours.
2. Turn control to high. Stir in cornstarch that has been dissolved in the 2 tablespoons cold water.
3. Cook on high for 15 minutes or until thickened.
4. During last 5 minutes of cooking, add water chestnuts, bamboo shoots, bean sprouts and pea pods. Serve over hot rice.

CROCK POT CUBED STEAK AND GRAVY

Ingredients:

2 to 2 1/2 lbs. steak (salted and peppered)
1 pkg. onion gravy mix
1 can cream of mushroom soup
2 cups water
Small amount of flour

Directions:

1. Dip steak in flour, fry until brown. Place in crock pot.
2. Add water, soup and gravy mix. Cover and cook on low 6 to 8 hours.

CROCK POT TORTILLA BEEF

Ingredients:

2 lbs. ground beef
1 medium onion
1 cup cream of mushroom soup
1 cup golden mushroom soup
1 cup Cheddar cheese soup
1 cup enchilada sauce (mild)
1 cup green chilies, chopped
10 corn tortillas (frozen)

Directions:

1. Brown ground beef and onion in top of stove and pour into crock pot - do not drain.
2. Add canned soups and chilies. Simmer all day on low setting 6 to 8 hours.
3. 30 minutes prior to serving, add 10 corn tortillas. Break into half dollar size pieces and poke each into mixture.

CROCK POT ROUND STEAK AND RICH GRAVY

Ingredients:

2 lbs. round steak
1 can cream of chicken soup
1 envelope dry onion soup mix
1/2 cup water

Directions:

1. Cut round steak into serving size pieces. Add rest of ingredients.
2. Cook on low 10-12 hours.

CROCK POT ROAST #1

Ingredients:
1 chuck roast
1 can stewed tomatoes (16 0zs)
1 onion chopped
2 cloves garlic, to taste
3 ribs celery sliced
3 carrots chunked
salt pepper and red pepper to taste
1/2 teaspoon EACH thyme, rosemary, basil, garlic powder
4 potatoes sliced
1 Tablespoon mustard
a dash of Worcestershire sauce
1/4 cup water

Directions:
1. In the bottom of a crockpot add the juice of the canned tomatoes, mustard,Worcestershire sauce, water, salt pepper, spices, and minced garlicup
2. Next add potatoes, tomatoes, carrots, onion and celery. Rub roast with salt and pepper and place on top of veggies.
3. Cook on low for 8 hours.

CROCK POT ROAST #2

Ingredients:
1 beef roast, 2-3 lbs.
1 chopped onion
2 Tablespoons fresh basil, chopped
1/3 cup sun dried tomatoes
clove of chopped garlic

Directions:
1. Put the beef roast in crockpot. Add chopped onion, fresh basil.
2. Soak 1/3 cups sun dried tomatoes in 1 cup of boiling water. Add a clove of chopped garlicup Soak for 10 minutes, then pour over roast.
3. Cook on low for 8 hours. Slice beef, serve with sauce, and sprinkle toasted pinenuts on top

CROCK POT RIO GRANDE MEATLOAF

Ingredients:
Cooking Spray
1 (15oz) can black beans, rinsed and drained
1/2 cup chopped onion
1/2 cups chopped green pepper
1/3 cup chopped fresh cilantro
2 Tablespoons seeded minced jalapeno
1 teaspoon salt
2 teaspoons ground cumin
2 teaspoons chili powder
1/2 teaspoon pepper
4 taco shells, finely crushed
2 large egg whites
3 large garlic cloves, minced
2 pounds ground round
1/2 cup salsa

Directions:
1. Coat slow cooker with spray.
2. Tear off two sheets of foil long enough to fit inbottom of cooker AND to extend 3 inches over each side of cooker. Fold each foil sheet lengthwise to form a 2 inch wide strip. Arrange strips in a cross fashion in cooker, pressing strips to bottom of cooker and extending ends over sides of cooker.
3. Combine beans, and next 11 ingredients in large bowl and stir well. Crumble beef over vegetable mixture and stir until just blended.
4. Shape into a loaf the shape of your cooker container. Place loaf in slow cooker over foil strips (foil stripsbecome handles to remove meat after cooked).

CROCK POT ROAST #3

Ingredients:

3 lb. tri-tip roast
5 large potatoes
1 large onion
1 envelope onion soup mix
1 can beef broth
2 cans water
2 teaspoons Worcestershire sauce
salt, pepper and garlic powder to taste

Directions:

1. Dice the potatoes and slice the onions and put in bottom of crockpot. Add remainder of ingredients after the roast is placed on the top of the potatoes and onions.
2. Cook on low 7 hours.

CROCK POT SAVORY BEEF STEW

Ingredients:

1 cup sun-dried tomatoes (not packed in oil)
1 1/2 pounds beef stew meat
12 small new potatoes (1 1/2 pounds), cut in half
1 medium onion, cut into 8 wedges
1 bag (8 ounces) baby-cut carrots (about 30)
2 cups water
1 1/2 teaspoons seasoned salt
1 dried bay leaf
1/4 cup water
2 Tablespoons Gold Medal all-purpose flour

Directions:

1. Rehydrate tomatoes as directed on package; drain and coarsely chop.
2. Mix tomatoes and remaining ingredients except 1/4 cups water and the flour in 31/2- to 4-quart slow cooker.
3. Cover and cook on low heat setting 8 to 9 hours or until vegetables and beefare tender.

4. Mix 1/4 cups water and the flour; gradually stir into beef mixture. Cover and cook on high heat setting 10 to 15 minutes longer or until slightly thickened. Remove bay leaf.

CROCK POT SAVORY SWISS STEAK

Ingredients:

1-1/2 lbs round steak
1/4 cup of flour
2 teaspoons dry mustard
salt & pepper to taste
1 teaspoon olive oil
1 onion - finely chopped
2 carrots peeled & grated
2 stalks celery - finely chopped
1 - 16 oz can tomatoes - undrained
2 Tablespoons Worcestershire sauce
2 teaspoons firmly packed brown sugar

Directions:

1. Cut steak into 6 serving size pieces. Coat with mixture of flour, mustard, salt &pepper.
2. In a large skillet, brown meat in oil. Transfer to a crock pot. In the same skillet, sauté onion, carrots, and celery until glazed.
3. Add tomatoes, Worcestershire sauce, and brown sugar. Heat, scraping up browned bits, and pour over meat.
3. Cover and cook on Low for 6-8 hours, or until tender. Spoon sauceover meat when serving.

CROCK POT SLOPPY JOES

Ingredients:

2 pounds ground beef
1 medium onion chopped
1 teaspoon salt
1/4 teaspoon pepper
1 can condensed chicken gumbo soup
1/4 cup ketchup
1 Tablespoon prepared mustard
8 hamburger rolls toasted

Directions:

1. In skillet brown ground beef, and drain well. Combine all ingredients except the hamburger rolls in crockpot.
2. Cover and cook on low setting for 6-9 hours oron HIGH for 2-3 hours.

CROCK POT SLOPPY GUISEPPES

Ingredients:

1 Tablespoon olive oil
1 large onion, diced
3/4 of 1 large green pepper, seeded and diced
3/4 pound lean ground beef
3/4 pound hot Italian sausage meat
2 cloves garlic, minced
1 medium carrot, peeled and grated
1 stalk celery, sliced thin
2 teaspoons dried parsley
1 teaspoon dried basil
1 teaspoon dried oregano
1 teaspoon chili powder, or to taste
1 teaspoon sugar
1/2 teaspoon salt
1/4 teaspoon pepper
1 jar (26 oz.) Garlic Chunky style spaghetti sauce

Directions:

1. In a large skillet over medium-high heat, heat oil and sauté onion and greenpepper until tender.
2. Stir in both meats and cook until no longer pink. As the meat cooks, break up the large pieces and stir to combine the meats.
3. Drain fat from meat. Return meat to skillet. Add garlic and stir gently until you begin to smell the garlic cooking (about 2 minutes).
4. Place meat in a 3-1/2 quart or larger crackpot.Add remaining ingredients. Stir to blend ingredients.
5. Cook on High for 1 hour then reduce to Low and cook for another 3 to 4 hours.

CROCK POT SMOKY BEEF N BEANS

Ingredients:

1 lb ground beef
1 cup chopped onion
12 bacon strips, cooked and crumbled
2 cans pork and beans
1 can kidney beans rinsed and drained
1 can butter beans, drained
1 cup ketchup
1/4 cup packed brown sugar
3 Tablespoons vinegar
1 teaspoon liquid smoke
1/2 teaspoon salt
1/4 teaspoon pepper

Directions:

1. In a skillet, cook the beet and onion until meat is no longer pink, drain.
2. Transfer to a slow cooker. Stir in the remaining ingredients.
3. Cover and cook on low for 6-7hours or until heated through.

CROCK POT SNOWY DAY BEEF STEW

Ingredients:

1 medium-size onion, finely chopped
2 medium-size carrots, cut into 1/4" thick slanting slices
1 pound small thin-skinned potatoes, scrubbed and cut lengthwise into quarters
8 ounces mushrooms, sliced
2 to 2 1/4 pounds lean boneless beef round, trimmed of fat and cut into 1 in. cubes
1/4 cup all-purpose flour
2 teaspoons dry thyme
1 can (about 14 1/2 oz.) stewed tomatoes
1/4 cup red wine or beef broth
1 package (about 10 oz.) frozen peas, thawed
salt

Directions:

1. In a 3 1/2-quart or larger electric slow cooker, combine onion, carrots, potatoes,and mushrooms.
2. Coat beef cubes with flour, then add to cooker and sprinkle with thyme. Add tomatoes and wine.
3. Cover and cook at low setting until beef is very tender when pierced (8 to 10 hours).
4. Skim and discard fat from stew, if necessary. Stir in peas. Increase cooker heat setting to high; cover and cook until peas are heated through (10 to 15 more minutes).

CROCK POT SOUR-CREAMED POT ROAST

Ingredients:

2 bacon slices
1 3-lb. beef chuck roast
3/4 cup chopped onion
1 teaspoon salt
1 bay leaf
1/4 teaspoon ground cumin
1/8 teaspoon pepper
1/2 cup dairy sour cream
3 Tablespoons all-purpose flour
2 Tablespoons snipped parsley
1/2 teaspoon Kitchen Bouquet
Hot cooked noodles

Directions:

1. In skillet cook bacon till crisp; drain, reserving drippings. Crumble bacon; wrap and refrigerate.
2. Trim fat from roast; cut in half to fit into crock pot.
3. In skillet brown meat in bacon drippings; drain. Place in cooker.
4. Stir together onion,salt, bay leaf, cumin, pepper, and 1/4 cups water; pour over meat.
5. Cover; cook on low-heat setting for 8-10 hours. Remove roast; discard bay leaf.
6. Skim fat from liquid; pour liquid into saucepan. Return roast to cooker; cover.
7. Blend sour cream and flour; stir into hot liquid. Cook and stir till thickened; do not boil. Stir in parsley and Kitchen Bouquet.
8. Season to taste. Serve meat garnished with bacon. Serve gravy over noodles.

CROCK POT SPICY BEEF AND POTATOES

Ingredients:

2 lb. stew beef
1 - 14 1/2 oz. can of Italian stewed tomatoes
1/2 cup red wine
1 - 2lb. bag of baby potatoes
3 cloves garlic minced
1 teaspoon each of oregano, cumin and chili powder
1/2 cup BBQ sauce
1/4 cups salsa
2 cups frozen corn
l teaspoon salt
1/8 teaspoon pepper
2 Tablespoons flour or cornstarch

Directions:

1. Mix salt/pepper/flour with beef and brown beef in 1 Tablespoon of oil in skillet.
2. When browned on all sides, remove from pan and set aside.
3. Place baby potatoes in the bottom of the crackpot. Combine all ingredients except corn and cook on low for 7 hours, high for 4 hours.
4. Add corn during the last hour. If it is too thin, thicken with cornstarch and water mixture.

CROCK POT SPICY POT ROAST

Ingredients:

5 lbs. blade, chuck or small shoulder roast
2 Tablespoons shortening
1/2 teaspoon thyme
2 Tablespoons sugar
1 Tablespoon vinegar
1 minced clove garlic, or 1/2 teaspoons garlic salt
2 cups tomato juice
1 cup chopped onion
1 bay leaf
1/2 teaspoon salt
1/4 teaspoon pepper

Directions:

1. Brown meat on all sides in shortening. Transfer to crockpot.
2. Combine remaining ingredients and pour over meat.
3. Cover and cook on high setting about 6 hours. Strain gravy and thicken with flour.

CROCK POT STUFFED PEPPERS #1

Ingredients:

6 large Green Bell Peppers -- tall shapes
1 pound Ground Beef, extra lean
1 cup Rice -- uncooked
1 large Onion -- chopped
1 large Carrot -- shredded
1 teaspoon Beef Bouillon granules
1/2 teaspoon Salt
1/2 teaspoon Pepper
1 can Condensed Tomato Soup
1 can Water

Directions:

1. Cut the top off and remove seeds from green peppers. Wash and set aside.
2. Combine ground beef, uncooked rice, onion, carrot, bouillon, salt and pepper in a large mixing bowl.
3. Stuff each pepper about 2/3 full (rice will need room to swell up). Stand the peppers side-by-side in the slow cooker
4. In a small mixing bowl, combine tomato soup and water, and pour mixture over the peppers. Cook on low for 6-8 hours.

CROCK POT
STUFFED PEPPERS #2
Ingredients:
1 1/2 lbs. ground beef or ground turkey
1 (6 oz.) package chicken-flavored rice mix
1 teaspoon salt
1 teaspoon garlic powder
1/2 cup raisin
6 medium size red or green bell peppers
1 (29 oz.) can tomato sauce
Directions:
1. Combine meat, rice mix, seasonings and raisins. Cut stem top of peppers off,hollow out the peppers and fill with the mixture.
2. Place peppers into the crockpot. Pour the tomato sauce over the stuffed peppers.
3. Cover and cook on Low for 8 hours or High for 4 hours.

CROCK POT SWISS BLISS
Ingredients:
2 pounds roast (chuck or bottom round), cut 1-inch thick
1 envelope onion soup mix
1 can (4 oz.) sliced mushrooms, drained
½ medium green pepper, sliced
1 can (20 oz.) tomatoes, drained and chopped, reserving liquid
salt and pepper to taste
1 Tablespoon steak sauce
1 Tablespoon cornstarch
1 Tablespoon dried parsley flakes
Directions:
1. Place meat in slow cooker and sprinkle with soup mix. Add mushrooms, green pepper slices, and tomatoes. Sprinkle with salt and pepper.
2. Combine remaining ingredients and add enough water to make 1½ cups of liquid. Pour over meat andvegetables, and sprinkle with parsley flakes.

3. Cover and cook for 8 to 10 hours.

CROCK POT SWISS STEAK #1
Ingredients:
1 1/2 lbs. round steak
1 chopped carrot
1 cup chopped celery
1 can tomato sauce
1 onion, sliced
2 Tablespoons flour
1 teaspoon salt
1/4 teaspoon black pepper
Directions:
1. Cut steak into serving pieces. Combine flour, salt & pepper & sprinkle over meat. Mix well & put into crock pot.
2. Add carrot, celery, & onion. Pour tomato sauce on top.
3. Cook on low for 8 to 10 hours.

CROCK POT SWISS STEAK #2
Ingredients:
2 lb. Round steak (cut in pieces)
3 Tablespoons Flour
2 Tablespoons Oil
1 can Tomatoes; 16 oz; chopped
1 large Onion; chopped fine
2 Celery stalks; chop fine
1 Tablespoon Dijon mustard
2 Tablespoons Wine vinegar
2 Beef bouillon cubes
1 Tablespoon Worcestershire sauce
1 Bay leaf
Salt and Pepper
Directions:
1. Season meat with salt and pepper. Dredge meat in flour. Heat oil in large skillet.Brown meat in batches so as not to crowd in pan.
2. Add to crockpot with remaining ingredients.
3. Cover pot and cook on low for 6 to 8 hours. Garnish with chopped parsley and serve with boiled, herbed potatoes.

CROCK POT SWISS STEAK #3

Ingredients:

2 pounds round steak
1 medium onion -- chopped
Flour
2 cups beef bouillon

Directions:

1. Cut round steak into serving-size pieces: Dredge in flour and brown in oil in largeskillet. Place browned meat in crockpot.
2. Sauté onion and add to crock-pot.
3. Pour bouillon over meat and cook for 6 to 8 hours on low (4 to 6 hours on high).

CROCK POT SWISS STEAK #4

Ingredients:

6 cube steaks
2 cans cream of mushroom soup
1 envelope onion soup mix
1/2 cup water

Directions:

1. Place all ingredients in crock pot; simmer on low all day; serve sauce over rice or mashed potatoes.

CROCK POT SWISS STEAK STEW

Ingredients:

1/4 cup all-purpose flour
1/2 teaspoon salt
1 1/2 pounds boneless round steak, cut into bite size pieces
1 (14.5 ounce) can Italian-style diced tomatoes
3/4 cup water
3 cups peeled and quartered new red potatoes
1 onion, diced
1 cup sweet corn

Directions:

1. In medium bowl combine flour and salt mix well. Add beef and coat well.
2. Coat a non-stick skillet with cooking spray and heat over medium heat. Add beef and cook until browned.
3. In a slow cooker layer potatoes, beef and onion.
4. Stir tomatoes with juice, water and any remaining flour mixture together. Pour over top.
5. Cover andcook on low setting for 7 to 8 hours or until beef is tender. Add corn, cover and cook an additional 25 minutes.

CROCK POT TANGY BARBECUE SANDWICHES

Ingredients:

3 cups chopped celery
1 cup chopped onion
1 cup ketchup
1 cup barbecue sauce
1 cup water
2 Tablespoons vinegar
2 Tablespoons Worcestershire sauce
2 Tablespoons brown sugar
1 teaspoon chili powder
1 teaspoon salt
1/2 teaspoons pepper
1/2 teaspoons garlic powder
1 3-4 lb boneless chuck roast -- trimmed
16 hamburger buns -- split

Directions:

1. In a slow cooker, combine the first 12 ingredients; mix well. Add roast.
2. Cover andcook on high for 6-7 hours or until tender.
3. Remove roast; cool. Shred meat and return to sauce; heat through. Use a slotted spoon to serve on buns.

CROCK POT FLANK STEAK

Ingredients:

1 1/2 to 2 lbs. Flank Steak
6 fresh tomatillos
1 (15 oz) can whole baby corn on the cob, drained
1/2 teaspoon of salt
1/4 teaspoon ground black pepper
1 small red onion, thinly sliced
1/4 chopped fresh cilantro
1/4 cup dry red wine

Directions:

1. Trim all visible fat from steak. Place steak in a 3 1/2 quart slow cooker.
2. Remove and discard husk and stem from tomatillos; chop and add to steak.
3. Top with baby corn, salt, pepper, cilantro, and onion. Pour in wine.
4. Cover and cook on low about6 hours or until steak is tender.
5. Slice steak crosswise into strips; spoon vegetables and sauce over sliced steak.

CROCK POT TIJUANA PIE

Ingredients:

1 1/2 lb. ground beef
1 onion, chopped
1 clove garlic, minced
1 teaspoon salt
1/4 teaspoon pepper
3-4 cups grated cheese
1 (10 oz.) can enchilada sauce
1 (8 oz.) tomato sauce
2 (16 oz.) cans chili beans
1 (16 oz.) can corn, drained
1 (6 oz.) can pitted olives, drained
6 corn or flour tortillas (size depends on size of crock pot)

Directions:

1. Brown beef, onion, garlic, and seasonings.
2. Wipe inside crock pot with oil. Place 1 tortilla in bottom. Spoon on meat mix a little sauce and cheese. Top with another tortilla and layer on a bean, cheese and corn section. Drop in a few olives. Continue layers, ending with cheese and olive top.
3. Cover and cook low 5-7 hours. Serve with additional hot tortillas.

CROCK POT TERIYAKI STEAK

Ingredients:

2 1/2 lb. Boneless chuck steak
2 Tablespoons Oil
1 teaspoon Ground ginger
1/2 cup Soy sauce
1 Tablespoon Sugar
1 Clove garlic, crushed

Directions:

1. Cut steak into 1/8" thick slices. Combine remaining ingredients in a small bowl. Place meat in a crock-pot. Pour sauce over.
2. Cover and cook on low for 6 to 8hours. Serve with rice.

CROCK POT TEXAS GOULASH

Ingredients:

2 lbs. ground beef
1 onion, chopped
1 can tomatoes
1 can whole kernel corn
2 cups uncooked macaroni
1 can beef broth
1/2 pkg. chili mix
1 Tablespoon sugar
Garlic, oregano, salt, and pepper to taste
Velveeta cheese (optional)

Directions:

1. Brown ground beef and onion. Add remaining ingredients, except cheese, and mix well.
2. Place in crock pot for 3 1/2 hours. Set on low.
3. Can add cut-up chunks of Velveeta cheese when the goulash is done, and steam until the cheese is melted

CROCK POT TEXAS HASH

Ingredients:
2 lbs. ground beef
2 small onions, chopped
2 green peppers, chopped
2 (16 oz.) cans tomatoes
1 cup rice
2 teaspoons Worcestershire sauce
2 1/2 teaspoons chili powder
2 1/2 teaspoons salt

Directions:
1. Brown ground beef in skillet, stirring until crumbly; drain. Place in crock pot.
2. Add remaining ingredients; mix well.
3. Cook, covered on low for 6 to 8 hours, adding water if necessary.

CROCK POT POT ROAST & POTATOES WITH SOUR CREAM GRAVY

Ingredients:
3 lbs. chuck or pot roast
2 Tablespoons flour
1 teaspoon salt
1/4 teaspoon pepper
1 Tablespoon oil
1/4 cup water
1 Tablespoon vinegar
1 teaspoon dill weed
5 or 6 small potatoes
5 or 6 carrots
1/2 teaspoons salt
1 large onion
1 Tablespoon flour
1 cup sour cream
1 teaspoon dill seed

Directions:
1. Coat roast with flour, salt and pepper. Brown in oil in skillet.
2. Put roast in crock pot, add water and vinegar. Sprinkle dill weed over meat, then add potatoes, carrots, onion and 1/2 teaspoons salt.
3. Cook on low for 10-12 hours or high for 6 hours.

4. To make gravy, pour off 3 tablespoons drippings, add flour and heat. Measure rest of drippings, add water to make 1 cup. Add to flour mixture and heat for 1 minute, stirring constantly. Add 1 cup sour cream and dill seed. Heat to boiling.

CROCK POT POT ROAST IN ONION GRAVY

Ingredients:
4-lb. boneless Round Beef Roast, fat trimmed and twine left on
Salt to taste
Freshly ground Black Pepper to taste
2 Tablespoons Olive Oil
2 large Onions, thinly sliced
4 cloves Garlic, minced
1 teaspoon dried Thyme
1/2 cups Brewed Coffee OR 1 teaspoon Instant Coffee dissolved in 1/2 cups boiling water
2 Tablespoons Balsamic Vinegar
1 Tablespoon Cornstarch
1 Tablespoon Water

Directions:
1. Season the beef roast with salt and pepper to taste.
2. In a large heavy skillet, warm one tablespoon of olive oil over medium-high heat. Add the beef roast and sear the outside until browned on all sides. Can take up to 5 minutes on each side.
3. Transfer the roast to a 3-1/2-quart slow cooker. Add the remaining tablespoon of oil to the same skillet and reduce the heat to medium.
4. Sauté the onions, stirring, for about 7 minutes or until they are soft and golden. Add the garlic and thyme; sauté, stirring, for abut a minute more. Pour in the coffee and balsamic vinegar, and allow to warm for about a minute.
5. Pour the mixture over the beef in the crock pot. Cover and cook on high setting

until the beef is tender, but not yet falling apart (about 4 1/2 hours).

5. Transfer the beef to a clean cutting board and tent with foil to maintain its heat. Let the roast rest for about 10 minutes.

6. Meanwhile, pour the juices from the slow cooking into a medium saucepan. Skim off the fat and bring the juices to a boil over medium-high heat.

7. In a small bowl, blend together the cornstarch and water. Add the mixture to the saucepan and cook, whisking constantly, until the gravy has thickened slightly. Season with salt and pepper to taste.

8. Remove the twine from the roast beef and carve. Serve warm with the gravy.

CROCK POT BARBEQUE BEEF STEW
Ingredients:
2 lbs. stew meat
3 Tablespoons oil
1 cup onion, sliced
1/2 cup green pepper, chopped
1 large clove garlic
1/2 teaspoon salt
1/8 teaspoon pepper
2 cups beef stock
1 can (8 oz.) tomatoes
1 can (4 oz.) mushrooms
1/3 cups barbecue sauce
3 Tablespoons cornstarch
1/4 cup cold water
Directions:
1. Saute onion, pepper and garlic in oil. Add salt, pepper, beef stock, tomatoes, mushrooms and barbecue sauce.
2. Cook in slow cooker/Crock Pot on low heat 8-10 hours.
3. Mix cornstarch, cold water and thicken before serving. Serve over hot cooked rice.

CROCK POT BRISKET
Ingredients:
1 3-5 lb. brisket - not too lean
1 can cranberry sauce jellied (soup can size)
1 envelope onion soup mix
1 12 oz. bottle beer or more as needed
Directions:
1. Place brisket in crock pot, use onion soup mix as a "dry rub" rub all over top andpress into roast with fingers.
2. Spoon out cranberry sauce and crumble with handsover top of brisket.
3. Slowly pour in beer so that the roast is covered. Cook on low for 8-10 hrs.

CROCK POT BARBECUE BRISKET
Ingredients:
First, make a batch of homemade Bar-Be-Que Sauce:
1 Tablespoon liquid smoke
1 Tablespoon crushed garlic (or less, we like lots)
1 large onion chopped (I use a small vidalia)
2 Tablespoons cider venegar
1 Tablespoon loose brown sugar (not packed)
3 Tablespoons fresh squeezed lemon juice
1-14 oz. bottle of ketchup
1/2 teaspoon chili powder
4 Tablespoons Worchestershire sauce
1 Tablespoon dry mustard powder
1 cup water or red wine
1 teaspoon salt
1/8 teaspoon black pepper
1 Tablespoon honey
Directions:
1. Mix ingredients together and heat on range.
2. Prep the brisket by removing all silver skin, place it in the crockpot, pour the homemade sauce over it and set on low.

3. The length of time cooking will depend on how large the brisket is (6-8 hours approx.).
4. When done, remove lid from CP and using two forks shred the brisket.

CROCK POT BARBECUED MEATBALLS I
Ingredients:
1 to 2 lbs. ground beef
2 teaspoons Worcestershire sauce
2/3 cup evaporated milk
1 envelope dry onion soup mix
Sauce:
2 cups ketchup
1 cup brown sugar, packed
1 Tablespoon Worcestershire sauce
Directions:
1. Mix beef, 2 teaspoonss Worcestershire sauce, evaporated milk and soup mix. Shape into balls the size of walnuts.
2. Broil 4 inches from broiler for 12 minutes or until done. Turn if necessary to keep from burning.
3. Mix sauce ingredients and boil 10 minutes. Pour over meatballs in slow cooker/Crock Pot turned on low.

CROCK POT BARBECUED MEATBALLS II
Ingredients:
2 pounds ground beef
1 cup bread crumbs
1 teaspoon garlic powder
2 packages onion soup mix
2 teaspoons Worcestershire sauce
2 eggs
Sauce:
2 onions, chopped
2 cans tomato paste (12 ounces total)
2 cloves garlic, minced
1/4 cup Worcestershire sauce
1/4 cup red wine vinegar
1/2 cup brown sugar
1/2 cup sweet pickle relish

1/2 cup beef broth
2 teaspoons salt
2 teaspoons dry mustard
Directions:
1. Combine first 6 ingredients and mix well. Shape into meatballs and brown in a skillet with 1 tablespoon of oil. Drain on paper towels.
2. Add all sauce ingredients to Crock Pot and stir well. Add meatballs and cook, covered, on low for 5 to 6 hours (high for 2 to 3).
3. Serve from the Crock Pot. Makes about 60 meatballs.

CROCK POT BAVARIAN POT ROAST
Ingredients:
3 to 4 lbs pot roast
1 teaspoon vegetable oil
1 teaspoon salt
1/8 teaspoon pepper
1/2 teaspoon ground ginger
3 whole cloves
4 medium apples -- cored and quartered
1 small onion -- sliced
1/2 cups apple juice or water
3 Tablespoons flour (up to 4 Tbs.)
3 Tablespoons water (up to 4 Tbs.)
Directions:
1. Wipe roast well and trim off excess fat. Lightly rub top of meat with oil. Dust with salt, pepper, and ginger. Insert cloves in roast.
2. Place apples and onions in Crock Pot and top with roast (cut roast in half, if necessary, to fit easily).
3. Pour in apple juice. Cover and cook on Low for 10 to 12 hours or on High for 5 to 6 hours.
4. Remove roast and apples to warm platter.
5. Turn Crock Pot to High setting. Make a smooth paste of the flour and water; stir into Crock Pot.
6. Cover and cook until thickened.

CROCK POT BEEF FOR SANDWICHES
Ingredients:
1 roast
1 packet Italian dressing mix or Ranch dressing mix OR 2 packages onion soup mix
1 cup water
Directions:
1. Place all in crock pot, cook on low 8 hours

CROCK POT BEER MEATBALLS
Ingredients:
1 can of beer
1 6 oz can spicy V-8 juice
1 teaspoon lemon juice
1 teaspoon hot sauce
1/2 cup Italian bread crumbs
1 cup onions
Salt and pepper to taste
1 large bottle ketchup
1 teaspoon horseradish
1 teaspoon Worcestershire sauce
2 to 3 lbs. ground beef
2 to 3 eggs
Directions:
1. Combine ground beef, 1/2 cups onions, Italian bread crumbs, eggs. Make the mixture into small meatballs. Then fry or bake the meat.
2. In saucepan combine remaining ingredients. Simmer for 15 minutes.
3. Put meatballs and sauce into slow cooker/Crock Pot. The sauce should cover the meat.
4. Allow to simmer in slow cooker/Crock Pot for at least 3 hours.

CROCK POT CHEESEBURGER SANDWICHES
Ingredients:
1½ lbs. lean ground beef
½ teaspoon garlic-pepper blend
1 pkg. pasteurized process cheese spread, (8 oz.) diced
2 Tablespoons milk
1 green bell pepper, chopped
1 small onion, chopped
2 cloves garlic, minced
8 sandwich buns
Directions:
1. In a large skillet, brown ground beef and garlic-pepper blend until thoroughlycooked. Drain.
2. In a 3½ to 4 quart crock pot, combine cooked ground beef and all remaining ingredients except buns; mix well.
3. Cover; cook on low setting for 6 to 7 hours. To serve: spoon mixture onto sandwich buns

CROCK POT CHOW MIEN
Ingredients:
4 oz. can mushrooms
1 1/2 lbs. cubed round steak
4 stalks celery
2 medium onions
1 cup hot water with 3 bouillon cubes
3 Tablespoons soy sauce
2 teaspoons Worcestershire sauce
1 lb. can Chinese vegetables
2 Tablespoons cornstarch and 2 Tablespoons water
Directions:
1. Cook 8 to 10 hours in crockpot - 1 hour before serving add Chinese vegetables and cornstarch and water.

CROCK POT CRANBERRY COCKTAIL MEATBALLS

Ingredients:

2 pounds Ground beef
1 cup Cornflake crumbs
2 Eggs
1/2 cup Chopped, fresh parsley
1/3 cup Ketchup
3 Tablespoons Minced onions
2 Tablespoons Soy sauce
1/4 teaspoon Garlic powder
1/4 teaspoon Pepper Sauce
16 ounces Can, jellied or whole cranberry sauce
12 ounces Chili sauce
1 Tablespoon Brown sugar
1 Tablespoon Lemon juice

Directions:

1. In a large bowl, combine ground beef, cornflake crumbs, parsley, eggs, ketchup, onion, soy sauce, garlic powder and pepper.
2. Mix well and form into small balls, from 1/2" to 3/4" in diameter. Place in a casserole or baking pan. Heat oven to 300 degrees F.
3. Meanwhile in a saucepan,combine cranberry sauce, chili sauce, brown sugar and lemon juice. Cook stirring over medium heat until smooth. Pour hot sauce over meatballs in casserole.
4. Bake for 30 to 45 minutes, depending on the size of the meatballs. Transfer to Crock Pot and keep on low for serving.

CROCK POT APPLE AND BROWN SUGAR CORNED BEEF

Ingredients:

1 corned beef brisket 1 quart apple juice 1 cup brown sugar
1 Tablespoon prepared mustard
8 small red potatoes
2 medium carrots, pared and cut into chunks
1 onion, peeled and cut into eights
1/2 head cabbage, cut into chunks

Directions:

1. Place all ingredients in large crock pot (cut meat in half if necessary). Stir to mix.
2. Cook on high for 4 to 5 hours on high or 8 to 10 hours on low.
3. Remove meat and vegetables and some of the cooking liquid. Slice meat thinly across the grain.
4. Serve with the vegetables and some of the liquid.

CROCK POT BARBECUED SHORT RIBS

Ingredients:

2 cups water
3 or 4 lbs. boneless short ribs
18 oz. bottle barbecue sauce
1 Tablespoon Worcestershire sauce
3 oz. Heinz 57 hickory smoke sauce
1/4 Tablespoon lemon pepper seasoning

Directions:

1. Combine water, barbecue sauce, Worcestershire, Heinz 57 sauce, lemon pepper and short ribs in crock pot.
2. Cook on low heat for 12 hours.

CROCK POT CARNE GISADA

Ingredients:
3 lbs. beef stew meat
2 cans diced ROTEL tomatoes with green chilies
salt and pepper to taste
3 cloves garlic minced
1 cup chopped onion
3 Tablespoons flour
1/2 teaspoon cumin
1/2 teaspoon oregano
1 teaspoon chili powder
1/4 cup water
1 diced bell pepper

Directions:
1. Place stew meat, 1/4 cups water, salt and pepper in crock pot. Turn heat to high and let simmer for 1 1/2 hours.
2. Drain juice from tomatoes into measuring cup. Add tomatoes garlic and onions to crock pot STIR let simmer on high for 30 minutes
3. Add cumin, oregano, and chili powder to crock pot and stir.
4. Blend juice and enough water to equal 1 1/2 cupss liquid and flour stir into meat/veggie mixture.
5. Let cook on LOW for 3-4 hours until sauce is nice and thick. Serve with warm flour tortillas.

CROCK POT BARBECUED POT ROAST

Ingredients:
1 teaspoon salt
2 lb. lean pot roast
1/2 cup tomato paste
24 peppercorns
1 small onion, chopped
1 teaspoon Worcestershire sauce

Directions:
1. Sprinkle salt over the roast and place in slow-cooker.
2. Spread tomato paste over meat; embed peppercorns into paste; top with onions and Worcestershire sauce.
3. Cover and cook on LOW 8-10 hrs. Serve meat with the gravy.

CROCK POT BEEF AND BEANS

Ingredients:
1 1/2 lbs. of stewing beef
1 Tablespoon prepared mustard
1 Tablespoon taco seasoning
1/2 teaspoon salt
1/4 teaspoon pepper
2 garlic cloves minced
1 can 16 oz diced tomatoes, undrained
1 med. onion chopped
1 can Kidney beans, rinsed and drained
1 can chili beans

Directions:
1. Combine mustard, taco seasonings, salt , pepper and garlic in a large bowl. Add beef and toss to coat.
2. Put the beef in your crock pot and add the rest of the ingredients. Cover and cook for 6 -8 hours on LOW.
3. Serve over hot rice.

CROCK POT BEEF AND BEANS #2

Ingredients:

Cut up left over roast beef in bite sized cubes
Large can beans
Large can diced tomatoes
1/2 cup finely chopped onion
1 cup mild or medium salsa
2/3 cup long grain rice
1 teaspoon salt
1/4 teaspoon pepper
1/4 teaspoon garlic
1 cup water

Directions:

1. Combine, stir, and cook on low for 8 - 9 hours, or high 4 - 4 1/2 hours.

CROCK POT BEEF AND BEAN BAKE

Ingredients:

3 bacon slices
1/2 pound ground round
1 cup finely chopped onion
1 (15.5 oz) can lima beans, drained
1 (15 oz) can pork and beans, undrained
1 (15oz) can light red kidney beans, drained
1/2 cup ketchup
1/2 cup barbecue sauce
1/4 cup firmly packed brown sugar
1 teaspoon dry mustard

Directions:

1. Cook bacon until crisp, crumble and set aside.
2. Cook beef and onion in skillet and crumble.
3. Place bacon, beef mixture and other ingredients in slow cooker. Stir well.
4. Cover and cook on high 1 hour. Reduce to low and cook 3-4 hours.

CROCK POT BEEF AND CHIPOTLE BURRITOS

Ingredients:

1 1/2 lb. boneless beef round steak, cut 3/4" thick
1 14 1/2 oz. can diced tomatoes
1 small onion, chopped
1 to 2 canned chipotle peppers in adobo sauce, chopped
1 teaspoon dried oregano, crushed
1/4 teaspoon ground cumin
1 clove garlic, minced
6 9-10" tomato-flavored or plain flour tortillas, warmed
3/4 cup shredded sharp cheddar cheese (3 oz.)
1 small jar of regular salsa
Dairy sour cream

Directions:

1. Trim fat from meat. Cut meat into 6 pieces.
2. In a 3 1/2 or 4 qt. crock pot place meat, undrained tomatoes, onion, peppers, oregano, cumin, and garlicup
3. Cover; cook on low-heat setting for 8 to 10 hours or on high-heat setting for 4 to 5 hours.
4. Remove meat from cooker. Using 2 forks, shred meat.
5. Spoon one-sixth of the meat onto each warm tortilla just below the center. Top with cheese, salsa, and sour cream. Roll up tortilla.

CROCK POT BEEF AND GRAVY

Ingredients:
2-3 pounds roast cut into bite sized pieces
1 packet Lipton's Onion soup mix
2 cans Cream of mushroom soup

Directions:
1. Place pieces of roast in crock pot. Sprinkle packet of onion soup on meat. Cover with cream of mushroom soup.
2. Let cook up to 9 hours. Stir about 1/2 way through cooking. Serve over mashed potatoes or pasta.

CROCK POT

BEEF BOURGUIGNON 1

Ingredients:
1 cup Dry red wine
2 Tablespoons Olive oil
1 Large Onion -- sliced
1/2 teaspoon Thyme
2 Tablespoons Parsley -- chopped
1 Bay leaf
1/4 teaspoon Pepper
2 Pounds stewing beef, cut into 1 1/2-inch cubes
3 Slices Bacon (thick-cut is possible) -- diced
12 Small White onions
1/2 Pound Sliced mushrooms
2 Cloves Garlic -- minced
1 teaspoon Salt

Directions:
1. Combine first seven ingredients, mix well, add beef. Marinate at least 3 hours (overnight if refrigerated).
2. Drain meat, reserving marinade. In skillet, saute bacon and remove. Brown meat in bacon fat.
3. Combine beef, bacon, vegetables and seasonings in slow cooker. Pour over enough marinade to cover.
4. Cook on low 8-10 hours.

CROCK POT BEEF BOURGUIGNON 2

Ingredients:
1 lb. bacon, cooked, reserve grease
3 lbs. beef, cubed
1 bottle red wine
1 lb. onion, chopped
1 lb. celery
1 lb. carrots, chopped
2 cloves garlic, chopped
Chopped shallots (optional)
1 bay leaf
Salt & pepper
Flour

Directions:
1. Slowly cook bacon in large baking pan; remove.
2. Dredge beef cubes in flour, brown in bacon fat. Transfer meat from skillet to heated platter.
3. Saute vegetable and garlic in bacon fat; remove. Drain fat from pan.
4. Gently combine beef, vegetables, bacon and half the wine. Add bay leaf and salt and pepper to taste.
5. Cook on low 8 – 10 hours.

CROCK POT BEEF BURGER STROGANOFF

Ingredients:
1 1/2 lbs. lean ground beef
3 slices bacon, diced
1 small onion, chopped
2 Tablespoons flour
1/4 teaspoon paprika
1 teaspoon salt
1 can (10 3/4oz) condensed cream of mushroom soup
2 Tablespoons dry red wine
1 cup dairy sour cream

Directions:
1. In large skillet, brown beef and bacon until red color disappears. Drain.
2. In crockpot, mix together drained beef, bacon, onion, flour, paprika, and salt. Stir in undiluted soup and wine.
3. Cover pot and cook on low 4 to 5 hours. Stir in sour cream.
4. Spoon mixture over toasted buns or egg noodles.

CROCK POT BEEF BURGUNDY 1

Ingredients:
2 slices bacon -- chopped
2 pounds sirloin tip or round steak -- cut in 1 inch cubes
1/4 cup flour
1 teaspoon salt
1/2 teaspoons seasoned salt
1/4 teaspoon marjoram
1/4 teaspoon thyme
1/4 teaspoon pepper
1 clove garlic -- minced
1 cube beef bouillon -- crushed
1 cup Burgundy wine
2 Tablespoons cornstarch

Directions:
1. In large skillet cook bacon several minutes. Remove bacon and set aside.
2. Coat beef with flour and brown on all sides in bacon mixture.
3. Combine steak, bacon drippings, cooked bacon, seasonings, bouillon and Burgundy in crock pot.
4. Cover and cook on low for 6 to 8 hours or until meat is tender.
5. Turn control to high. Add cornstarch (dissolved in 2 tablespoons water); cook on high 15 minutes.

CROCK POT BEEF BURGUNDY 2

Ingredients:
3 lbs beef, cut in large cubes-can use stew beef or round steak 1 can Minestrone Soup
1 can Tomato Bisque Soup
1 can Cream of Mushroom soup
1 envelope dry onion soup mix
1 soup can Burgundy wine

Directions:
1. Flour and brown meat. Place in crockpot.
2. Mix remaining ingredients and pour over meat.
3. Cook on low 6-8 hours. Serve over noodles or rice.

CROCK POT
BEEF BURGUNDY #3
Ingredients:
1 10 oz. pkg fresh pearl onions
1 2 pound top round steak
2 1/2 cups sliced onions
1 minced garlic clove
Cooking Spray
1/3 cup all purpose flour
1 10.5 oz can condensed beef broth, undiluted
1/2 cup dry red wine
2 Tablespoons tomato paste
1/2 teaspoon dried thyme
1/2 teaspoon salt
1/4 teaspoon pepper
1 bay leaf
1 8oz package fresh mushrooms
3 cups hot cooked egg noodles (6oz uncooked)
Directions:
1. Drop pearl onions in boiling water 1 minute. Drain and peel.
2. Trim fat from steak and cut until 1 1/2" cubes. Place large nonstick skillet on medium high heat and sauté steak 5 minutes or until browned. Place steak in slow cooker.
3. Add sliced onion and garlic to skillet. Coat with spray and sauté 5 minutes or until tender. Sprinkle flour over onion mixture and cook 1 minute stirring constantly.
4. Gradually add broth, wine and tomato paste stirring constantly. Cook 1 minute or until thick. Add pearl onions, thyme, salt, pepper, bay leaf and mushrooms.
3. Pour wine mixture over beef in slow cooker. Cover with lid, cook on high 1 hour and low 4-5 hours. Discard bay leaf. Serve over noodles.

CROCK POT
BEEF BURGUNDY #4
Ingredients:
2lbs. beef cubed into 1" pieces
1 envelope dry onion soup mix
1 can cream of mushroom soup
1 (4oz) can whole mushrooms
1/2 cup red wine
Directions:
1. Combine all of the above in a crock pot. Stir together well then cover.
2. Cook on lowfor 8 hours. Makes its own gravy. Serve over noodles

CROCK POT BEEF CASSEROLE
Ingredients:
1 1/2 lbs. stewing steak
1 oz. flour
2 Tablespoons oil
2 large onions
3 medium carrots
1 pint beef stock
salt and pepper
Directions:
1. Cut the steak into 1 inch cubes and toss in the flour seasoned with saltand pepper.
2. Brown on all sides in the oil, then remove from the pan.
3. Cut the onions into thin slices and cook in the oil until soft and golden.
4. Slice the carrots thinly and put into the crock pot. Top with the onions and the meat. Add any remaining flour to the fat in the pan and cook for 2 minutes.
5. Work in the stock and stir over low heat until the liquid comes to the boil.
6. Pour into the crock pot, cover and cook on HIGH for 30 minutes, then on LOW 6-7 hours.

CROCK POT BEEF FAJITAS

Ingredients:

1 1/2 pounds beef flank steak
1 cup chopped onion
1 green sweet pepper, cut into 1/2 inch pieces
1 jalapeno pepper, chopped
1 Tablespoon cilantro
2 garlic cloves, minced (or 1/4 teaspoon garlic powder)
1 teaspoon chili powder
1 teaspoon ground cumin
1 teaspoon ground coriander
1/2 teaspoon salt
1 can (8oz) chopped tomatoes
12 8inch flour tortillas
Toppings: sour cream, guacamole, shredded cheddar cheese and salsa

Directions:

1. Cut flank steak into 6 portions.
2. In any size crock pot combine meat, onion, green pepper, jalapeno pepper, cilantro, garlic, chili powder, cumin, coriander and salt. Add tomatoes.
3. Cover and cook on low 8-10 hours or high 4-5 hours.
4. Remove meat from crockpot and shred. Return meat to crockpot and stir.
5. To serve, spread meat mixture into flour tortillas and top with toppings. Roll up.

CROCK POT FAJITAS #1

Ingredients:

2 lbs. flank steak cut crosswise into 6 pieces
1/4 cup flour
2 red or green peppers sliced
1 onion, thinly sliced
2 Tablespoons packed brown sugar
3 cloves garlic, chopped
2 teaspoons cumin
2 teaspoons ground coriander
1 teaspoon salt
1/2 teaspoon pepper
juice of 1 lime
2 Tablespoons Worcestershire sauce
1 pint of cherry tomatoes
8 flour tortillas
2 Tablespoons chopped fresh coriander
Prepared salsa and cilantro, optional

Directions:

1. Coat meat with the flour and place in the bottom of the crock pot.
2. Mix first10 ingredients and layer on top of meat in 4 qt crock pot.
3. On low, cook for 8-10 hoursstirring in tomatoes during last 30 mins.
4. Warm tortillas. Remove meat from crockpot and shred. Mix with pepper mixture and sprinkle with cilantro.
5. Serve in tortillas and garnish with salsa.

CROCK POT FAJITAS #2

Ingredients:
1 to 1 1/2 lb. stew meat -- well browned
1 16-24 oz. jar Pace picante sauce
1 green pepper cut into julienne strips
1 medium to large onion cut into rings

Directions:
1. Layer meat, pepper, onion, salsa until all ingredients are used.
2. Cook on low heat until done. Serve on flour tortillas with lettuce, cheese, etcup

CROCK POT BEEF FOR SANDWICHES

Ingredients:
1 roast
1 packet Italian dressing mix
1 cup water

Directions:
1. Place all in crockpot, cook on low 8 hours.

CROCK POT BEEF POT ROAST

Ingredients:
1 1/2 lb- 2lb. pot roast meat
1 dry package of Good Seasons Garlic Dressing
1 dry pkg of Italian (or Zesty Italian) Dressing
1 can of beer (your choice-not dark)

Directions:
1. Place one envelope of Good Seasons in bottom of crock pot.
2. Place meat on top, top with other package of dressing and pour beer over all.
3. Let cook 8-10 hours on low.

CROCK POT BEEF POT ROAST #2

Ingredients:
Beef bottom round rump roast, about 2 lb.
4 - 6 carrots, peeled and cut into 1-2" chunks
1 - 2 onions cut into wedges
1/4 - 1/2 cup canned beef broth
1 can Campbell's Cream of Chicken & Mushroom Soup
Mashed potatoes

Directions:
1. Put carrot chunks and onion wedges in bottom of greased 3-1/2 quart crockpot.
2. Brown rump roast on all sides in frying pan and put in crock pot on top of thevegetables.
3. Pour beef broth over meat (more liquid will accumulate as the roast cooks); put lid on and cook on Low for 8 hours.
4. About 45 minutes before it's done, boil the potatoes.
5. Just before you're ready to mash them, take roast out of crock pot and slice it up. Open canned soup and putit in small batter bowl; add just enough juices from the crock pot to stir it and getthe lumps out.
6. After you've done so, pour it back into the crock pot and stir to mix. Add the beef slices and stir to cover with gravy. Put the lid back on.
7. Mash the potatoes, then add some margarine and stir until it's melted.
8. Heat 1/4 cups milk in the microwave (in a glass measuringcup), then stir it into the potatoes along with salt, pepper, and about 1/2 teaspoons of horseradish.
9. Serve with the potatoes.

CROCK POT BEEF STEW 1

Ingredients:
2 lbs. stew beef
1/4 cup flour
1 teaspoon paprika
4 large carrots
3 large potatoes
1 cup condensed beef broth
1 1/2 teaspoons salt
1/2 teaspoon pepper
1/3 cup soy sauce
1 large onion
1 can tomato sauce (8 oz.)

Directions:
1. Layer potatoes, then carrots. Top with meat; sprinkle meat with soy sauce, salt, paprika, pepper and flour.
2. Spread with chopped onions. Combine beef broth and tomato sauce, pour over all.
3. Cover and cook on low 7 - 8 hrs. or high 4 - 5 hrs.

CROCK POT BEEF STEW 2

Ingredients:
1 lb. beef bourguignon
3 large sweet potatoes (cut into 1" thick slices)
2 cans beef bouillon (or broth or consommée)
2 small cans tomato paste
3-4 handfulls of assorted veggies
1 lb. fresh mushrooms (quartered)
1 large onion (diced)
2 cloves garlic (minced)
1/4 cups flour

Directions:
1. Mix bite sized pieces of meat in flour, brown in some oil along with the diced garlicup
2. While meat is browning, combine beef bouillon & tomato paste in a crock pot, mix well.
3. Pre-cook the sweet potatoes until just tender, add to crock pot along with onions and any raw veggies that you may use. Add enough water to cover and cook on low for about 5 hours.

CROCK POT BEEF STEW 3

Ingredients:
1 package stew beef
1 can cream of potato soup
1 can cream of mushroom soup
1 - 1 1/2 cans of water

Directions:
1. Cook on high all day (7-8) hours. Serve over white rice.

CROCK POT BEEF STEW 4

Ingredients:
2 lbs. beef stew meat, cut into 1 inch pieces
1/4 cup flour
1/2 teaspoon pepper
1 teaspoon Worcestershire sauce
1 bay leaf
3 potatoes, diced
1 stalk celery, sliced
1 1/2 teaspoons salt
1 1/2 cups beef broth
1 clove garlic
1 teaspoon paprika
2 onions, chopped
2 teaspoons Kitchen Bouquet (optional)

Directions:
1. Place meat in crock pot.
2. Mix flour, salt, pepper and pour over meat. Stir to coat meat with flour.
3. Add remaining ingredients and stir to mix well.
4. Cover and cook on low for 10 to 12 hours or high for 4 to 6 hours. Stir stew thoroughly before serving.

CROCK POT BEEF STEW 5

Ingredients:
1 ½ pounds stew beef
Handful of Baby carrots
3 white potatoes
1 large onion cut into wedges
1 can of beef broth
1 clove of garlic minced
2 teaspoons of kitchen bouquet
1 teaspoon of Worcestershire sauce

Directions:
1. Add water to fill crock-potCut stew beef into bite size pieces, dredge in four with salt and pepper. Place into crock-pot.
2. Add beef broth, garlic, onion, carrots and potatoes, add kitchen bouquet and Worcestershire sauce.
3. Add water just to top turn crock pot on high and cook for 5-6 hours. Stir occasionally.

CROCK POT BEEF STEW 6

Ingredients:
4 lb. stew beef, cut into small pieces
2 envelopes dry onion soup mix
2 cans cream of mushroom soup
4 oz. jar sliced mushrooms, drained
2 cups Ginger Ale
1 lb. carrots, sliced

Directions:
1. Mix all ingredients in Crock pot. Cover and cook on low 8-10 hours. Serve with noodles or rice.

CROCK POT BEEF STROGANOFF 1

Ingredients:
2 lbs. top round steak, sliced thin across the grain
1 lb. fresh mushrooms, sliced
1 medium onion, sliced
1/4 teaspoon thyme
3/4 cup dry sherry
3/4 cup beef broth (
3/4 teaspoon dry mustard
1/4 teaspoon garlic salt

Directions:
1. Put everything in the crockpot, stir well and cook on low for 8 hours.
2. Turn heat to high and mix in 1-1/2 cups sour cream and 1/2 cups cake flour.
3. Heat on high for 40 minutes. Serve over rice or noodles.

CROCK POT BEEF STROGANOFF 2

Ingredients:
1 1/2 lb. lean ground beef
1 medium onion, chopped
1 clove garlic, minced
3 Tablespoons tomato paste
1/2 cup beef broth
3 Tablespoons sherry
1 teaspoon salt
Dash pepper
1 can mushrooms, drained
1 cup sour cream

Directions:
1. Brown ground beef with onion and garlic; drain. Add to crock pot with remaining ingredients except for sour cream.
2. Cover and cook on low for 5 to 7 hours. Stir in sour cream. Heat through. Serve over egg noodles.

CROCK POT BEEF STROGANOFF 3

Ingredients:
3 lb. beef round steak, 1/2 inch thick
1/2 cup flour
2 teaspoons salt
1/8 teaspoon pepper
1/2 teaspoons dry mustard
2 medium onions, thinly sliced and separated into rings
2 (4 oz. each) cans sliced mushrooms, drained or 1/2 lb. mushrooms, sliced
1 (10 1/2 oz.) can condensed beef broth
1/4 cup dry white wine (optional)
1 1/2 cups sour cream
1/4 cup flour

Directions:
1. Trim all excess fat from steak and cut meat into 3 inch strips about 1/2 inch wide.
2. Combine 1/2 cups flour, the salt, pepper and dry mustard; toss with steak strips to coat thoroughly.
3. Place coated steak strips in crock pot; stir in onion rings and mushrooms. Add beef broth and wine; stir well.
4. Cover and cook on low setting for 8- 10 hours.
5. Before serving, combine sour cream with 1/4 cups flour; stir into crock pot. Serve stroganoff over rice or noodles.

CROCK POT BEEF STROGANOFF 4

Ingredients:
1 can cream of mushroom soup 1 package onion soup mix
1 package mushroom
1 onion cut in rings
1 package beef stew meat
salt
pepper

Directions:
1. Put in crock pot and cook all day. Add 16 oz sour cream before serving. Serve over Egg Noodles.

CROCK POT BEEF TIPS

Ingredients:
1/2 cup Flour
1 teaspoon Salt
1/8 teaspoon Pepper
4 lb. Beef or sirloin tips
1/2 cup Chopped green onions
2 cups Sliced mushrooms (4 oz. can, drained) OR
1/2 lb. Mushrooms, sliced
1 can Condensed beef broth, (10 1/2 oz.)
1 teaspoon Worcestershire sauce
2 teaspoons Tomato paste or ketchup
1/4 cup Dry red wine or water
3 Tablespoons Flour
1 Buttered noodles

Directions:
1. Combine 1/2 cups flour with the salt and pepper and toss with beef cubes to coat thoroughly. Place in crock-pot.
2. Add green onions and drained mushrooms. Combine with beef broth, Worcestershire sauce and tomato paste or ketchup.
3. Pour over beef and vegetables; stir well. Cover and cook on LOW setting for 7 to 12 hours.
4. One hour before serving, turn to HIGH setting.
5. Make a smooth paste of red wine and 3 tablespoons flour; stir into crock-pot, mixing well.

CROCK POT BEEF BBQ

Ingredients:

2 1/2 lbs. lean chuck roast
1 large onion, chopped
1/2 cup chopped celery
2 Tablespoons vinegar
4 Tablespoons lemon juice
3 Tablespoons Worcestershire sauce
1 cup ketchup

Directions:

1. Combine all ingredients in crock pot. Cook on medium for at least 1 1/2 hours.
2. Use two forks to break apart beef and to remove any strips of fat.

CROCK POT BBQ

Ingredients:

4 lb. pork or beef roast
1 medium onion, sliced
1/2 cup hickory smoke flavored BBQ sauce
3 cups water
3/4 cup regular BBQ sauce

Directions:

1. Cook meat and onion in crock pot on high for 4 to 6 hours or on low overnight. Drain water and throw out onion.
2. Add BBQ sauces and cook on low for more 1 hour.

CROCK POT BRACIOLE

Ingredients:

2 1/2 pounds Round steak
1/4 to 1/2" thick 1/2 pound Bulk Italian sausage
1 Tablespoon Dried parsley flakes
1/2 teaspoon Leaf oregano
2 cloves Garlic -- minced
1 large Onion -- finely chopped
1 teaspoon Salt
1 can Italian style tomatoes -- 16 0z
1 can tomato paste -- (6 oz)
1 teaspoon Salt
1 teaspoon Leaf oregano
10 large Tomatoes or 2 28 oz cans
tomatoes
5 cloves Garlic -- chopped
1 tablespoon Worcestershire sauce
2 teaspoons Salt
2 large Onions -- chopped
1 Tablespoon Flour
1 Tablespoon Vegetable oil
1 teaspoon Oregano
1 teaspoon Thyme
1 Tablespoon Wine vinegar
1 Tablespoon Sugar

Directions:

1. Trim all excess fat from round steak. Cut into 8 evenly shaped pieces.
2. Pound steak pieces between waxed paper until very thin and easy to roll.
3. In skillet, lightly brown sausage. Drain well and combine with parsley, 1/2 teaspoons oregano, garlic, onion, and salt; mix well.
4. Spread each steak with 2 to 3 tablespoons of sausage mixture. Roll up steaks and tie.
5. Stack steak rolls in crock pot. Combine tomatoes, tomato paste, salt, and 1 teaspoon oreagno; pour over rolls.
6. Cover and cook on low setting for 8 to 10 hours. Serve steak rolls with sauce.

Directions For Sauce:

1. Place all ingredients except flour, oil, and vinegar in crockpot; stir well.
2. Cover and cook on low setting for 8 to 10 hours. Remove cover and turn to high setting for the last hour to reduce excess moisture.
3. Before removing sauce from crock pot, stir in flour, oil, and vinegar. Allow to cool.
4. Pour 3 cupss of sauce at a time into blender container; blend until smooth.

CROCK POT CABBAGE AND BEEF CASSEROLE

Ingredients:

2 lb. ground beef
1 head cabbage, shredded
1 small onion, chopped
1 (16oz) can tomatoes
broth or tomato juice to cover bottom of pot
Garlic salt, thyme, red pepper and a bit of oregano

Directions:

1. Brown ground beef and drain. Shred cabbage and chop onion. Put in broth or other liquid to cover bottom of pot.
2. Layer cabbage, onion, spices, meat, and garlic salt.
3. Repeat layers ending with beef. Top with tomatoes, undrained and a dusting of oregano.
4. Cook on high for 1 hour. Stir all together. Cook on low heat until ready to eat, 8-10 hours.

CROCK POT CABBAGE BURGER BAKE

Ingredients:

6 cups shredded cabbage and carrots
3/4 pound lean ground beef
1/2 teaspoon salt
1/4 teaspoon ground black pepper
1 medium onion -- finely chopped
1 cup long-grain rice
1 26 oz. can chunky low-fat spaghetti sauce
1/2 cup water
1/4 teaspoons dried basil leaves -- crushed
1/4 teaspoon seasoned salt

Directions:

1. Place 1/2 of the cabbage and carrots in a slow cooker. Crumble ground beef over top. Sprinkle 1/4 teaspoons of the salt and 1/8 teaspoon of the pepper.

2. Evenly distribute onion, then rice over all. Top with remaining cabbage, salt, and pepper.
3. Combine spaghetti sauce, water, basil, and seasoned salt; pour over cabbage.
4. Cover and cook on LOW 5 to 6 hours or until rice is tender.

CROCK POT CAMP STEW

Ingredients:

1 can bar-b-que beef
1 can bar-b-que chicken
1 can bar-b-que pork
1 can stewed tomatoes
1 can corn
3 cups cubed potatoes
1 onion, chopped

Directions:

1. Cube potatoes, chopped onion. Cook until partly tender. Place in slow cooker/Crock Pot.
2. Open all cans and add to slow cooker/Crock Pot, stir. Cook for at least an hour. Serve with corn sticks or bread sticks.

CROCK POT MEXICAN FIESTA

Ingredients:

1 bag white corn tortilla chips
1 pound lean ground beef
1 can ranch style beans
3 cups cheddar cheese -- grated
1 can cream of mushroom soup
1 can cream of chicken soup
1 can Mild rotel tomatoes and chiles
2 teaspoons chili powder
1/2 cup onion -- chopped

Directions:

1. Spray crock pot with non-stick spray and cover the bottom with slightly crushed chips.
2. Combine soups, rotel, chili powder, and onion in a separate bowl and blend well with a whisk.
3. Brown ground beef in a skillet, drain fat, and add ranch style beans to it and mix together. (Do not drain the beans).
4. Layer half of the beef mixture over the chips, then half of the soup mixture over the beef, ending with half the cheese over the beef. Repeat these layers once more beginning with chipsand ending with cheese.
5. Cook on high in crock pot for three hours.

CROCK POT BEEF WITH MUSHROOMS AND RED WINE GRAVY

Ingredients:

1 1/2 lbs. well-trimmed beef stew meat, cut into one inch pieces
2 medium onions cut into half inch wedges
1 pkg. sliced fresh mushrooms (8oz)
1 envelope beefy onion soup mix
3 Tablespoons cornstarch
salt and pepper to taste
1 1/2 cups dry red wine

Directions:

1. Place beef, onions and mushrooms in a 4qt or larger crock pot. Add dry soup mix. Sprinkle with cornstarch and salt and pepper.
2. Pour wine over all. Cover and cook on low 10-12 hours or high 5-6 hours. Stir well before serving.

CROCK POT CARNE GISADA 2

Ingredients:

3 lbs. beef stew meat
2 cans diced ROTEL tomatoes with green chilis
salt and peper to taste
3 cloves garlic minced
1 cup chopped onion
3 Tablespoons flour
1/2 teaspoon cumin
1/2 teaspoon oregeno
1 teaspoon chili powder
1/4 cup water
1 diced bell pepper

Directions:

1. Place stew meat, 1/4 cups water, salt and pepper in crockpot.
2. Turn heat to high and let simmer for 1 1/2 hours.
3. Drain juice from tomatoes into measuring cup. Add tomatoes, garlic, and onions to crock pot.
4. STIR, let simmer on high for 30 minutes.
5. Add cumin, oregeno, and chili powder to crock pot and stir.
6. Blend juice and enough water to equal 1 1/2 cupss liquid and flour stir into meat/veggie mixture.
7. Let cook on LOW for 3-4 hours until sauce is nice and thick . Serve with warm flour tortillas.

CROCK POT CHILI COKE ROAST

Ingredients:
3-5 lb. roast (beef or pork)
1 jar chili sauce or Manwich
1 pkg. onion soup mix
1 can coke

Directions:
1. Place roast in crock pot and pour remaining ingredients over it.
2. Cook on low for 6-7 hours

CROCK POT CHINESE PEPPER STEAK

Ingredients:
1-1 1/2 lbs. boneless beef round steak
1 clove garlic minced
1/2 teaspoon salt
1/4 teaspoon pepper
1/4 cup soy sauce
1 Tablespoons hoisin sauce
1 teaspoon sugar
1 tomato, seeded, peeled & diced
2 red or green bell peppers, cut into strips
3 Tablespoons cornstarch
3 Tablespoons water
1 cup fresh bean sprouts
4 green onions, finely chopped
Cooked Rice

Directions:
1. Trim fat from steak; slice into thin strips.
2. Combine steak, garlic, salt, pepper, soy sauce, hoisin sauce and sugar in slow cooker.
3. Cover and cook on LOW about 4 hours.
4. Turn control to HIGH. Add tomato and bell peppers. Dissolve cornstarch with water in a small bowl and stir into steak mixture.
5. Cover and cook on HIGH 15-20 minutes or until thickened. Stir in bean sprouts, sprinkle with onions. Serve with rice.

CROCK POT CHINESE PIE

Ingredients:
1 to 1 1/2 pounds ground beef
3/4 cup diced bell pepper (green AND red if possible)
3/4 cup diced onion
1 package (dry) brown gravy
4 to 6 medium red or round white potatoes, diced (about 4 cupss)
2 Tablespoons butter, melted
1 (15 oz) can whole kernel corn, drained (or 2 cupss frozen)
1 (15 oz) can creamed corn
salt and pepper to taste

Directions:
1. Brown ground beef with diced peppers and onion. Drain well. Place ground beef mixture in crockpot.
2. Toss diced potato with melted butter to coat and add to crockpot; add whole kernel corn and creamed corn.
3. Cover and cook on low for 7 to 9 hours.

CROCK POT CORNED BEEF AND CABBAGE

Ingredients:
3 lb. uncooked corned beef brisket (in pouch with pickling juice is okay)
2 carrots, chopped into 2" pieces
5 small red potatoes, halved
1 onion, quartered
1 small turnip, chopped into 2" pieces
3/4 cup malt vinegar
1/2 bottle (6 oz) Irish stout
1 teaspoon mustard seed
1 teaspoon coriander seed
1 teaspoon black peppercorns (whole)
1 teaspoon dill seed
1 teaspoon allspice (whole)
1 bay leaf
1 small (2 Lb) head cabbage, cut into wedges

Directions:
In a LARGE (6.5 qt) Crock-Pot, place the carrots, spuds, onion and turnip in bottom. Add the liquids.
2. Spice rub the brisket. Place on top. Cover and cook on LOW for 8 hours.
3. Add cabbage wedges. Cook an additional 3 hours on LOW. Serve with Coarse Grain Mustard and Horseradish Sauce.

CORNED BEEF AND CABBAGE

Ingredients:
4 1/2 lb. Corned beef brisket
2 medium onions, quartered
1 cabbage head, cut in small wedges
1/2 teaspoon pepper
3 Tablespoons vinegar
3 Tablespoons sugar
2 cups water

Directions:
1. Combine ingredients in removable liner with cabbage on top. Cut meat to fit, ifnecessary. Place liner in base.
2. Cover and cook on low 10-12 hours or high 6-7 hours.

CROCK POT CORNED BEEF HASH

Ingredients:
1 can of corned beef (Or 2 cups cooked corned beef)
1 medium onion, shredded
2 medium celery sticks, chopped
5 potatoes, chopped
2 Tablespoons butter
1 diced green pepper
garlic to your taste
1 cup mushrooms
1 Tablespoon Worcestshire sauce
a dash or two of italian seasoning
salt and pepper to taste
2- 10 oz cans of chicken broth

Directions:
1. Grind up or chop corned beef and place in the crock pot with all the other ingredients.
2. Cook in crock pot on low for 8 hours.

CROCK POT CORNED BEEF HASH 2

Ingredients:
1 can of corned beef hash
3 large potatoes
3 ribs of celery chopped
1 large onion chopped
2 large cloves of garlic
salt and pepper to taste
dash of basil
2 cans of chicken broth

Directions:
1. Fry the Garlic, celery, onion, and salt and pepper in a tbsp of garlic until veggies are tender.
2. Pour everything in the crock pot and turn on low for about 5-6 hours.

CROCK POT GROUND BEEF & POTATO DINNER

Ingredients:
1 1/2 lb. ground beef
1 large clove garlic
1/4 teaspoon pepper
1/2 teaspoon thyme
6 medium potatoes
2 large onions
1 can cream of mushroom soup (10 3/4 oz.)
1/2 cup water

Directions:
1. Cook ground beef and garlic in skillet until lightly browned. Stir in pepper and thyme.
2. Peel and slice potatoes and onions. Put 1/2 potatoes and onions into buttered crock pot. Add browned beef and top with remaining potatoes and onions.

3. Mix mushroom soup with water and spread over top of contents.
4. Cover and cook on low for 8 to 10 hours or on high for 3 to 4 hours.

CROCK POT HAMBURGER CASSEROLE
Ingredients:
2 lbs. browned ground beef
3 carrots, peeled and sliced
2 onions, sliced
4 potatoes, peeled and sliced
1 can peas, drained
2 stalks celery, diced
1 can cream of chicken soup
1 can water
Directions:
1. Place potatoes in bottom of crockpot, top with carrots and other vegetables.
2. Place ground beef on top. Combine soup and water and pour over ground beef.
3. Cover and cook on low for 6 to 8 hours.

CROCK POT MEATBALLS
Ingredients:
2 pounds Hamburger
1 cup Breadcrumbs
1 each Egg
Grated Parmesan cheese
Parsley and oregano
Onion and garlic powder
Milk
1 can Beer
1 bottle Ketchup, regular size
Directions:
1. Mix hamburg, breadcrumbs, egg, seasonings and milk together. Make small meatballs.
2. Mix ketchup and beer in the Crock Pot and start to heat. You can put the raw meatballs into the sauce and simmer for several hours or bake the meatballs first to get out most of the grease.

CROCK POT GARLIC POT ROAST
Ingredients:
3 lb. pork roast
1 Tablespoon vegetable oil
1 teaspoon salt
1/2 teaspoon pepper
1 medium onion, sliced
3 cloves garlic, peeled
1 cup chicken broth
Directions:
1. Brown pork roast in vegetable oil and sprinkle with salt and pepper.
2. Peel garlic and slice onion, place in bottom of Crock Pot. Place pork on top then pour broth over pork.
3. Cover and cook on low 8 to 10 hours.

CROCK POT GERMAN BEEF STEW
Ingredients:
1 1/2 lbs. beef chuck, cut in 2" cubes
2 Tablespoons flour
1/2 teaspoon celery salt
1/2 teaspoon garlic powder
1/2 teaspoon ground ginger
1/4 teaspoon ground black pepper
1 can (16 oz.) diced tomatoes, undrained
2 cups thinly sliced carrots
1 large potato, cut into chunks
1/4 cup sherry
1/4 cup dark molasses
1 cup water
Directions:
1. Place beef in slow cooker .
2. In a small bowl combine flour, celery salt, garlic powder, ground ginger, and pepper; sprinkle over beef.
3. In a medium bowl, combine tomatoes, carrots, potatoes, sherry, molasses, and water; pour over beef.
4. Cook on low setting for 6 to 8 hours. If desired, add 1/4 cups raisins 30 minutes before serving.

CROCK POT SWISS STEAK

Ingredients:
1 1/2 - 2 lb. round steak
2 Tablespoons flour
1 sliced green pepper
1 teaspoon salt
1/8 teaspoon pepper
2 Tablespoons salad oil
1 large onion, sliced
1 (16 oz.) can tomatoes, cut up
1 stalk celery, thinly sliced
1 Tablespoon thick bottled steak sauce

Directions:
1. Cut steak into serving size pieces. Coat with flour, salt and pepper.
2. In large skillet or slow cooking pot with browning unit, brown meat in oil. Pour off excessive fat.
3. In slow cooking pot, combine meat with tomatoes, onion, green pepper and steak sauce.
4. Cover pot and cook on low for 6 to 8 hours or until tender. Thicken juices with additional flour, dissolved in a small amount of water, if desired.

CROCK POT EASY SWISS STEAK

Ingredients:
2 to 2 1/2 lbs. round steak
1 pkg. onion soup mix
1/4 cup water
1 (10 oz.) can cream of mushroom soup

Directions:
1. Cut steak into 5 to 6 serving size pieces. Place in crock pot.
2. Add dry onion soup mix, water and soup. Cover and cook for 6 to 8 hours.

CROCK POT GRAPE JELLY MEATBALLS

Ingredients:
1 1/2 cups chili sauce
1 cup grape jelly (can use currant jelly)
1 to 3 teaspoons Dijon mustard
1 pound lean ground beef
1 egg, lightly beaten
3 Tablespoons fine dry bread crumbs
1/2 teaspoon salt

Directions:
1. Combine chili sauce, jelly, and mustard in Crock Pot and stir well. Cook, covered, on high while preparing meatballs.
2. Combine remaining ingredients and mix thoroughly. Shape into 30 meatballs.
3. Bake meatballs in a preheated 400 degree oven for 15 to 20 minutes; drain well.
4. Add meatballs to sauce, stir to coat, cover and cook on low for 6 to 10 hours.

CROCK POT GREEK STEW

Ingredients:
3 pounds of stewing beef
1 1/2 pounds small onions (about 7) 3 cloves garlic, minced
1- 28 oz. can tomatoes
1/2 cups beef stock
1- 5 1/2 oz. can tomato paste
2 Tablespoons red wine vinegar
2 teaspoons dried oregano
1/2 teaspoon each salt & pepper
1/2 cup all purpose flour
1/2 cup cold water
1 sweet green pepper, chopped
1/2 cup crumbled feta cheese
2 Tablespoons chopped fresh parsley

Directions:
1. Cut beef into 1 inch cubes, trimming off any fat.
2. Cut onions into wedges leaving root end intact.
3. Put meat and onions into slow cooker along with garlic and tomatoes.

4. Combine beef stock, vinegar, oregano, salt and pepper and add to slow cooker, stirring gently to blend.
5. Cook on Low for 8-9 hours or High for 6 hours.
6. Add flour and water mixture and chopped green pepper. Cook on high for 15 minutes or until thickened. Serve sprinkled with feta cheese and parsley.

CROCK POT MEXICAN POT ROAST

Ingredients:
3 lb. well trimmed boneless beef bottom round roast
1/2 teaspoon each salt and pepper
2 cupss bottled salsa
1 can (4 oz) chopped green chiles
1 can (16 oz) tomato paste
1/2 cup water
1 envelope (1.25 oz) taco seasoning mix

Directions:
1. Rub the roast with the salt and pepper and set aside. Mix remaining ingredients ina small bowl.
2. Pour half of the sauce into a 4 qt. or larger crockpot. Add the roast. Pour remaining sauce over the roast.
3. Cover and cook on low 8 to 10 hours or until meat is very tender. Remove roast from crock pot, skim fat off top of sauce.
4. Slice meat against the grain and serve with the sauce.

CROCK POT MEXICAN STYLE POT ROAST

Ingredients:
4 pounds chuck roast
1 teaspoon salt
1 teaspoon ground black pepper
2 Tablespoons olive oil
1 onion, chopped
1 1/4 cups diced green chile pepper
1 teaspoon chili powder
1 teaspoon ground cayenne pepper

3/4 cups hot pepper sauce
1 teaspoon garlic powder
water as needed

Directions:
1. Trim the roast of any excess fat and season with the salt and pepper.
2. Heat olive oil in a large skillet over medium high heat, then sear the meat on all sides. Transfer the roast to a slow cooker.
3. Add the onion, chile peppers, chili powder, cayenne pepper, hot pepper sauce and garlic powder.
4. Add enough water to cover 1/3 of the roast.
5. Cover slow cooker and cook on high setting for 6 hours, checking to make sure there is always at least a small amount of liquid in the bottom.
6. Reduce heat to low setting for 2 to 4 hours, or until meat is totally tender and falls apart.
7. Reserve any remaining liquid for a sauce and thicken, if desired.

CROCK POT SWEDISH MEATBALLS

Ingredients:
1 1/2 lbs. ground chuck
3/4 cup seasoned bread crumbs
1 small onion, diced
1 egg
1 1/2 teaspoons salt
3/4 teaspoon pepper
1 pkg. Lipton onion soup mix
1 can cranberry jelly sauce
1 bottle chili sauce

Directions:
1. Mix all ingredients above and form into balls. Brown in oven at 350 degrees for approximately 30 minutes.
2. Place meatballs into crock pot on low.
3. Make sauce by combining 1 can cranberry jelly sauce and 1 bottle chili

sauce, simmer on top of stove until melted together.
4. Pour sauce over meatballs. Slow cook for 2 to 3 hours

CROCK POT MANHATTAN MEATBALLS

Ingredients:
1 lb ground beef
1 lb. mild pork sausage (or use all beef)
2 cups soft bread crumbs or 1 1/2 cups oatmeal
2 eggs
1/2 cup chopped onion
2 Tablespoons parsley
2 teaspoons salt
1/2 teaspoons garlic salt Sauce:
1 (12 oz) jar apricot preserves
1/2 cup barbecue sauce

Directions:
1. Mix first 8 ingredients together and form meatballs. Brown in skillet, or in oven at 450 degrees for 15 minutes.
2. Heat sauce, pour over meatballs. Bake at 350 degrees for 25 minutes or cook in Crock Pot. Can be served over rice or as an appetizer with toothpicks.

CROCK POT MEATBALLS

Ingredients:
2 pounds Ground beef
1 medium Onion-grated or minced
20 Ritz crackers, crushed
1/4 teaspoon Black pepper
1/4 teaspoon Garlic salt
1/2 teaspoon Dry mustard
2 large Eggs, beaten
1 1/2 cups Bottled Barbecue Sauce
3/4 cup Tomato paste
1 teaspoon Liquid smoke
1/3 cup Catsup
1/3 cup Brown sugar
1/2 cup Water or as needed

Directions:
1. In a large bowl combine the ground beef, onion, crushed crackers, pepper, garlic salt, dry mustard and eggs.
2. Squish the mixture together by hand until well mixed and form into walnut sized balls.
3. Place them on a flat wire rack in a roasting pan or a large cake pan. Bake the meatballs in a 350 degree oven for 15 minutes, turn and bake for 15 minutes more.
4. In a Crock Pot combine the remaining ingredients. Cook on high 30 minutes. Add the meatballs and simmer for several hours.

CROCK POT LAYERED BEEF AND TATERS

Ingredients:
1 lb. ground beef
1 can tomato sauce
1 can mexi-corn drained
1/4 cup minced onion
1 teaspoon salt
Dash of pepper
1 1/2 cupss dried mashed potato flakes
1 1/2 cups sour cream
1/3 cup water
1 1/2 cups grated cheddar

Directions:
1. In skillet brown hamburger, and drain well.
2. Place beef in the crockpot add tomato sauce, corn, onion, salt and pepper. Mix well.
3. In bowl mix the potato flakes, with sour cream and water. Spread potato mixture over the beef. Top with grated cheese.
4. Cover and cook on Low for 7-10 hours.

CROCK POT LAYERED STEW

Ingredients:
Place in order in crock pot:
6 large potatoes, cubed
6 large carrots, diced
3 lbs. beef cubes
3 Tablespoons flour, sprinkled
3 diced onions
3 large celery ribs, diced
Heat together and pour over above

Ingredients:
1/3 cup soy sauce
1 teaspoon salt
1/2 teaspoon pepper
1 Tablespoon paprika
3 beef bouillon cubes or 3 teaspoons instant beef bouillon
1 (8 oz.) can tomato sauce
1 cup water
Cook on high 4-5 hours.

CROCK POT LAYERED ENCHILADA CASSEROLE

Ingredients:
1 can whole tomatoes
1 small onion, cut into pieces
1 clove garlic, minced
1/2 teaspoon ground red pepper
1/2 teaspoons salt
1 (6 oz.) can tomato paste
1 lb. ground beef, browned
2 cups shredded cheddar cheese
9 corn tortillas

Directions:
1. Blend tomatoes (undrained), onion and garlic in blender or food processor. Pour into med sauce pan.
2. Add red pepper, salt and tomato paste. Heat to a boil; simmer for 5-10 min.
3. Place 3 tortillas in bottom of crockpot. Layer on tortillas 1/3 of the ground beef, 1/3 of the sauce and 1/3 of the cheddar. Repeat layers two more times.
4. Cover and cook on Low 6-8 hours

CROCK POT SPICY MARMALADE MEATBALLS

Ingredients:
Meatballs:
2 lbs. ground beef (chuck)
1/2 cup bread crumbs
1 teaspoon Worcestershire sauce
1/2 teaspoon salt
1/4 teaspoon pepper
1 small onion, minced
1/2 teaspoon chili powder
1/4 teaspoon garlic powder
3 eggs
Sauce:
2 cups ketchup
1/4 cup Worcestershire sauce
1 jar orange marmalade (10 to 12 ounces)
dash cayenne, more or less to taste
1 teaspoon chili powder

Directions:
1. Combine sauce ingredients in slow cooker/Crock Pot; cover and cook on high while preparing meatballs.
2. Combine meatball ingredients. Heat a large skillet over medium high heat. Add meatballs; brown on all sides.
3. Place browned meatballs in a 325° oven and bake for 45 minutes.
4. Transfer meatballs to slow cooker/Crock Pot with a slotted spoon or drain on brown paper first.
5. Cover and reduce to LOW for 2 to 4 hours.

CROCK POT BEEF AND BRATWURST

Ingredients:
1 lb. beef roast, cubed
1 bratwurst
3 potatoes, cubed skin on
1/2 small white onion
3 medium portabello mushrooms quartered
1 packet of beef au jus mix
5 cups water

Directions:
1. Put water and au ju powder in crock pot first, stir it up so it's mixed properly,
then place everything else in the pot.
2. Cook on low until the meat is cooked, about 5 hours.
3. Turn up to high for 20-30 minutes before serving so it's nice and hot.

CROCK POT BEER BRAISED BEEF IN CROCK POT

Ingredients:
3 lb. lean beef stew meat cut into 1 1/2-inch pieces
1 teaspoon salt
1/2 teaspoon pepper
2 medium onions, thinly sliced
1 can mushrooms (or pieces) undrained (8-oz.)
1 can beer (12 oz.) dark or light, your choice
1 Tablespoon vinegar
2 beef bouillon cubes
2 teaspoons sugar
2 cloves garlic, minced
1 teaspoon thyme
2 bay leaves

Directions:
1. Put the beef in the crock pot. Combine all the other ingredients and pour over the beef.
2. Cook on low for 8-10 hours or on high for 4-5 hours.

CROCK POT BLACK FOREST POT ROAST

Ingredients:
3 lbs. Top Round Pot Roast
1 small onion
1 pack button mushrooms
3 Tablespoons water
1/4 cup ketchup
1/4 cup red wine
2 Tablespoons Dijon Mustard
1 Tablespoon Worcestershire Sauce
1/2 teaspoons table salt
1/8 teaspoon black pepper
1 clove garlic
2 Tablespoons cornstarch
3 Tablespoons water

Directions:
Trim all visible fat from meat; place in slow cooker.
2. In a small bowl, combine onion, water, mushrooms, ketchup, wine, mustard, Worcestershire Sauce, salt, pepper, and garlicup Pour over meat.
3. Cover and cook on LOW about 8 hours. Remove meat and slice. Keep meat warm and turn control to HIGH.
4. Dissolve cornstarch in water; stir into cooker. Cover and cook on High until thickened. Serve with Sauce.

CROCK POT BURRITOS

Ingredients:
2 lb. beef roast
1 chopped onion
1 can chopped peppers (10 oz.)
2 cans tomato sauce (4 oz. each)
1 Tablespoon chili powder
salt and pepper to taste

Directions:
1. The night before you plan to serve, put roast in crock pot and leave on low all night. Next morning, add the rest of the ingredients.
2. Cook on low all day.

3. Pre-heat oven to 350°. Spread cooked filling on extra large fat-free flour tortillas. You can add refried beans, sour cream, grated cheese and shredded lettuce as you prefer.

4. Fold and wrap in aluminum foil. Bake in preheated oven 10 to 15 minutes.Your favorite salsa can be added before or after baking.

CROCK POT GLAZED CORNED BEEF

Ingredients:

4 lb. Corned beef
1 1/2 teaspoons Horseradish
Water
2 Tablespoons Red wine vinegar
2 Tablespoons Prepared mustard
1/4 cup Molasses

Directions:

1. In crockpot cover corned beef with water. Cover and cook on low for 10 to 12 hours.

2. Drain cooked corned beef; place on broiler pan or oven proof platter.

3. Combine mustard, horseradish, wine vinegar, and molasses. Brush on all sides of meat.

4. Brown in 400°F oven for 20 minutes or until it begins to brown; brush with sauce several times while browning.

CROCK POT YANKEE POT ROAST AND VEGETABLES

Ingredients:

1 beef chuck pot roast (2½ pounds)
3 medium. baking potatoes unpeeled and cut into quarters (about 1 pound)
2 large carrots, cut into ¾-inch slices
2 ribs celery, cut into ¾-inch slices
1 medium onion, sliced
2 bay leaves
1 teaspoon dried rosemary leaves
½ teaspoon dried thyme leaves
½ cup reduced-sodium beef broth

Directions:

1. Trim excess fat from meat and discard. Cut into serving pieces; sprinkle with saltand pepper.

2. Combine vegetables, bay leaves, rosemary and thyme in crock pot.Place beef over vegetables in crock pot. Pour broth over beef.

3. Cover and cook onlow 8½ to 9 hours or until beef is fork-tender. Remove beef to serving platter. Arrange vegetables around beef. Remove and discard bay leaves

CROCK POT SWEET SAUERBRATEN

Ingredients:

3 lb. Rump or chuck pot roast
3 Potatoes, peeled & cubed
3 Carrots, peeled & sliced
2 Onions, sliced
10 1/2 oz. Can condensed consommé
1 cup Dry red wine
1/2 cup Red wine vinegar
1 Dill pickle, chopped
1/4 cup Water
1/4 cup Flour
6 Ginger snaps, crumbled
Salt and pepper to taste

Directions:

Put pot roast into crockpot. Arrange vegetables around meat. Add consommé, redwine, vinegar and pickle.

2. Cover and cook on high 6 to 8 hours.

3. Remove meat and vegetables from crockpot. Slice meat. Keep meat and vegetables warm.

4. In saucepan, blend flour and water, stir in juices from crockpot along with gingersnaps, and cook and stir over medium heat until sauce comes to boil and thickens.

5. Season to taste with salt and pepper. Spoon sauce over meat.

CROCK POT MEAT LOAF

Ingredients:
3 lbs. ground turkey or chicken
1 lb. ground hamburger
1 cup instant rice
1/4 cup A-1 steak sauce
2 whole eggs
1/4 cup flour, bread crumbs or crushed crackers or chips
Salt, pepper, onion powder, garlic powder to taste

Directions:
1. Combine all ingredients. Form into ball. Wrap well in foil. Poke small holes in bottom side of ball.
2. Place in crock pot on canning lids or something that will keep the meat above any drippings. Cook on low 8 hours.

CROCK POT MEATLOAF #1

Ingredients:
1 1/2 lb. ground beef
1 egg, beaten
1/2 cup bread crumbs
1/2 cup tomato juice
3 Tablespoons chopped onion
3 Tablespoons chopped bell pepper
3 Tablespoons chopped celery
2 Tablespoons seasoned salt
1/4 Tablespoon Thyme
Catsup or Chili Sauce
5 pepper rings

Directions:
1. Using a fork, mix all the ingredients, except catsup and pepper rings. Shape into a loaf and put into greased crockpot.
2. Top with catsup and pepper rings. Cover and cook on high for 1 hour, then on low 6-8 hours

CROCK POT MEATLOAF #2

Ingredients:
1 slice of bread
1/4 cup of milk
1 egg, beaten
1 medium onion, chopped
1-1/2 teaspoons curry powder
2 teaspoons lemon juice
1/4 cup chopped almonds
8 dried apricots, soaked and chopped
1/4 cup chutney
salt and pepper
1-1/2 lb. ground beef
2 bay leaves, broken in several places

Directions:
1. Soak bread in milk, squeeze dry. Mix egg with milk.
2. Add all ingredients, except bay leaves to ground beef; blend well. Shape into a loaf. Insert bay leaves in top of meat loaf.
3. Place in crockpot on sliced vegetables or accessory meat rack. Cover and cook on low setting for 8 to 10 hours. Remove bay leaves before serving.

CROCK POT MEATLOAF #3

Ingredients:
1 egg
1/4 cup milk
1/2 cup bread crumbs
1/4 cup finely chopped onion
2 Tablespoons finely chopped green pepper
saltpepper
1 1/2 lbs. ground beef
1/4 cup ketchup

Directions:
1. In a bowl, beat egg and milk. Stir in the bread crumbs, onion, green pepper, saltand pepper. Add the beef and mix well.
2. Shape into a loaf. Place in crockpot andspread ketchup on top of loaf.

3. Cover and cook on high one hour; reduce heat to low and cook another 7-8 hours.

CROCK POT PEPPERED BEEF BRISKET IN BEER

Ingredients:
1 (4 lb.) beef brisket
1 large onion sliced and separated into rings
3/4 teaspoon pepper
3 Tablespoons all-purpose flour
3 Tablespoons brown sugar
2 garlic cloves, minced
3/4 cup beer
1/2 cup chili sauce

Directions:
1. Trim fat from brisket; cut in half. Place onion rings in slow cooker. Sprinkle with pepper evenly over brisket.
2. Place brisket halves over onion rings.
3. Place flour, brown sugar and garlic in a small bowl, gradually add beer and chili sauce, stirring until well blended. Pour over brisket.
4. Cover with lid and cook on high setting for 1 hour then reduce to low setting and cook 6-8 hours our until tender.

CROCK POT PEPPER STEAK WITH RICE

Ingredients:
3 cups hot cooked rice
1 lb. round steak, cut into 1/2" thick strips
1 Tablespoon paprika
2 Tablespoons butter
1 1/2 cloves garlic, crushed
1 1/2 cups beef broth
1 cup onion, sliced
2 green peppers, sliced
2 Tablespoons cornstarch
1/4 cup each of water and soy sauce
2 large tomatoes, cut

Directions:
1. Sprinkle meat with paprika, and brown meat in butter. Add garlic and broth and cornstarch and cover until thickens.
2. Add everything (except the rice) to the crock pot, cook for 4-6 hours. Serve over rice.

CROCK POT LEMON PEPPER ROUND STEAK

Ingredients:
1-1/2 to 2 lbs round steak
2 Tablespoons vegetable oil
1/2 cup flour
1/4 teaspoon lemon pepper seasoning
1/2 teaspoon seasoned salt
1/3 cups water
1 can cream of celery soup

Directions:
1. Cut steak into cubes. Mix flour & seasonings. Coat meat thoroughly.
2. Heat oil in skillet and brown meat. Place browned meat in crockpot.
3. Combine water & soup. Pour over meat. Shake on additional lemon pepper and seasoned salt if desired.
4. Cook on low for 7-8 hours.

CROCK POT LEMON POT ROAST

Ingredients:
2 1/2 lb. Chuck roast
1 1/2 cups Water
1/2 cup Lemon juice
1 Onion, chopped
1 teaspoon Salt
1 teaspoon Celery salt
1 teaspoon Onion salt
1/4 teaspoon Black pepper
1/4 teaspoon Marjoram, ground
1 Garlic clove, crushed

Directions:
1. Put roast in a shallow pan or marinating container. In a medium bowl, combine remaining ingredients. Pour over roast.
2. Cover; refrigerate at least 4 or up to 24 hours. Remove roast from marinade; place in a crock pot.
3. Cover and cook on low 8 hrs, high 4 hrs, or until tender when pierced with fork.

CROCK POT
FRENCH DIP ROAST
Ingredients:
1 large onion, quartered and sliced
1 beef bottom round roast (about 3 lbs.)
1/2 cup dry white wine or water
1 pkg. (3/4 oz) au jus gravy mix
1/8 teaspoon seasoned pepper
Directions:
1. Place onion in crackpot. Trim excess fat from roast. Cut meat in half if needed to fit in crock pot. Place meat in crock pot over onions.
2. In a small bowl, combine wine (or water), au jus mix and pepper until blended. Pour over roast.
3. Cover andcook on high for 6 hours or on low for 12 hours (until very tender).
4. Remove meat from liquid. Let stand 5 minutes before thinly slicing across grain. Strain broth, if desired; taste for salt. Serve with hard French rolls for sandwiches... use liquid for dipping.

CROCK POT FRENCH DIP
SANDWICH #1
Ingredients:
1 lean beef roast (3 to 4 pounds)
1/2 cups light soy sauce
1 low-sodium beef bouillon cube
1 bay leaf
3 to 4 whole peppercorns
1 teaspoon each of dried rosemary, crushed, dried thyme and garlic powder
Bread OR rolls of your choice

Directions:
1. Remove and discard all visible fat from roast. Place in a slow cooker.
2. Combine soysauce, bouillon and spices; pour over roast. Add water to almost cover roast.
3. Cover and cook over low heat 10 - 12 hours or until meat is very tender.
4. Remove meat from broth; shred with a fork. Serve on bread or rolls.

CROCK POT FRENCH DIP
SANDWICH #2
Ingredients:
3-4 lb rump roast
1 pkg. au jus mix (dry)
1 pkg. Italian dressing mix (dry)
1 (10.5 oz) can beef broth
1 1/2 cups water
Green pepper, sliced thin (optional)
Onion, sliced thin (optional)
Hoagie buns, sourdough buns or your choice
Swiss Cheese (optional)
Directions:
1. Place roast in crock-pot. Mix next 4 ingredients and pour over meat.
2. Cook on LOWfor 8-10 hours.
3. Remove roast and if adding peppers and onions put those in thecrockpot and turn on HIGH until peppers just start to get limp.
4. Remove veggies and set aside. Reserve juice for serving.
5. Slice meat thinly or pull apart. Pile meat on buns with optional veggies and cover with cheese. Wrap in foil.
6. Heat in 350°F oven for 10 minutes. Serve on plate with cup of juice for dipping.

Crock Pot Chicken

CROCK POT CHICKEN CASSEROLE

Ingredients:
4 large chicken breasts
1 small can cream of chicken soup
1 small can cream of celery soup
1 small can cream of mushroom soup
1/2 cup diced celery
1 cup Minute Rice

Directions:
1. Mix in crock pot the soups and rice. Place chicken on top of mixture, then sprinkle diced celery over chicken.
2. Cook on low for 4 hours.

CROCK POT STUFFED CHICKEN BREAST

Ingredients:
3-4 boneless whole chicken breasts
Stuffing of your choice

Directions:
1. Prepare dressing. If using package mix, 1/2 of package should be enough. (May use applesauce instead of water in dressing.)
2. Roll dressing up in breast and close with toothpick.
3. Brown in butter or margarine in hot pan. When brown, cover with paprika and place in crock pot.
3. Cover chicken with 2 cans cream of celery soup. Turn on high for 5 or more hours.

CROCK POT ZESTY CHICKEN

Ingredients:
1 chicken, cut to suit
1 can Campbell's mushrooms
1 can tomato soup
1 cup milk

Directions:
1. Cut chicken and brown in skillet or oven. Prepare mixture of soups and milk; combine ingredients.
2. Simmer in a crock pot 2 hours. Serve with mashed potatoes and green beans.

CROCK POT CHICKEN AND CORNMEAL DUMPLINGS

Ingredients:
1 (9 oz.) pkg. frozen cut green beans
2 cups cubed, cooked chicken
2 cups diced potatoes
1 (13 3/4 oz.) can chicken broth
1 (12 oz.) can vegetable juice cocktail (1 1/2 cup)
1 teaspoon chili powder
6 drops bottled hot pepper sauce
1/3 cup yellow cornmeal
2 Tablespoons snipped parsley
1/2 cup sliced celery
1/2 cup chopped onion
1/2 teaspoon salt
1 1/4 cups packaged biscuit mix
1 cup sharp shredded American cheese
2/3 cup milk

Directions:
1. Thaw beans by placing in strainer and run hot water over beans. Transfer to crock pot.
2. Add chicken, potatoes, chicken broth, vegetable juice, celery, onion, chili powder, salt and hot pepper sauce, mixed together. Cover.
3. Cook on low for 4 hours. Turn to high heat and heat until bubbly. Add water at this point if needed.
4. Combine biscuit mix, cornmeal, 1/2 cup cheese and parsley. Add milk and stir until just moistened.

5. Drop by tablespoons onto stew; cover. Cook 2 1/2 hours more (don't lift cover). Sprinkle dumplings with rest of cheese.

CROCK POT CHICKEN
Ingredients:
1 can cream of chicken soup
1/2 can milk
1/2 can water
Salt & pepper
Poultry seasoning
Directions:
1. Brown chicken, place in crock pot.
2. Combine cream of chicken soup, milk, water, salt, pepper and poultry seasoning.
3. Pour over chicken. Cook 4 to 6 hours on low. Serve over noodles or rice.

CROCK POT CHICKEN TORTILLAS
Ingredients:
Meat from 1 whole chicken OR canned chicken or parts
1 can cream of chicken soup
1/2 cup green chili salsa
2 Tablespoons quick cooking tapioca
1 medium onion, chopped
1 1/2 cup grated cheese
1 dozen corn tortillas
Black olives
Directions:
1. Tear chicken into bite size pieces, mix with soup, chili, salsa and tapioca.
2. Line bottom of crock pot with 3 corn tortillas, torn into bite size pieces.
3. Add 1/3 of the chicken mixture. Sprinkle with 1/3 of the onion and 1/3 of the grated cheese. Repeat layers of tortillas topped with chicken mixture, onions and cheese.
4. Cover and cook on low 6 to 8 hours or high for 3 hours. Garnish with sliced black olives.

CROCK POT RUBY CHICKEN
Ingredients:
2 lb. chicken pieces
1 medium onion, chopped
2 Tablespoons Oil
2 teaspoons salt
1 teaspoon pumpkin pie spice
1 can Orange juice, concentrated
2 teaspoons grated orange peel
1 lb. whole cranberries
1 cup sugar
Directions:
1. Night before: Chop onions, thaw orange juice and chicken, measure spices.
2. In the morning: Add ingredients to crockpot. Cook on low 8-10 hours, till done. Serve over hot cooked rice.

CROCK POT ROAST CHICKEN
Ingredients:
1 whole chicken
salt & pepper
parsley
dried seasoning, i.e. oregano, basil, rosemary
butter
Directions:
1. Rinse chicken thoroughly. Sprinkle cavity with salt, pepper and parsley.
2. Put in crock pot breast side up. Sprinkle a little salt & pepper on it with seasoning of your choice. Dot breast with butter.
3. Do not add any liquid. Cook on high one hour and low for 10-12 hours.

CROCK POT ROAST STICKY CHICKEN

Ingredients:

4 teaspoons salt
2 teaspoons paprika
1 teaspoon cayenne pepper
1 teaspoon onion powder
1 teaspoon thyme
1 teaspoon white pepper
1/2 teaspoon garlic powder
1/2 teaspoon black pepper
1 large roasting chicken
1 cup chopped onion

Directions:

1. In a small bowl, thoroughly combine all the spices. Remove giblets from chicken, clean the cavity well and pat dry with paper towels.
2. Rub the spice mixture into the chicken, both inside and out, making sure it is evenly distributed and down deep into the skin.
3. Place in a resealable plastic bag, seal and refrigerate overnight.
4. When ready to cook chicken put the onions into the cavity, put the chicken into thecrockpot and do not add any liquid (as the cooking process goes on it will produce it's own juices).
5.   Cook on low 8 to 10 hours.

CROCK POT ROBUSTO CHICKEN

Ingredients:

2-4 boneless, skinless chicken breasts
1 bottle Seven Seas Robusto Italian dressing
1 lb. bag egg noodles
4 oz. sour cream
1/2 cup Parmesan cheese

Directions:

1. Place chicken breasts in crock pot. Pour Italian dressing over.
2. Cover and cook on low 7 hours or high 3 1/2 hours.

3. Remove chicken from crock pot and leave turned on. Add 1/2 the sour cream and stir until dissolved.
4. Cook noodles and drain. Add remaining sour cream and the Parmesan cheese to noodles and mix until dissolved.
5. Serve chicken over the noodles. Pour warm Italian dressing over top. Sprinkle with Parmesan cheese to taste

CROCK POT ROSEMARY CHICKEN WITH PASTA

Ingredients:

2 medium onions, sliced or chopped
2 teaspoons bottled minced garlic or 4 cloves garlic, minced
3/4 lb. skinless, boneless chicken breasts or thighs
1 (14.5 oz) can diced tomatoes
1 (6 oz) can tomato paste
2 Tablespoons wine vinegar
2 bay leaves
1 teaspoon sugar
1/2 teaspoon dried rosemary, crushed or
1 Tablespoon fresh
1/4 teaspoon salt
1/4 teaspoon pepper1 (4 oz) can sliced mushrooms, drained
1 pkg. (8 oz) dried pasta (penne, mostaccioli, or elbow macaroni)
Grated Parmesan cheese

Directions:

1. In a 3-1/2 to 4-1/2 quart crockpot, place the onions and garlicup Add chicken to crockpot.
2. In a mixing bowl combine undrained tomatoes, tomato paste, vinegar,bay leaves, sugar, rosemary, salt, and pepper; mix well.
3. Pour over chicken. Cover and cook on LOW heat setting for 7 hours. Or, cook on HIGH heat settingfor 3-1/2 hours.
4. When ready to serve, remove bay leaves. Stir mushrooms into chicken mixture; cook for 5 to 10 minutes more to

heat through.

5. Cook pasta according to package directions. Serve the chicken and sauce over the hot cooked pasta; sprinkle with Parmesan cheese.

CROCK POT SAUCY CHICKEN

Ingredients:

6 drumsticks (skinned)
6 thighs (skinned)
1 (14 oz.) can of diced tomatoes with garlic (undrained)
1 can tomato paste
2 teaspoons chicken bouillon granules
1/4 cup chopped onion, dried
1/4 teaspoon crushed red pepper
1/2 teaspoon Italian seasoning
1/2 teaspoon garlic powder

Directions:

1. Mix ingredients and pour over chicken. Heat in crock pot for 1 hour on high heat then on low for 4 to 5 hours or until chicken is tender.

CROCK POT SAUCY CHICKEN THIGHS

Ingredients:

3 lbs. bone in/skinless chicken thighs
1 can Italian style diced tomatoes
1 can tomato sauce
1 chopped onion
2 cloves minced garlic
salt and pepper to taste
1 teaspoon Italian Seasoning

Directions:

1. Layer all ingredients in crock pot and cook on high 1 hour then low 6 hours.
2. Serve with spinach fettuccini, mashed potatoes or rice.

CROCK POT SMOTHERED CHICKEN

Ingredients:

4 chicken breasts, skinless & boneless
12 oz. Baby Bella mushrooms, sliced

1 can Cream of Chicken Soup
1 can Cream of Mushroom Soup
1 can French Onion Soup
1 large onion, sliced
assortment of vegetables

Directions:

1. Cut the chicken into bite size chunks and quickly brown in a small amount of olive oil.
2. Remove from pan, set aside and brown onion until almost soft. Add mushrooms and sauté for additional 5 minutes.
3. Layer vegetables in bottom of crock, add some of the onion/mushrooms, then all of the chicken. Top with rest of onions/mushrooms.
4. Empty all three soups into sauté pan. Stir and deglaze thoroughly then pour over chicken.
5. Cook on high for 2 hours, then on low for another 2-1/2 hours.

CROCK POT SOUR CREAM SALSA CHICKEN

Ingredients:

4 skinless boneless chicken breast halves
1 package taco seasoning mix
1 cup salsa
2 Tablespoons cornstarch
1/4 cup light sour cream

Directions:

1. Spray the crockpot with cooking spray. Add the chicken breasts. Sprinkle withTaco Seasoning. Top with salsa.
2. Cook on low for 6-8 hours.
3. When ready to serve, remove the chicken from the pot.
4. Place about 2 Tablespoons cornstarch in a small amount of water. Stir well. Stir the cornstarch mixture into salsa sauce.
5. Stir in 1/4 cup of sour cream. Serve.

CROCK POT SOUTHWESTERN CHICKEN STEW

Ingredients:
3 boneless skinless chicken breasts
1 can Rotel tomatoes
1 can black beans or 1 can of red beans
2 cans cream of mushroom or cream of chicken soup
2 cans of corn or one bag of frozen corn
2 cups of water or chicken broth

Directions:
1. Put all ingredients in crock pot. Do not drain cans of corn and beans.
2. Cook on low for about 8 hours. If using whole pieces of chicken, take them out, cut them up, and put them back into the crock pot.

CROCK POT SOY CHICKEN #1

Ingredients:
1 whole chicken, cut into 8 pieces
2 cups chicken broth
1/4 cup soy sauce
1/4 cup Worcestershire sauce
5 or 6 small to mededium potatoes
2-4 carrots
1/2 onion, chopped
1 garlic clove, chopped
1/2 teaspoon oregano
1 Tablespoon oil

Directions:
1. Brown chicken in oil in a skillet. Chop potatoes into bite size pieces, dice carrots and onion.
2. Put veggies, including garlic cloves, into crock pot; add seasonings, soy and Worcestershire sauce. Mix.
3. Add chicken and pour broth over all. Cook on high about 5 hrs, low about 8.

CROCK POT SOY CHICKEN #2

Ingredients:
5 lbs. skinless chicken thighs
1 cup ketchup
1 cup soy sauce
1 cup sugar

Directions:
1. In the crock pot mix together the ketchup, soy sauce and sugar.
2. Wash the chicken and add to the sauce and mix well.
3. Cook on low heat 7-8 hours.

CROCK POT SWEET AND SOUR CHICKEN

Ingredients:
2 Tablespoons ketchup
1 cup water
1/2 cup white vinegar
1 Tablespoon soy sauce
1 cup brown sugar, packed
1 1/2 lbs. chicken breasts (boneless skinless, cubed)
2 Tablespoons Cornstarch
2 Tablespoons water

Directions:
1. Combine first 5 ingredients in the crock pot and mix well.
2. Add chicken and cook on lowfor 6-8 hours OR on high for 3-4 hours.
3. Combine cornstarch and water in small bowl. Stir into slow cooker. Cook on high setting for about 15-20 minutes, stirring often, until thickened.

CROCK POT SWEET AND TANGY CHICKEN

Ingredients:

8 skinless, boneless chicken breasts, divided
2 (18 ounce) bottles prepared barbecue sauce
1 (15 ounce) can pineapple chunks, juice reserved
1 green bell pepper, sliced
1 onion, chopped
2 cloves garlic, minced

Directions:

1. Place 4 of the chicken breasts in the bottom of a slow cooker.
2. In a large bowl, combine the barbecue sauce, pineapple, green bell pepper, onion and garlicup
3. Mix well and pour half of this mixture over the chicken in the slow cooker.
4. Place the remaining chicken in the slow cooker and top with the remaining sauce.
5. Cook on low setting for 8 to 9 hours.

CROCK POT SWISS CHICKEN CASSEROLE

Ingredients:

6 chicken breasts, boneless and skinless
6 slices Swiss cheese
1 can cream of mushroom soup
1/4 cup milk
2 cups stuffing mix
1/2 cup butter or margarine, melted

Directions:

1. Lightly grease crock pot or spray with cooking spray. Place chicken breasts in pot.Top with cheese.
2. Combine soup and milk, stirring well. Spoon over cheese; sprinkle with stuffing mix. Drizzle melted butter over stuffing mix.
3. Drizzle melted butter over stuffing mix.
4. Cook on low 8 to 10 hours or high 4 to 6 hours.

CROCK POT VEGGIE AND CHINESE CHICKEN

Ingredients:

Chicken breast - (chopped)
Cabbage - 2 cups chopped
Red and green peppers - 1 each (chopped)
White onion - 1 (chopped)
Chinese peppercorn - 1 teaspoon (ground)
Honey - 1 Tablespoon
Soy sauce - 2 Tablespoons
Salt - 1 to 2 teaspoons
Diced ginger - 1 Tablespoon
Chicken soup stock - 1 to 2 cups
Corn starch - 2 Tablespoons + 1/4cup water

Directions:

1. Mix all the ingredients in the slow cooker (but not the starch and water), and cook on low for 6 to 8 hours.
2. In the last 30 minutes mix the starch and water into the pot. Serve.

CROCK POT ANGEL CHICKEN

Ingredients:

6 boneless chicken breasts
1/2 cup butter
1 pkg. dry Italian salad dressing mix
1 can golden mushroom soup
1/2 cup white wine (cooking wine or regular drinking wine)
4 oz. onion & chive cream cheese
1 pkg angel hair pasta (cook according to box directions)

Directions:

1. Place chicken in crock pot.
2. In sauce pan melt butter. Stir in Italian salad dressing mix, soup, cream cheese & wine. Pour over chicken.
3. Cook on low for 4-5 hours. Pour over cooked angel hair pasta.

CROCK POT HOMESTYLE CHICKEN

Ingredients:
1 frying chicken, cut up
Salt & pepper
1 can cream of mushroom soup
1/2 cup sauterne or sherry
2 Tablespoons butter or margarine, melted
2 Tablespoons dry Italian salad dressing mix
2 (3 oz.) pkgs. cream cheese, cut in cubes
1 Tablespoon onion, chopped

Directions:
1. Wash chicken and pat dry. Brush with butter. Sprinkle with salt and pepper.
2. Place in crock pot. Sprinkle with dry salad mix.
3. Cover and cook on low for 5 to 6 hours.
4. About 3/4 hour before serving, mix soup, cream cheese, wine, and onion in small saucepan. Cook until smooth.
5. Pour over chicken in pot. Cover and cook for 30 minutes on low. Serve with sauce. Serve with rice or noodles.

CROCK POT CHICKEN IN MUSHROOM GRAVY

Ingredients:
3 whole chicken breasts, halved
1/4 cup dry white wine or chicken broth
1 can cream of chicken soup
1 (4 oz.) can mushrooms, sliced
Salt & pepper

Directions:
1. Place chicken pieces in crock pot. Season with salt and pepper.
2. Mix wine and soup, pour over chicken. Add mushrooms.
3. Cover and cook on low for 7 to 9 hours or high 3 to 4 hours.

CROCK POT BARBECUE CHICKEN I

Ingredients:
1 Chicken, cut up and skin removed
1 cup ketchup
3/4 cup brown sugar
3 Tablespoons Worcestershire sauce

Directions:
1. Place chicken in crockpot. Combine remaining ingredients and pour over chicken.
2. Cook 4 hours on high or 8-10 hours on low.

CROCK POT BARBECUE CHICKEN II

Ingredients:
4-6 pieces chicken
1 bottle BBQ sauce
1/2 cup white vinegar
1/2 cup brown sugar
1 teaspoon mesquite seasoning
1/2 teaspoon garlic powder
1/2-1 teaspoon red pepper flakes

Directions:
1. Mix BBQ sauce with all other ingredients. Place chicken in crockpot. Pour sauce over all.
2. Cook slowly on low heat in crockpot about 4-6 hours. Serve with baked beans, potato salad and coleslaw.

CROCK POT BARBECUE CHICKEN III

Ingredients:
1 frying chicken cut up or quartered
1 can condensed tomato soup
3/4 cup chopped onion
1/4 cup vinegar
3 Tablespoons brown sugar
1 Tablespoon Worcestershire sauce
1/2 teaspoon salt
1/4 teaspoon sweet basil
1/4 teaspoon thyme

Directions:
1. Place chicken in slow cooker. Combine all other ingredients and pour over chicken.
2. Cover tightly and cook on low for 6-8 hours.

CROCK POT CHEESY CHICKEN
Ingredients:
3 whole boneless chicken breasts
2 cans cream chicken soup
1 can chedder cheese soup
Directions:
1. Remove all fat and skin from chicken; rinse and pat dry, sprinkle with salt, pepper and garlic powder.
2. Put in crockpot and add the three soups straight from the cans.
3. Cook on low all day (at least 8 hrs) do not lift the lid. Serve over rice or noodles.

CROCK POT CHICKEN CACCIATORE
Ingredients:
one whole chicken, cut up
one large undrained can of cut-up tomatoes
one cut-up onion
one cut-up green pepper
minced garlic (to taste)
one Tablespoon Italian herbs
red pepper flakes to taste
Directions:
1. Place cut up chicken in slow cooker/Crock Pot.
2. Cover with all ingredients.
3. Cook all on low 6-8 hours until falling apart.

CROCK POT CHICKEN CASSEROLE
Ingredients:
1 8 oz. pkg noodles
3 cups diced cooked chicken
1/2 cup diced celery
1/2 cup diced green pepper
1/2 cup diced onion
1 4 oz. can mushrooms
1 4 oz. jar pimiento
1/2 cup parmesan cheese
1 1/2 cups cream style cottage cheese
1 cup grated charp process cheese
1 can cream of chicken soup
1/2 cup chicken broth
2 Tablespoons melted butter
1/2 teaspoon basil
Directions:
1. Cook noodles according to pkg. directions and drain and rinse thoroughly.
2. In a large bowl, combine remaining ingredients with noodles until well mixed.
3. Pour mixture into greased crockpot. Cover and cook on low for 6-8 hours or high 3-4 hours.

CROCK POT CHICKEN TORTILLAS
Ingredients:
meat from 1 whole chicken
1 can cream of chicken soup
1/2 cup green chili salsa
2 Tablespoons quick cooking tapioca
1 medium onion, chopped
1 1/2 cup grated cheese
1 dozen corn tortillas
Black olives
Directions:
1. Tear chicken into bite size pieces, mix with soup, chili, salsa and tapioca.
2. Line bottom of crock pot with 3 corn tortillas, torn into bite size pieces. Add 1/3 of the chicken mixture. Sprinkle with 1/3 of the onion and 1/3 of the grated cheese.
3. Repeat layers of tortillas topped with chicken mixture, onions and cheese.
4. Cover and cook on low 6 to 8 hours or high for 3 hours. Garnish with sliced black olives.

CROCK POT CHICKEN WINGS IN BBQ SAUCE

Ingredients:

3 pounds chicken wings (16 wings)
salt and pepper to taste
1 1/2 cups any variety barbecue sauce
1/4 cup honey
2 teaspoons prepared mustard or spicy mustard
2 teaspoons Worcestershire sauce
Tabasco to taste, optional

Directions:

1. Rinse chicken and pat dry. Cut off and discard wing tips. Cut each wing at joint to make two sections.
2. Sprinkle wing parts with salt and pepper. Place wings on a broiler pan. Broil 4-5 inches from the heat for 20 minutes, 10 minutes for each side or until chicken is brown.
3. Transfer chicken to slow cooker/Crock Pot.
4. For sauce, combine barbecue sauce, honey, mustard, Worcestershire sauce and if more heat is desired...Tabasco to taste in a small mixing bowl.
5. Pour over chicken wings. Cover and cook on low for 4-5 hours or on High 2 -2 1/2 hours. Serve directly from slow cooker/Crock Pot.

CROCK POT CHICKEN WINGS IN TERIYAKI SAUCE

Ingredients:

3 pounds chicken wings (16 wings)
1 large onion, chopped
1 cup soy sauce
1 cup brown sugar
2 teaspoons ground ginger
2 cloves garlic, minced
1/4 cup dry cooking sherry

Directions:

1. Rinse chicken and pat dry. Cut off and discard wing tips. Cut each wing at joint to make two sections.

2. Place wing parts on broiler pan. Broil 4-5 inches from the heat for 20 minutes, 10 minutes for each side or until chicken is brown.
3. Transfer chicken to slow cooker/Crock Pot. Mix together onion, soy sauce, brown sugar, ginger, garlic and cooking sherry in bowl.
4. Pour over chicken wings. Cover and cook on Low 5-6 hours or on HIGH 2-3 hours. Stir chicken wings once to ensure wings are evenly coated with sauce.
5. Serve from Slow Cooker.

CROCK POT CHICKEN AND STUFFING

Ingredients:

4 Chicken Breasts, Boned and Skinned
4 Slices Swiss Cheese
1 Can Cream of Chicken soup
1 Can Cream of Mushroom soup
1 Cup Chicken Broth
1/4 Cup Milk
2 Cups Pepperidge Farm Herb Stuffing Mix
1/2 Cup Melted butter
Salt and pepper to taste

Directions:

1. Season chicken breasts with salt and pepper and place chicken breasts in crockpot.
2. Pour chicken broth over chicken breasts. Put one slice of Swiss cheese oneach breast.
3. Combine both cans of soup and milk. Cover chicken breasts with soup mixture.
4. Sprinkle stuffing mix over all. Drizzle melted butter on top.
5. Cook on low for 6-8 hours.

CROCK POT CHICKEN CHILI
Ingredients:
2 whole chicken breasts, skinned, deboned, cut in 1/2" chunks
Celery heart
1 medium onion
2 cans stewed tomatoes, sliced
16 oz. medium salsa or picante sauce
1 can chick peas (or 1 pkg. pkg. white kidney beans)
6 oz. mushrooms
Olive oil
Directions:
1. Brown chicken in 1 tablespoon olive oil.
2. Chop celery, onion and mushrooms. Combine all ingredients in large slow cooker/Crock Pot, stir and simmer on low heat for 6-8 hours.
3. Serve with bread or taco chips.

CROCK POT CHICKEN CURRY
Ingredients:
2 whole chicken breasts, boned
1 can cream of chicken soup
1/4 cup dry sherry
2 Tablespoons butter or margarine
2 green onions with tops, finely chopped
1 teaspoon curry powder
1 teaspoon salt
Dash of pepper
Fluffy rice
Directions:
1. Cut chicken into small pieces, place in crock pot. Add all remaining ingredients except rice.
2. Cover and cook on high setting 2 1/2 to 4 hours. Serve over hot rice.

CROCK POT CHICKEN MERLOT WITH MUSHROOMS
Ingredients:
2 1/2 to 3 lbs. meaty chicken pieces, skinned
3 cups sliced fresh mushrooms

1 large onion, chopped
2 cloves garlic, minced
3/4 cup chicken broth
1 6-ounce can tomato paste
1/4 cup dry red wine (such as Merlot) or chicken broth
2 Tablespoons quick-cooking tapioca
2 Tablespoons snipped fresh basil or 1 1/2 teaspoon dried basil, crushed
2 teaspoons sugar
1/4 teaspoon salt
1/4 teaspoon pepper
2 cups hot cooked noodles
2 Tablespoon finely shredded Parmesan cheese
Directions:
1. Rinse chicken; set aside. In a 3 1/2-4- or 5-quart crock pot place mushrooms, onion, and garlic.
2. Place chicken pieces on top of the vegetables. In a bowl combine broth, tomato paste, wine or chicken broth, tapioca, dried basil (if using), sugar, salt, and pepper. Pour over all.
3. Cover; cook on low-heat setting for 7 to 8 hours or on high-heat setting for 3 1/2 to 4 hours. If using, stir in fresh basil.
4. To serve, spoon chicken, mushroom mixture, and sauce over hot cooked noodles. Sprinkle with Parmesan cheese.

CROCK POT CHICKEN OR TURKEY PIE
Ingredients:
3 cups diced cooked chicken or turkey
2 cans (14 1/2 ounce each) chicken broth
1/2 teaspoon salt
1/2 teaspoon pepper
1 stalk celery, thinly sliced
1 medium onion, chopped
1 bay leaf
3 cups potatoes, peeled and cubed
1 package frozen mixed veggies (16 oz.)
1 cup milk
1 cup flour

1 teaspoon pepper
1/2 teaspoon salt
1 9-inch refrigerated pie crust
Directions:
1. In Crock Pot, combine chicken, broth, 1/2 teaspoon salt, 1/2 teaspoon pepper, celery, onion, bay leaf, potatoes, and mixed vegetables.
2. Cover and cook on low 8 to 10 hours or on high 4 to 6 hours. Remove bay leaf.
3. Preheat oven to 400 degrees.
4. In a small bowl, mix milk and flour. Gradually stir flour and water mixture into Crock Pot. Stir in pepper, poultry seasoning, and salt.
5. Remove the liner from Crock Pot base and carefully place 9-inch pie crust over the mixture.
6. Place the crock pot liner inside preheated oven and bake (uncovered) for about 15 minutes, or until browned.
*If your liner is not removable, put the mixture in a casserole dish, cover with the pie crust and bake as above.

CROCK POT CHICKEN WITH CHEESE SAUCE
Ingredients:
2 chicken breast halves
1 can cream of chicken soup
white wine
Directions:
1. Place two chicken breast halves in crock pot (frozen or thawed).
2. Mix together one can cream of chicken soup & half soup can of white wine; pour over chicken.
3. Place two slices Swiss cheese over top of chicken breasts (processed cheese melts and blends more easily).
4. Cook in crock pot for 2-3 hours (on high) or 3-4 hours (on low). Serve over steamed rice.

CROCK POT CHILI CHICKEN
Ingredients:
3 whole chicken breasts (1 1/2 to 2 lbs, cut in 1 inch pieces)
1 cup chopped onion
1 cup chopped bell pepper
2 garlic cloves
2 Tablespoons vegetable oil
2 cans Mexican stewed tomatoes (16 ounce each)
1 can chili beans
2/3 cup picante sauce
1 teaspoon chili powder
1 teaspoon cumin
1/2 teaspoon salt
Directions:
1. Saute chicken, onion, pepper, garlic in vegetable oil until vegetables are wilted.
2. Transfer to slow cooker/Crock Pot and add remaining ingredients. Cook, covered, on low, for 4 to 6 hours. Serve over rice.

CROCK POT CREAM CHEESE CHICKEN
Ingredients:
1 frying chicken, cut up
2 Tablespoons melted butter
salt and pepper to taste
1 package of dry Italian seasoning mix
1 can cream of chicken soup
1 8 oz brick of cream cheese, cut up in cubes
1/2 cup chicken broth
1 large onion
crushed garlic to taste
Directions:
1. Brush chicken with butter and sprinkle with the dry Italian seasoning mix.
2. Cover and cook on low for 6-7 hours.
3. About 45 minutes before done, brown the onion in the butter and then add the cream cheese, soup, and chicken broth to the saucepan.

4. Add the crushed garlic and stir all ingredients until smooth. Add salt and pepper to taste.

5. Pour sauce mixture over chicken in crock pot and cook an additional 30-45 minutes.

6. Remove chicken to platter and stir sauce before putting in gravy.

CROCK POT CHIPOTLE CHICKEN

Ingredients:

4 boneless chicken breasts
1 can of enchilada sauce
2 or 3 regular jars of salsa (you can add a chipotle chili or two in the sauce)

Directions:

1. Cook on high for 5 hours when chicken is frozen.

2. Take meat out and shred.

3. Stir box of instant rice into salsa, let cook, and serve as the side dish.

4. Serve the chicken on tortillas with whatever toppings you'd like.

CROCK POT COUNTRY CAPTAIN CHICKEN BREASTS

Ingredients:

2 medium-size Granny Smith apples
1 small onion, finely chopped
1 small green bell pepper, seeded and finely chopped
3 cloves garlic, minced or pressed
2 Tablespoons dried currants
1 Tablespoon curry powder
1 teaspoon ground ginger
1/4 teaspoon ground red pepper (cayenne)
1 can (about 14 1/2 oz.) diced tomatoes
6 small skinless, boneless chicken breast halves (about 1 3/4 lbs. total)
1/2 cup chicken broth
1 cup long-grain white rice
1 pound large raw shrimp, shelled and deveined
1/3 cup slivered almonds
Salt
Chopped parsley

Directions:

1. Quarter, core, and dice unpeeled apples. In a 4-quart or larger electric slow cooker, combine apples, onion, bell pepper, garlic, currants, curry powder, ginger, and red pepper; stir in tomatoes. Rinse chicken and pat dry; then arrange, overlapping pieces slightly, on top of tomato mixture. Pour in broth. Cover and cook at low setting until chicken is very tender when pierced (6 to 7 hours).

2. Carefully lift chicken to a warm plate, cover lightly, and keep warm in a 200 degree oven. Stir rice into cooking liquid. Increase cooker heat setting to high; cover and cook, stirring once or twice, until rice is almost tender to bite (30 to 35 minutes). Stir in shrimp, cover and cook until shrimp are opaque in center; cut to test (about 10 more minutes).

3. Meanwhile, toast almonds in a small nonstick frying pan over medium heat until golden brown (5 to 8minutes), stirring occasionally. Set aside.

4. To serve, season rice mixture to taste with salt. Mound in a warm serving dish; arrange chicken on top. Sprinkle with parsley and almonds.

CROCK POT CRANAPPLE CHICKEN BREAST BAKE

Ingredients:

4 to 6 boneless, skinless chicken breast halves
4 to 6 green onions
1/2 cup dried sweetened cranberries
1/2 cup chopped dried apple
1 clove garlic very thinly sliced
2 Tablespoons brown sugar
2 Tablespoons water
1 teaspoon lemon juice
2 teaspoons butter

Directions:

1. Place chicken breasts in a 2-quart (or larger) crockpot.
2. Add remaining ingredients in the order given, dotting evenly with the butter last.
3. Cover and cook on low for 6to 7 hours. Serve over rice.

CROCK POT CRANAPPLE SAUCE

Ingredients:

10-12 medium apples
1-2 cups cranberry juice
lemon juice, 1/4 to 1/2 lemon
2 Tablespoons sugar
1/4 to 1/2 cup dried cranberries

Directions:

1. Wash the apples and chop them up without peeling. Squeeze lemon juice over them as you cut them.
2. Put apples in crockpot with cranberry juice -- use 1 cup if you want the applesauce thick, more if you want it thin.
3. Stir in sugar to suit your taste. Let apples stew on low for 6-8 hours.
4. About an hour or two before serving, stir in cranberries or craisins.

CROCK POT CREAMY CHICKEN AND RICE

Ingredients:

chicken tenders (3 per person)
cream of mushroom soup (1 can for 2-3 people, 2 for 4-6)
Mrs. Grass Onion Soup Mix (1 per each can of soup)
1 Tablespoon olive oil
long grain brown rice (1 cup per can of soup)
1 Tablespoon whole thyme, crushed
salt and pepper to taste
broccoli florettes (optional)
diced red pepper (optional)

Directions:

1. Heat olive oil in a saute pan, and add rice until it begins to crackle, but not brown.
2. Whisk together the soups and additional water, herbs and seasonings.
3. Combine all ingredients (except veggies) in crock pot, and cook on high 4-6 hours, or 8-10 hours on low.
4. During last 30-45 minutes, add desired veggies.

CROCK POT ARROZ CON POLLO

Ingredients:

4 Chicken breast halves, skin and excess fat removed
1/4 teaspoon salt
1/4 teaspon pepper
1/4 teaspoon paprika
1 tablespoon oil
1 medium onion, chopped
1 small red pepper, chopped 1 clove of garlic, minced
1/2 teaspoon dried rosemary leaves
1 14 1/2 ounce can crushed tomatoes
1 10 oz package frozen peas

Directions:
1. Season chicken with salt, pepper, and paprika.
2. In a medium skillet, heat oil over medium-high heat. Add chicken and brown. Put chicken in the crock pot.
3. In a small bowl, combine remaining ingredients except the peas. Pour over chicken.
4. Cover, cook on Low 7-9 hours (High 3-4 hours). One hour before serving, add peas.

CROCK POT ARTICHOKE, CHICKEN AND OLIVES
Ingredients:
1 1/2 lbs skinless, boneless chicken breast halves and/or thighs
2 cups sliced fresh mushrooms
1 (14.5 oz) can diced tomatoes
1 (8 or 9 oz) pkg frozen artichokes
1 cup chicken broth
1 medium onion, chopped
1/2 cup sliced pitted ripe olives (or 1/4 cup capers, drained) 1/4 c dry white wine or chicken broth
3 Tablespoons quick cooking tapioca
2-3 teaspoons curry powder
3/4 teaspoon dried thyme, crushed
1/4 teaspoon salt
1/4 teaspoon pepper
4 cups hot cooked couscous
Directions:
1. Rinse chicken & set aside. In a 3 1/2 qt crock pot combine mushrooms, undrained tomatoes, frozen artichoke hearts, chicken broth, onion, olives, & wine/broth.
2. Stir in tapioca, curry powder, thyme, salt, & pepper. Add chicken. Spoon some of the tomato mixture over chicken.
3. Cover & cook on LOW for 7 to 8 hours or on HIGH for 3 1/2 to 4 hours. Serve with hot cooked couscous.

CROCK POT AUTUMN CHICKEN
Ingredients:
2 large or 4 small chicken breasts
2 parsnips - 2 carrots
1 acorn squash
1 14.5 oz. can of chicken broth
garlic
salt
pepper
nutmeg
honey
Directions:
1. Peel and chop carrots and parsnips and place them in the bottom of the crockpot.
2. Sprinkle with garlicup Place chicken on top. Pour in broth.
3. Cut squash into chunks and slice off the skin. Place on top of chicken. Sprinkle desired amounts of salt, pepper and nutmeg on top of squash and drizzle enough honey on top to lightly cover the squash.
4. Cook on low 8-10 hours.

CROCK POT BOURBON BREAST OF CHICKEN
Ingredients:
4 chicken breasts halves
1/4 cup flour
1/2 teaspoon paprika
Salt
2 Tablespoons butter
2 Tablespoons oil
2 Tablespoons onion, chopped
2 Tablespoons parsley, chopped
1/4 teaspoon dried chervil
1/4 cup bourbon
1 (4 oz.) can mushrooms, undrained
1 (10 oz.) can tomatoes
1/4 teaspoon sugar
Salt & Pepper

Directions:

1. Dredge chicken in flour which has been mixed with paprika and a little salt.
2. Heat butter and oil in a skillet and saute chicken on both sides until lightly browned.
3. Stir in onion, parsley and chervil and cook a moment. Remove from heat.
4. Place chicken in crock pot. Combine remaining ingredients and pour over chicken.
5. Cover and cook on LOW for 6 to 7 hours. Serve with noodles of rice.

CROCK POT BUFFALO CHICKEN BREASTS

Ingredients:
4 Boneless, Skinless Chicken Breasts
1/4 cup hot sauce
2 Tablespoons vinegar
2 Tablespoons melted butter
Paprika

Directions:
1. Place chicken in crockpot. Mix together remaining ingredients and pour over chicken. Sprinkle with paprika.
2. Cook on Low for 6 to 8 hours.

CROCK POT BRAISED CHICKEN CURRY WITH YAMS

Ingredients:
Canola oil
2 lbs. chicken legs and thighs
2 large white onions, chopped
1 Tablespoon minced garlic
1 Tablespoon minced ginger
1/3 cup madras curry powder
1 banana
2 bay leaves
4 cups chicken stock
3 large yams, peeled and chopped
salt and black pepper to taste

Directions:

1. In a hot stock pot coated with oil, season the chicken and brown on all sides. Put chicken aside.
2. In the same stockpot, remove all chicken fat, leaving only a coating of oil and saute onions, garlic and ginger. Caramelize well, then add curry powder. Mix quickly for 2 minutes making sure not to burn the curry powder.
3. Add back the chicken, banana, bay leaves,yams and chicken stock. Check for seasonings. Bring to a boil and then simmer slowly for 1 1/2 - 2 hours. Serve on basmati rice.

CROCK POT BRAISED CHICKEN

Ingredients:
Chicken legs or thighs - 1.5lbs
Celery - 3 stalks (cubed)
White onion - 1 (cubed)
Garlic - 4 to 6 cloves (crushed)
Ginger - 1 Tablespoon (diced)
Red chilies - 3 to 5 (diced, optional)
5 spices powder - a pinch (optional)
Light soy sauce - 2 Tablespoon
Sugar - 2 teaspoons
Chicken soup stock - 1 to 2 cups

Directions:
1. Cut the chicken in bite sized pieces. Mix with the diced ginger and red chilies.
2. Add the celery, white onions, garlic in to the slow cooker. Add in the chicken, andthe rest of the ingredients.
3. Cook for 6 to 8 hours on low.

CROCK POT CHICKEN CASABLANCA

Ingredients:
1 large onion, sliced
1 teaspoon fresh ginger, grated
2 cloves garlic, minced
3 large carrots, diced
2 large potatoes, peeled and diced
1 medium zucchini, sliced 1" thick
1 15 oz. can garbanzo beans, drained
3 lbs. Boneless, skinless chicken breast pieces
1/2 teaspoon cumin
1/2 teaspoon turmeric
1/2 teaspoon salt
1/2 teaspoon pepper
1/4 teaspoon cinnamon
1/4 teaspoon cayenne pepper
1 (14 1/2 oz.) can chopped tomatoes
2 Tablespoons chopped parsley
1 Tablespoon chopped cilantro

Directions:
1. Combine first eight ingredients in crock pot. Combine spices in small bowl andsprinkle over ingredients in crock pot.
2. Add chopped tomatoes. Cover; cook on Low 8 to 10 hours (High 4 to 5 hours).
3. Stir in parsley and cilantro before serving. Serve over cooked rice.

CROCK POT BROWN RICE AND CHICKEN

Ingredients:
1 cup diced cooked chicken
2 onions, chopped
2 stalks celery, chopped
2 cups cooked brown rice
1/4 cup dry white wine
2 cups chicken broth
1 cup sliced almonds

Directions:
1. Combine all ingredients in slow cooker.
2. Cook on low 6 to 8 hours. Serve with sliced almonds lightly toasted.

CROCK POT CARROT CHICKEN

Ingredients:
skinless, boneless chicken breasts
1 medium head cabbage, quartered
1 pound carrots, cut into 1" pieces
water to cover
4 cubes chicken bouillon
1 teaspoon poultry seasoning
1/4 teaspoon Greek-style seasoning
2 Tablespoons cornstarch
1/4 cup water

Directions:
1. Rinse chicken and place in slow cooker. Rinse cabbage and place on top of chicken, then add carrots.
2. Add enough water to almost cover all. Add bouillon cubes and sprinkle liberally with poultry seasoning. Add Greek seasoning to taste (as you would salt and pepper).
3. Cook on low for 8 hours OR on high for 4 hours.
To Make Gravy:
When you're nearly ready to eat, pour off some of the juice and place in a saucepan. Bring to a boil.
Dissolve cornstarch in about 1/4 cup water (depending on how thick you like your gravy).
Add to saucepan and simmer all together until thick. If desired, season with additional Greek seasoning.
Serve gravy over chicken and potatoes, if desired.

CROCK POT CHEESY CHICKEN BAKE

Ingredients:
1 can mushroom soup
1 can cream of broccoli soup
1 can broccoli cheese soup
2 pkgs. Chicken Breasts (boneless, skinless)
1 can Mixed vegetables
1-2 Tablespoons Tapioca for thickening
1 cup shredded cheddar cheese

Directions:
1. Dice chicken put in crockpot sprinkle with salt and pepper. Pour all three cans of soup over chicken and stir.
2. Cover and cook on low about 4-6 hours.
3. About an hour before serving add mixed veggies, cheese and thicken with tapioca.

CROCK POT CHICKEN I

Ingredients:
1 frying chicken, cut up Salt & pepper
1 can cream of mushroom soup
1/2 cup sauterne or sherry
2 Tablespoons butter or margarine, melted
2 Tablespoons dry Italian salad dressing mix
2 (3 oz.) pkgs. cream cheese, cut in cubes
1 Tablespoon onion, chopped

Directions:
1. Wash chicken and pat dry. Brush with butter. Sprinkle with salt and pepper. Place in crock pot.
2. Sprinkle with dry salad mix. Cover and cook on low for 5 to 6 hours.
3. About 3/4 hour before serving, mix soup, cream cheese, wine, and onion in small saucepan. Cook until smooth.
4. Pour over chicken in pot. Cover and cook for 30 minutes on low. Serve with sauce. Serve with rice or noodles.

CROCK POT CHICKEN II

Ingredients:
1 large chicken, cut-up
2 cups soy sauce
2 cups vinegar

Directions:
1. Put in crockpot and cook on high 4-5 hours.

CROCK POT CHICKEN ALA KING

Ingredients:
1 can cream of chicken soup
3 Tablespoons flour
1/4 teaspoon pepper
Dash of cayenne pepper
1 lb. boneless, skinless chicken breasts, cut into cubes
1 celery rib, chopped
1/2 cup chopped green pepper
1/4 cup chopped onion
1 package (10 oz.) frozen peas, thawed
2 Tablespoons diced pimentos, drained
Hot cooked rice

Directions:
1. Combine soup, flour and peppers in crock pot, stir until smooth. Stir in chicken, celery, onion and green pepper.
2. Cover and cook on low 7-8 hours or until meat is cooked through.
3. Stir in peas and pimentos. Cook 30 minutes longer. Serve over rice.

CROCK POT CHICKEN AND DUMPLINGS

Ingredients:
4 Tablespoons butter
1 Tablespoon vegetable oil
1 onion, chopped
3 pounds chicken parts, cut up
2 cups chicken broth
2 stalks celery
1 Tablespoon minced parsley
2 carrots, peeled, sliced
1 teaspoon black pepper
Salt to taste
1/2 teaspoon ground allspice
1 cup dry white wine (optional)
1 can refrigerated biscuits
1/2 cup heavy cream
2 Tablespoons flour

Directions:
1. In a large skillet, brown onion in butter and oil just until tender, then brown chicken parts and place all in a 6-quart crock pot.
2. Add remaining ingredients except heavy cream, flour and biscuits.
3. Cook on high 2-1/2 to 3 hours, or on low 5 to 7 hours.
4. When chicken is done, remove pieces to plate and let cool, then debone.
5. While chicken is cooling, mix flour and cream together, then stir into crock pot.
6. Open biscuits and cut each biscuit into 4 pieces. Drop into crockpot and turn on high. These will need to cook about 30 minutes, until they are firm.
7. Return chicken meat to crockpot after deboning and serve. You can use your own homemade biscuit recipe for canned if you prefer.

CROCK POT CHICKEN & NOODLES

Ingredients:
4 carrots, sliced
4-5 pieces chicken
1 small onion, chopped
2 cups water
4 chicken bouillon cubes
1 teaspoon garlic salt
salt & pepper, to taste
1 lb. egg noodles

Directions:
1. Place carrots in crockpot, followed by all ingredients except noodles.
2. Cook on LOW for 8 hours.
3. At the end of cooking time, cook egg noodles on stovetop.
4. While noodles cook, remove chicken from crockpot & cut into bite-size pieces. Return chicken & noodles to crockpot.

CROCK POT CHICKEN AND RICE 1

Ingredients:
Boneless, skinless chicken breast (2-3 lbs)
Chicken Flavored Rice
Cream of Celery soup
Cream of Chicken soup
1 cup water
salt

Directions:
1. Put rice in crockpot, and water. Combine soups and layer on top of rice. Salt chicken and layer chicken in pot.
2. Set on high for 4-5 hours or low or auto shift for 7-10 hours.

CROCK POT CHICKEN AND RICE 2

Ingredients:
3/4 cup rice
1 can cream of celery soup
1 can cream of mushroom soup
1 small can whole mushrooms
1 small jar pimento strips, drained
1/2 green pepper, chopped
1/2 onion, chopped
1 can water chestnuts, drained, sliced
8 to 12 chicken breasts, halved
Grated Parmesan cheese

Directions:
1. Place rice in crock pot. Combine remaining ingredients except chicken and cheese in bowl. Mix well.
2. Pour half of mixture over rice. Place chicken on top. Pour remaining soup mixture over all.
3. Cook on high for 3 hours or until chicken is tender. Garnish with cheese.

CROCK POT CHICKEN AND SAUSAGE PAELLA

Ingredients:
2 1/2 to 3 lbs. meaty chicken pieces
1 Tablespoon cooking oil
8 oz. cooked smoked turkey sausage, halved lengthwise and sliced
1 large onion, sliced
3 cloves garlic, minced
2 Tablespoons snipped fresh thyme or 2 teaspoon dried thyme, crushed
1/4 teaspoon black pepper
1/8 teaspoon thread saffron or 1/4 teaspoon ground turmeric
1 14 1/2 oz. can reduced-sodium chicken broth
1/2 cup water
2 cups chopped tomatoes
2 yellow or green sweet peppers, cut into very thin bite-size strips
1 cup frozen green peas
3 cups hot cooked rice

Directions:
1. Skin chicken. Rinse chicken; pat dry. In a large skillet brown chicken pieces, half at a time, in hot oil. Drain off fat.
2. In a 3 1/2, 4, or 5 quart crock pot place chicken pieces, turkey sausage, and onion. Sprinkle with garlic, dried thyme (if using), black pepper, and saffron or turmericup Pour broth and water over all.
3. Cover; cook on low-heat setting for 7 to 8 hours or on high-heat setting for 3 1/2 to 4 hours.
4. Add the tomatoes, sweet peppers, peas, and if using, the fresh thyme to the cooker. Cover; let stand for 5 minutes. Serve over the hot rice.

CROCK POT CHICKEN BREASTS & MUSHROOMS

Ingredients:
4 chicken breasts
1 can cream of mushroom soup
1 can cream of chicken soup
8 oz. jar sliced mushrooms
1 teaspoon sugar
1 teaspoon garlic powder
salt & pepper to taste
1 teaspoon Greek seasoning
1 pkg. egg noodles, cooked

Directions:
1. Combine soups, sugar, & mushrooms & place in crock pot.
2. Wash chicken breasts &sprinkle with garlic powder, Greek seasoning, salt, & pepper. Put in crock pot.
3. Cook on high 4-5 hours or low 8-10 hours.
4. Cook noodles according to pkg.directions & add margarine as desired. Serve with prepared chicken breasts.

CROCK POT CHICKEN CACCIATORE

Ingredients:
1 large onion, thinly sliced
1 1/2 lb. skinless, boneless chicken breasts
2 (6 oz each) cans tomato paste
8 oz. fresh sliced mushrooms
1/2 teaspoon salt
1/4 teaspoon pepper
2 cloves garlic, minced
1 teaspoon oregano
1/2 teaspoon basil
1 bay leaf
1/4 cup dry white wine
1/4 cup water

Directions:
1. Put sliced onion in bottom of crock pot. Add chicken pieces.
2. Stir together tomato paste, mushrooms, salt, pepper, garlic, herbs, white wine and water. Spread over chicken.
3. Cover; cook on Low 7 to 9 hours (High: 3 to 4 hours). Serve chicken pieces over hot spaghetti or vermicelli.

CROCK POT CHICKEN CACCIATORE 2

Ingredients:
1 small can tomatoes, diced
2 cans (small ones) tomato paste
1/2 cup dry white wine
1 can mushrooms
1 small onion, sliced
4 cloves garlic, sliced
1 Tablespoon Italian Seasoning
1 teaspoon basil
1 teaspoon oregano

Directions:
1. Mix all ingredients together and pour over the top of the chicken.
2. Cook on LOW all day.

CROCK POT CHICKEN CACCIATORE 3

Ingredients:
1 chicken (5 pounds), cut into pieces
1/4 cup olive oil
1 cup flour
1 cup chopped onions
1 cup sliced mushrooms
1 cup julienned carrot
1 cup julienned green pepper
2 Tablespoons minced garlic
8 cups chopped, peeled tomatoes
1/2 cup tomato paste
3/4 cup red or Marsala wine
1 teaspoon oregano
1 teaspoon basil
1 1/2 teaspoons salt
1 teaspoon pepper
freshly grated Romano cheese

Directions:
1. Wash and drain the chicken pieces. Heat the oil in a deep skillet.
2. Roll and coat each chicken piece in the flour and brown each piece on all sides to a golden brown. Transfer the chicken to paper towels to drain.
3. Saute the onion, mushrooms, carrots, green peppers, and garlic in the same skillet for 10 minutes. Add the tomatoes and saute for another 5 minutes.
4. Stir in the tomato paste, wine, herbs, salt and pepper, and cook over medium heat for another 5 minutes.
5. Add all the chicken pieces and mix well. Turn down the heat very low, and simmer, covered, for 1 hour.

CROCK POT CHICKEN CASSEROLE

Ingredients:
4 large chicken breasts
1 small can cream of chicken soup
1 small can cream of celery soup
1 small can cream of mushroom soup
1/2 cup diced celery
1 cup Minute Rice

Directions:
1. Mix in crockpot the soups and rice. Place chicken on top of mixture, then sprinkle diced celery over chicken.
2. Cook on low for 4 hours.

CROCK POT CHICKEN CORDON BLEU

Ingredients:
4-6 chicken breasts (pounded out thin)
4-6 pieces of ham
4-6 slices of swiss cheese
1 can cream of mushroom soup(can use any cream soup)
1/4 cup milk

Directions:
1. Put ham and cheese on chicken. Roll up and secure with a toothpick.
2. Place chicken in crock pot so it looks like a triangle /_\ Layer the rest on top.
3. Mix soup and milk. Pour over top of chicken. Cover and cook on low for 4 hours or until chicken is no longer pink.

CROCK POT CHICKEN ENCHILADAS I

Ingredients:
boneless, skinless chicken (can still be frozen)
1 large can enchilada sauce (green or red)
medium or large flour tortillas
shredded cheese

Directions:
1. Empty enchilada sauce into the crockpot and place chicken filets into the sauce.
2. Cook on low setting all day. Scoop out chicken and cut or shred onto a plate.
3. Spread a tortilla on another plate and arrange some chicken into a "stripe" down the middle. Sprinkle liberal shredded cheese, and ladle some sauce over it.
4. Roll the tortilla up, ladle more sauce over it, and sprinkle more cheese. Place in the microwave for about 20 seconds on High to melt the cheese. More microwave time may be needed for multiple enchiladas on one plate.

CROCK POT CHICKEN ENCHILADAS II

Ingredients:
1 large can Enchilada sauce
4 chicken breasts
2 cans cream of chicken soup
1 small can sliced black olives
2 dozen corn tortillas
1 chopped onion
1 pkg. sharp cheddar cheese

Directions:
1. Cook chicken and shred. Mix soup, olives and onions. Cut tortillas in wedges.
2. Layer crockpot with sauce, tortillas, soup mix, chicken and cheese all the way to top, ending with cheese on top.
3. Cook on low temp all day.

CROCK POT CHICKEN FRICASSEE

Ingredients:
1 can cream of chicken soup
1/2 soup can water
1/2 cup chopped onions
1 teaspoon paprika
1 teaspoon lemon juice
1 teaspoon rosemary
1 teaspoon thyme
1 teaspoon salt
1/4 teaspoon pepper
4 skinless boneless chicken breast
non-stick cooking spray

Chive Dumplings *Ingredients:*
3 Tablespoons shortening
1 1/2 cups flour
2 teaspoons baking powder
3/4 teaspoon salt
3 Tablespoons fresh, chopped chives, or
2 Tablespoons dried chives
3/4 cup skim milk

Directions:
1. Spray crockpot with non-stick cooking spray. Place chicken in crockpot.
2. Mix remaining ingredients together and pour over chicken. Cover and cook on low 6-8 hours.
3. 1 hour before serving, prepare chive dumplings by mixing dry ingredients and shortening. Add chives and milk, combine well. Drop by teaspoonsful onto hot chicken and gravy. Cover and cook on high for 45-60 minutes.

CROCK POT CHICKEN FRICASSEE

Ingredients:
1/2 cups all purpose flour
2 teaspoons salt
1 1/2 teaspoons ground mustard
1/2 teaspoon garlic powder
6 pork chops, trimmed
2 Tablespoons vegetable oil
1 can condensed cream of chicken soup, undiluted
1/3 cup water

Directions:
1. In a shallow bowl, combine flour, salt, mustard and garlic powder; dredge porkchops.
2. In a skillet, brown the chops on both sides in oil. Place in a crockpot. Combine soup and water; pour over chops.
3. Cover and cook on low for 6-8 hours or until meat is tender. If desired, thicken pan juices and serve with the pork chops.

CROCK POT GLAZED CHICKEN

Ingredients:
4 skinless boneless chicken breasts
6 oz. frozen concentrated orange juice
1/2 teaspoon thyme
salt pepper

Directions:
1. Place chicken in crockpot. Mix the thyme and orange juice and pour over.
2. Cook about 4-5 hours on low. Season to taste.

CROCK POT CHICKEN IN A POT

Ingredients:
3 lb. whole chicken
2 carrots, sliced
2 onions, sliced
2 celery stalks with leaves,
1 teaspoon basil
2 teaspoons salt
1/2 teaspoon black pepper
1/2 cup chicken broth or wine

Directions:
1. Put carrots, onions, and celery in bottom of crock pot. Add whole chicken. Top with salt, pepper, liquid. Sprinkle basil over top.
2. Cover and cook until done-low 8 to 10 hours. (High 3 to 4 hours, using 1 cup water).
3. Remove chicken and vegetables with spatula.

80

CROCK POT CHICKEN IN SPICY SAUCE

Ingredients:
1/2 cup tomato juice
1/2 cup soy sauce
1/2 cup brown sugar
1/4 cup chicken broth
3 cloves garlic minced
1 whole chicken, cut in skinless serving size pieces or favorite parts

Directions:
1. Combine all ingredients except chicken in a bowl. Dip each peice of chicken in the sauce. Place in the slow cooker.
2. Pour remaining sauce over the top. Cook on low for 6-8 hours or high 3-4 hours.

CROCK POT CHICKEN AND NOODLES

Ingredients:
2 1/2 to 3 1/2 pound broiler/fryer chicken cut up
1 cup chicken broth
2 cups water
1 package (8 ounces) egg noodles
Salt and pepper to taste

Directions:
1. Place chicken in crock-pot. Season with salt and pepper; add all liquid.
2. Cover and cook on Low 8 to 10 hours (High 4 to 5 hours).
3. Remove chicken from broth. Turn crockpot to high and add noodles.
4. Bone chicken and cut up meat. Stir chicken into noodles. Cover and cook 30 to 45 minutes, stirring occasionally.

CROCK POT CHICKEN PARMIGIANA

Ingredients:
3 Chicken breasts
1 Egg
1 teaspoon Salt
1/4 teaspoon Pepper
1 cup Dry bread crumbs
1 1/4 cups Butter
1 can Pizza sauce (10 1/2 oz.)
6 slices Mozarella cheese
Parmesan cheese

Directions:
1. If using whole chicken breasts, cut in to halves. In bowl beat egg salt and pepper dip chicken into egg. Then coat with crumbs.
2. In large skillet saute chicken in butter. Arrange chicken in pot. Pour pizza sauce over chicken.
3. Cover and cook on low 6 to 8 hours. Add mozzarella cheese, sprinkle parmesan cheese on top. Cover and cook 15 minutes.

CROCK POT CHICKEN PIZZA

Ingredients:
4 skinless, boneless chicken breast- cut into bite size pieces
1 onion, chopped
1 green bell pepper, chopped
2 large cans tomato sauce
2 large cans diced tomatoes
1 Tablespoon dried parsley
1 Tablespoon dried oregano
1 Tablespoon dried basil
1 teaspoon thyme
4 cloves garlic, pressed
1 bay leaf

Directions:
1. Place all ingredients in slow cooker. Stir to make sure all chicken is coated well.
2. Cook on Low setting for 8 hours, until chicken and vegetables are tender.

CROCK POT CHICKEN/ SAUSAGE CASSOULET

Ingredients:
1 package Frozen lima beans
1 cup Tomato juice
1 Carrot, 1/2 inch pcs
1 Stalk celery, 1/2"pcs
1 Onion, chopped
1 Clove garlic, minced
1 Bay leaf
1 teaspoon Chicken bouillon granules
1/2 teaspoon Dried basil, crushed
1/2 teaspoon Dried oregano, crushed
3 Boneless chicken breasts
3 Chicken drumsticks
8 ounces Smoked kielbasa

Directions:
1. Place carrots, limas, celery and onions on bottom of crock pot which has been sprayed with Pam.
2. Combine herbs, juice and bouillon and add to vegetables. Place chicken on top of vegetables.
3. Cut sausage into pieces. Put chicken and sausage on top of veggies.
4. Cover crockpot and cook on Low heat for 10 hours or on high for 5 hours. Remove bay leaf before serving.

CROCK POT CHICKEN STEW

Ingredients:
2 lb. Chicken breasts/skinless Boneless/ cut in 1" cubes
2 cups Fat-free chicken broth
3 cups Potatoes; peeled, cube
1 cup Onion; chopped
1 cup Celery; sliced
1 cup Carrots; sliced thin
1 teaspoon Paprika
1/2 teaspoon Pepper
1/2 teaspoon Rubbed sage
1/2 teaspoon Dried thyme
6 oz. no-salt-added tomato paste
1/4 cup Cold water
3 Tablespoon Cornstarch

Directions:
1. In a slow cooker, combine the first 11 ingredients; cover and cook on HIGH for 4 hours.
2. Mix water and cornstarch until smooth; stir into stew. Cook, covered, 30 minutes more or until the vegetables are tender.

CROCK POT CHICKEN STEW MEXICAN STYLE

Ingredients:
2 lbs. skinless boneless chicken breasts cut into 1 1/2" peices
4 medium russet potatoes, peeled and cut very small
1 (15 oz.) can mild salsa
1 (4 oz.) can diced green chilies
1 (1 1/4 oz.) package taco seasoning mix
1 (8oz.) can tomato sauce

Directions:
1. Mix all ingredients together in crockpot, cook 7-9 hours on low. Serve with warm flour tortillas.

CROCK POT CHICKEN STEW

Ingredients:
2 or 3 uncooked boneless, skinless chicken breasts
1 can of white beans, undrained
1 can of petite diced tomatoes, undrained chopped onion to taste
1 yellow pepper, diced
1 cup cooked instant rice

Directions:
1. Place chicken on bottom of crock pot.
2. Pour over can of white beans.
3. Pour over can of diced tomatoes.
4. Sprinkle chopped onion and yellow pepper. Sprinkle over all S&P, and other favorite spices to taste.
5. Cook on high for 5 hours.
6. 1 hour before serving, break up chicken pieces into bite sized chunks and mix in cooked instant rice.
7. Stir and reduce to Low for last hour.

CROCK POT CHICKEN STROGANOFF

Ingredients:
1 cup sour cream
1 Tablespoon Gold Medal all-purpose flour
1 envelope (.87 to 1.2 oz) chicken gravy mix
1 cup water
1 lb. boneless, skinless chicken breast halves, cut into 1" pieces
1 (16 oz.) bag frozen stew vegetables, thawed
1 (4 oz.) jar sliced mushrooms, drained
1 cup frozen peas, thawed
1 1/2 cups Bisquick Original or Reduced Fat baking mix
4 green onions, chopped
1/2 cup milk

Directions:
1. Mix sour cream, flour, gravy mix and water in 3 1/2 to 4-quart Crock pot until smooth.
2. Stir in chicken, stew vegetables and mushrooms.
3. Cover and cook on low heat setting 4 hours or until chicken is tender and sauce is thickened.
4. Stir in peas.
5. In separate bowl, mix baking mix and onions. Stir in milk just until moistened.
6. Drop dough by rounded tablespoonfuls onto chicken-vegetable mixture.
7. Cover and cook on high heat setting 45 to 50 minutes or until toothpick inserted in center of dumplings comes out clean.

CROCK POT CHICKEN THIGHS

Ingredients:
6 chicken thighs (remove skin)
1 can Italian-style diced tomatoes (28 oz.)
salt and pepper

Directions:
1. Place all ingredients into the crockpot and cook on high for about 3 hours. Serve with egg noodles.

CROCK POT CHICKEN WINGS

Ingredients:
5 lb. chicken wings
2 cups brown sugar
1 cup French's mustard
4 Tablespoons soy sauce

Directions:
1. Cut each wing into 3 pieces - throw away the tip.
2. Brown in skillet until golden brown and put in slow cooker, turn on low heat.
3. Mix brown sugar, mustard and soy sauce in saucepan and heat until it becomes liquid. Pour over the wings and cook on low 4-8 hours.

CROCK POT CHICKEN WITH CHEESE SAUCE FOR TWO

Ingredients:
2 chicken breast halves
1 can cream of chicken soup
white wine
2 slices swiss cheese

Directions:
1. Place chicken in crockpot (frozen or thawed).
2. Mix together can of cream of chicken soup & half soup can of white wine; pour over chicken.
3. Place swiss cheese over top of chicken breasts.
4. Cook in crockpot for 2-3 hours (on high) or 3-4 hours (on low)

CROCK POT COQ AU VIN 1

Ingredients:
12 small White onions, peeled
4 lb. Roasting chicken, cut up
1/2 teaspoon Salt
1/4 teaspoon Black pepper
1/4 cup Brandy or cognac
2 Cloves garlic, peeled and crushed
1/4 teaspoon Ground thyme
1 Bay leaf
1 1/2 cup Dry red wine
5 Tablespoons All purpose flour
1 cup Chicken bouillon
3/4 lb. Fresh mushrooms, wiped and stemmed
1 Tablespoons Butter or margarine
1/4 teaspoons Salt
1 Tablespoon Chopped fresh parsley

Directions:
1. Place the onions in the slow cooker.
2. Remove the fat from the vent of the chicken and dice it. In a large skillet over medium heat, heat the fat until it is rendered. Discard the shriveled bits and saute the chicken until well browned. Season with 1/2 teaspoon salt and the pepper.
3. Warm the brandy in a ladle or a small saucepan; light it with match and pour it over the chicken. When the flame dies, lift the chicken into the slow cooker and add the garlic, thyme, and bay leaf.
4. Pour the wine into the hot skillet and scrape up the pan juices. Dissolve the flour in the bouillon, turn it into the skillet and bring to simmering, stirring briskly to prevent lumps. Turn into the slow cooker.
5. Cover and cook on Low 7-9 hours.
6. Before serving: About 10 minutes before serving, in a medium skillet, saute the mushrooms in the butter over medium high heat. In about 5 minutes, they will be tender and the moisture will have evaporated from the skillet.
7. Season with 1/4 teaspoon salt and add to the chicken casserole. If the sauce seems thin, simmer it in the mushroom skillet long enough to thicken to the consistency of heavy cream.
8. Garnish the Coq au Vin with parsley before serving.

CROCK POT COQ AU VIN 2

Ingredients:
2-1/2 lb. chicken cut up or boneless, skinless chicken breasts
1 clove garlic crushed
1 teaspoon salt
1/4 teaspoon pepper
1/2 teaspoon dried thyme
6 bacon slices, diced
2/3 cups sliced green onions
1 cup chicken broth
8 small white onions, peeled
1 cup burgundy wine
1/2 lb. whole mushrooms
chopped parsley
8 small new potatoes scrubbed

Directions:
1. In large skillet, saute dieced bacon and green onions until bacon is crisp. Remove and drain on paper towel.
2. Add chicken pieces to skillet and brown well on all sides. Remove the chicken when it has browned and set aside.
3. Put peeled onions, mushrooms, and garlic in crock pot. Add browned chicken pieces, bacon and green onions, salt, pepper, thyme, pototales and chicken broth.
4. Cover and cook on Low 6 - 8 hours (High 3-4).
5. During the last hour add burgundy and cook on high. Garnish with chopped parsley.

CROCK POT COQ AU VIN WITH SHIITAKE MUSHROOMS

Ingredients:

2 Tablespoons olive oil
3 lb. chicken pieces, rinsed & patted dry
1/3 cup finely chopped shallot
1/3 cup finely chopped onion
2 carrots, quartered lengthwise & cut crosswise into 1/4" pieces (about 1/2 cup)
1/2 lb. pearl onions, blanched in boiling water for 3 minutes, drained, & peeled
1 bay leaf
3/4 teaspoon thyme, crumbled
2 Tablespoons Cognac
1 cup dry white wine
2 cup chicken broth
1/4 lb. shiitake mushrooms, stems discarded & caps sliced thin
1/4 cup cornstarch
Freshly ground nutmeg to taste

Directions:

1. In a heavy kettle, heat the oil over moderately high heat until it is hot but not smoking and in it saute the chicken pieces, seasoned with salt and pepper, in batches, turning them once, for 8 to 10 minutes, or until they are browned.
2. Transfer the chicken pieces as they are browned to a plate and keep them warm, covered.
3. Place the shallot, onions, carrots, pearl onions, bay leaf, and thyme in a crockpot.
4. Place the browned chicken on top of the vegetables.
5. Combine the Cognac, white wine and 1 3/4 cup of chicken broth and add to the cooker.
6. Cover and cook on LOW for 5 hours or until chicken is tender.
7. Turn control to HIGH and add the mushrooms. Dissolve the cornstarch in the remaining 1/4 cup chicken stock. Stir into the mixture.
8. Cover and cook for 20 minutes more, or until sauce is thickened, stirring once.
9. Transfer the chicken to a plate, and keep warm. Discard the bay leaf, and season the sauce with freshly ground nutmeg and salt and pepper to taste.

CROCK POT COUNTRY CHICKEN STEW WITH BASIL DUMPLINGS

Ingredients:

12 small white onions
water
1 pound boneless skinless chicken thighs
1 pound bonless skinless chicken breasts halves
1/2 Tablespoon chopped fresh basil leaves (or 1/2 teaspoon dried, crumbled)
salt and pepper to taste
1 large red bell pepper cut into 1" squares
4 cloves garlic - thinly sliced
2 cups canned chicken broth
1/3 cup dry white wine
2 Tablesppons all purpose flour
2 Tablespoons butter - room temperature
1 pound fresh asparagus - cut into 1-1/2" lengths
DUMPLINGS:
1 cup buttermilk and baking mix
1/3 cup whole milk
1/4 cup chopped fresh basil leaves (or 1 Tablespoon dried, crumbled)

Directions:

1. Using a sharp knife, make a small X in the root end of each onion. Bring a saucepan of water to boil. Add the onions, lower the heat, and simmer for 5 minutes. Drain and rinse under running cold water. Slip skins off onions.
2. Rinse chicken and pat dry. Quarter the thighs and chicken breast halves. Stir in basil and seaons with salt and pepper.
3. Put chicken pieces in a 3-1/2 quart or larger crockery slow-cooker. Top with onions, bell peppers, and garlicup Pour in stock, and wine. DO NOT sitr. Cover and

cook on LOW for 6 - 8 hours or HIGH for 2- 2-1/2 hours.

4. Stir the stew. If cooking on LOW, change setting to HIGH. In a small bowl, blend together the flour and butter. Stir into slow-cooker. cook, stirring until sauce begins to thicken, about 5 minutes. Stir in asparagus.

5. In medium bowl, combine dumpling ingredients until evenly moistened. Drop by Tablespoons onto hot stew in 6 small rounds. Cover and cook for another 25 to 30 minutes, until dumplings are cooked through.

CROCK POT CRANBERRY CHICKEN

Ingredients:
1 small onion, thinly sliced
1 cup fresh or frozen (unthawed) cranberries
12 skinless, boneless chicken thighs (about 2 1/4 lbs. total)
1/4 cup catsup
2 Tablespoons firmly packed brown sugar
1 teaspoon dry mustard
2 teaspoons cider vinegar
1 1/2 Tablespoons cornstarch blended w/2 Tablespoons cold water
salt

Directions:
1. In a 3-quart or larger electric slow cooker, combine onion, cranberries. Arrange chicken on top. In small bowl, mix catsup, sugar, mustard and vinegar and pour over chicken. Cover. Cook at low setting until chicken is very tender when pierced (6 1/2 to 7 1/2 hours).

2. Lift out chicken when done, blend cornstarch mixture into cooking liquid. Increase cooker heat setting to high; cover and cook, stirring 2 or 3 times until sauce thickens (10 to 15 more minutes). Season to taste with salt; pour over chicken.

CROCK POT CREAM CHEESE CHICKEN

Ingredients:
1 frying chicken -- cut up
2 Tablespoons melted butter or margarine
salt & pepper -- to taste
2 Tablespoons dry Italian salad dressing
1 can condensed mushroom soup
6 ounces cream cheese; -- cut in 1" cubes
1/2 cup sauterne wine or sherry
1 Tablespoon onion -- minced

Directions:
1. Brush chicken with butter and sprinkle with salt and pepper. Place in a crock pot and sprinkle dry mix over all.

2. Cover and cook on low for 6 - 7 hours.

3. About 45 minutes before done, mix soup, cream cheese, wine, and onion in a small saucepan. Cook until smooth.

4. Pour over the chicken and cover and cook another 45 minutes. Serve with sauce.

CROCK POT CREAMY CHICKEN DINNER

Ingredients:
4 boneless/skinless chicken breasts seasoned with garlic powder, onion powder and
seasoned salt
1 large can cream of chicken soup
2 cans cream of mushroom soup
3/4 cup frozen cut carrots
3/4 cup frozen green beans

Directions:
1. Place all ingredients in the crockpot and cook it about 7 hours on low.

2. Add 2 cups of minute rice to it the last 5 minutes before dinner.

CROCK POT CREOLE CHICKEN

Ingredients:
8 chicken thighs
1 can diced tomatoes
1 can tomato paste
1 chopped bell pepper
1 chopped onion chopped ham
diced sausage
Tabasco sauce to taste

Directions:
1. Place all ingredients in the crock pot and cook on low 4-5 hours.

CROCK POT GARLIC BROWN SUGAR CHICKEN

Ingredients:
Chicken pieces-enough to feed your family-legs, thighs
1 cup packed brown sugar
2/3 cup vinegar
1/4 cup lemon-line soda
2-3 Tablespoons minced garlic
2 Tablespoons soy sauce
1 teaspoon pepper

Directions:
1. Place chicken in crockpot. Mix all remaining ingredients and pour over chicken.
2. Cook on low for 6-8 hours. Serve over rice or noodles.

CROCK POT GARLIC CHICKEN

Ingredients:
3 lb. Frying Chicken, cut into serving pieces
Salt and Black Pepper to Taste
2 Tablespoons Olive Oil
1/2 cup Dry White Wine
1/8 cup (2 Tbs.) Vermouth
2 Tablespoons fresh Parsley, chopped
2 Tablespoons fresh Basil, chopped
1 Tablespoon fresh Oregano, chopped
Dash of Crushed Red Pepper Flakes
20 cloves Garlic, peeled (20 is correct)
2 stalks Celery, sliced
Juice of 1 Lemon
Peel of 1 Lemon

Directions:
1. Remove the skin from the chicken pieces, if so desired. Sprinkle the chicken pieces with salt and pepper.
2. Warm the olive oil in a heavy skillet over medium-high heat. Brown the chicken on all sides, and remove to a platter when golden.
3. In a large mixing bowl, blend together the white wine, vermouth, parsley, basil, oregano, and red pepper flakes.
4. Add the garlic and celery, and mix to coat. With a slotted spoon, transfer the coated vegetables to a slow cooker.
5. Add the chicken pieces to the remaining herb and wine mixture and coat well.
6. Place the chicken on top of the vegetables in the slow cooker. Sprinkle the lemon juice and peel over the top of the chicken.
7. Pour the rest of the wine and herbmixture over the top of the chicken.
8. Cover and cook on low for 6 hours, or until the chicken is no longer pink in the thickest cuts. Discard the celery and garlic and serve warm.

CROCK POT BARBECUED CHICKEN

Ingredients:
1 reg. size bottle BBQ sauce (any flavor)
10 oz. Coke
Chicken (pieces or whole)

Directions:
1. Mix BBQ sauce and Coke in crock pot. Add chicken.
2. Cook on low 8 hours.

CROCK POT FIESTA CHICKEN

Ingredients:

2 Tablespoons oil
3 pounds boneless, skinless chicken breasts, cut into 1-inch pieces
1 medium onion, chopped
1 teaspoon oregano
1 small jalapeno pepper, finely chopped
3 cloves garlic, minced
1 can (14 1/2 ounce) Mexican style diced tomatoes
1/4 teaspoon ground cumin

Directions:

1. Heat oil in skillet. Cook chicken pieces until browned. Remove and drain.
2. Place onion, green bell pepper, garlic and jalapeno pepper in skillet and saute until slightly cooked.
3. Add all ingredients to crockpot and stir to combine.
4. Cover; cook on LOW 8 hours (HIGH 4 hours). Serve on flour tortillas.

CROCK POT GARLIC PEPPER CHICKEN PARMESAN

Ingredients:

4 chicken leg quarters
2 Tablespoons Mrs. Dash's Gallant Garlics Roasted Garlic Pepper seasoning
1 can Del Monte Zucchini with Tomato Sauce
3 oz. shredded mozzarella cheese

Directions:

1. Put chicken in pot. Sprinkle with seasoning. Pour zucchini with tomato sauce over chicken.
2. Cook for 6 hours on high.
3. Sprinkle with cheese and cook until cheese melts - about 30 mins.

CROCK POT GREEK CHICKEN

Ingredients:

6 skinless chicken breasts
1 large can tomato sauce
1 small can tomato puree
1 can sliced mushrooms
1 can ripe olives
1 Tablespoon garlic
1 Tablespoon lemon juice
1 teaspoon oregano
1 onion, chopped
1/2 cup wine or brandy (optional)
2 cups rice
Salt to taste

Directions:

1. Wash and remove fat from chicken. Bake in 350 degree oven for about an hour.
2. Combine all other ingredients except rice. Put chicken and sauce in a slow cooker/Crock Pot on low heat and cook for at least 4 hours to blend flavors.
3. Before serving, cook rice according to directions on box. Serve chicken and sauce over rice.

CROCK POT GREEN CHILE-STUFFED CHICKEN BREASTS

Ingredients:

4 boneless, skinned chicken breast halves, pounded thin
3 ounces cream cheese
3/4 cups shredded Cheddar or Monterey Jack cheese
4 ounces green chiles
1/2 teaspoon chili powder
salt and pepper to taste
1 can cream of mushroom soup
1/2 cup hot enchilada sauce

Directions:

1. Combine cream cheese, shredded cheese, chiles, chili powder and salt and pepper.
2. Place a generous dollop on each flattened chicken breast, then roll up.
3. Place chicken rolls in the slow cooker/Crock Pot, seam-side down. Top chicken breast rolls with remaining cheese mixture, soup, and enchilada sauce.
4. Cover and cook on LOW for 6 to 7 hours

CROCK POT HEALTHY CHICKEN CREOLE

Ingredients:
3 lbs. chicken thighs or breasts, skinned
1 cup celery, diced
1 red bell pepper, sliced
1 green bell pepper, sliced
1 onion, sliced
1 can sliced mushrooms
1 can tomatoes
1 teaspoon garlic powder
3 pkg. sugar substitute
1 teaspoon Cajun seasoning
1/2 teaspoon paprika
salt & pepper to taste
Louisiana hot sauce to taste
2 cups minute rice, cooked

Directions:
1. Place chicken in bottom of slow cooker/Crock Pot. Combine remaining ingredients (except rice) & add to slow cooker/Crock Pot.
2. Cook on high 4 to 5 hours or on low 7-8 hours.
3. Cook rice according to package direction. Spoon Creole mixture over hot cooked rice.

CROCK POT HONEYED CHICKEN WINGS

Ingredients:
3 lb. chicken wings
Salt and pepper, to taste
1 cup honey
1/2 cup soy sauce
2 Tablespoons vegetable oil
2 Tablespoons ketchup
1/2 garlic clove, minced

Directions:
1. Cut off and discard chicken wing tips. Cut each wing into 2 parts and sprinkle with salt and pepper.
2. Combine remaining ingredients and mix well.

3. Place wings in slow cooker and pour sauce over. Cook 6 to 8 hours on low.

CROCK POT HOT CHICKEN SANDWICHES

Ingredients:
12 eggs
1 loaf of bread (cubed)
2 large (or 3 small) boiler chickens (reserve some broth for use in recipe)
salt to taste
pepper to taste

Directions:
1. Boil the chickens until done and let cool.
2. When the chicken meat is completely cool to the touch, pick the chicken meat from the bones and set aside.
3. Reserve a little of the broth for later.
4. Cube the loaf of bread and put it in a large bowl. Mix in the 12 eggs with the cubed bread.
5. Add the chicken meat you picked from the bone and enough broth from the chicken to moisten. Add salt and pepper to your own taste.
6. Mix well. Pour mixture into a lightly greased slow cooker/Crock Pot.
7. Cook on low for about 6 hours. Serve by scooping onto buns.

CROCK POT JERK CHICKEN

Ingredients:

1 large onion, cut into 8 pieces
1 generous Tablespoon chopped crystallized ginger
1/2 to 1 habanero pepper, seeded, deveined, and finely minced (wear gloves!)
1/2 teaspoon ground allspice
2 Tablespoons dry mustard
1 teaspoon freshly ground black pepper
2 Tablespoons red wine or balsamic vinegar
2 Tablespoons soy sauce
2 cloves garlic, crushed and minced
3 to 4 pounds chicken tenders

Directions:

1. Combine onion and ginger in a food processor; process until finely chopped.
2. Add remaining ingredients, except chicken, and pulse until well combined.
3. Place chicken in a 3 1/2-quart (or larger) slow cooker/Crock Pot and cover with sauce.
4. Cover, set on low, and cook for 6 to 8 hours. or until chicken is tender (3 to 4 hours on high).

CROCK POT LAZY CHICKEN

Ingredients:

1 package boneless chicken breasts
1 can cream of mushroom soup
1/4 cup flour
1 jar sliced mushrooms
Salt, pepper and paprika

Directions:

1. Rinse chicken breasts. Put salt, pepper and paprika on both sides. Place in Crock Pot.
2. Mix other ingredients together. Add to Crock Pot.
3. Cook on LOW all day. Serve over noodles, rice, or mashed potatoes.

CROCK POT LEMON BAKED CHICKEN

Ingredients:

16 ounces skinned and boned uncooked chicken breasts, cut into 4 pieces
1 lemon
1 teaspoon lemon pepper
1 teaspoon paprika

Directions:

1. Place chicken pieces in a slow cooker. Squeeze juice of half a lemon over chicken. Sprinkle lemon pepper and paprika over top.
2. Cut remaining lemon half into thin slices. Arrange slices around chicken.
3. Cover and cook on HIGH for 4 hours.

CROCK POT CHICKEN LASAGNA FLORENTINE

Ingredients:

2 (10.5oz) cans condensed reduced-fat cream of chicken
1 pkg. frozen chopped spinach (10oz) thawed, drained and squeezed
1 (9oz) package frozen diced cooked chicken
1 (8oz) carton reduced fat sour cream
1 cup milk
1/2 cup (2oz) Parmesan cheese
1/3 cup chopped onion
1/2 teaspoon salt
1/4 teaspoon pepper
1/8 teaspoon ground nutmeg
9 uncooked lasagna noodles
Cooking Spray
1 cup shredded part skim mozzarella

Directions:

1. Combine first 10 ingredients in large bowl and stir well.
2. Coat Crock Pot with spray and place 3 uncooked lasagna noodles in bottom of cooker. Break noodles in half as necessary to fit.
3. Spread 1/3 spinach mixture over noodles; sprinkle with 1/3 cup mozzarella.

Layer 3 more noodles, half remaining spinach mixture, and 1/3 cup mozzarella. Top with remaining noodles and spinach. Sprinkle with remaining cheese.
4. Cover with lid; cook on high 1 hour and reduce to low 5 hours or until done.

CROCK POT LEMON-GARLIC CHICKEN
Ingredients:
3 pounds Chicken
1/2 cup Lemon juice
1/2 cup Garlic cloves, crushed
1 teaspoon Seasoned salt
1 teaspoon Poultry seasoning
2 dashes Tabasco
1 cup White wine
Directions:
1. Skin and cut up chicken. Combine with other ingredients in slow cooker/Crock Pot.
2. Cook on low for 8 hours.
3. When chicken is done, debone chicken. Serve over rice. I

CROCK POT LEMON PEPPER CHICKEN
Ingredients:
5 boneless skinless chicken breasts (or any chicken pieces)
Lemon Pepper seasoning
2 Tablespoons melted or squeeze margarine
Directions:
1. Put chicken in slow cooker/Crock Pot. Sprinkle generously with seasoning. Pour margarine over chicken.
2. Cook on low for 10 hours or on high for 6 hours.

CROCK POT LEMON-ROSEMARY CHICKEN
Ingredients:
1/2 cup lemon juice
1 Tablespoon vegetable oil

1 garlic clove, crushed
1 teaspoon dried rosemary
1/4 teaspoon salt
1/4 teaspoon pepper
1 1/2 to 2 lbs.boneless, skinless chicken breasts
Directions:
1. In a large food storage bag, place lemon juice, oil, garlic, rosemary, salt and pepper. Add chicken.
2. Close bag and marinate in refrigerator 4 hours or overnight, turning bag frequently.
3. Place chicken in the slow cooker/Crock Pot and pour marinade over. Cover and cook for 6 to 8 hours, or until tender, basting occasionally with the marinade, if possible.
4. You may add frozen broccoli and carrots about 1 to 1 1/2 hours before done.

CROCK POT LEMON TARRAGON CHICKEN WITH ASPARAGUS
Ingredients:
1 pound frozen chicken breasts, boneless
1/4 cup lemon juice
1/4 cup chicken stock
1 teaspoon tarragon (dried)
1 package frozen asparagus (or fresh partially cooked)
2 Tablespoons flour
1/2 cup heavy or whipping cream
salt and pepper to taste
Directions:
1. Put frozen chicken breasts in Crock Pot and add lemon juice, broth, and tarragon. Cook on low 6 hours.
2. Add asparagus; whisk cream and flour together and add.
3. Cook another hour on high or until asparagus is tender and sauce is thickened. Serve over noodles or rice.

CROCK POT LOW CAL CHICKEN

Ingredients:
2 medium onions, thinly sliced
2-3 lb. chicken, cut up and skinned
2 cloves garlic, minced
1 large can tomatoes
1 teaspoon salt
1/4 teaspoon pepper
1/2 teaspoon oregano, crushed
1/2 teaspoon basil
1/2 teaspoon celery seed
1 bay leaf

Directions:
1. Layer ingredients in the crock pot in order listed and cook on low 6-8 hours, or on high 2 1/2 - 4 hours.

CROCK POT LOW FAT GLAZED CHICKEN

Ingredients:
6 ounces orange juice, frozen concentrate-thawed
3 chicken breasts, split
1/2 teaspoon marjoram
1 dash ground nutmeg
1 dash garlic powder (optional)
1/4 cup water
2 Tablespoons cornstarch

Directions:
1. Combine thawed orange juice concentrate (not regular orange juice) in bowl along with the marjoram, garlic powder and nutmeg.
2. Split the chicken breasts to make 6 serving sizes. Dip pieces into the orange juice to coat completely. Place in crockpot.
3. Pour the remaining orange juice mixture over the chicken. Cover and cook on low for 7-9 hours, or cook on high for 4 hours.
4. When chicken is done, remove to serving platter. Pour the sauce that remains into a saucepan.

5. Mix the cornstarchand water and stir into the juice in pan. Cook over medium heat, stirring constantly, until thick and bubbly. Serve the sauce over the chicken.

CROCK POT LOW-FAT CHICKEN & VEGGIE BAKE

Ingredients:
8 boneless, skinless chicken breasts
2 cans whole potatoes, drained
1 teaspoon garlic powder
1 bottle fat free Italian salad dressing
1 pkg. frozen veggies
1 can water chestnuts (optional)
salt & pepper

Directions:
1. Sprinke chicken breasts with salt, pepper and garlicup Put chicken in bottom of slow cooker/Crock Pot. Add remaining ingredients.
2. Cook on high for 4-6 hours or on low for 8-10 hours.

CROCK POT MAPLE-FLAVORED BARBECUE CHICKEN

Ingredients:
1 cup ketchup
1/2 cup maple flavored syrup
2 Tablespoons prepared mustard
2 Tablespoons Worcestershire sauce
2 teaspoons lemon juice
1/2 teaspoon chili powder
1/4 teaspoon garlic powder
4 boneless, skinned chicken breasts

Directions:
1. Place all ingredients in slow cooker/Crock Pot and cook on low for about 7 to 8 hours or until chicken is done.
2. Remove meat, shred and return to sauce. Place on buns for sandwiches or serve over hot rice.

CROCK POT MEDITERRANEAN STYLE CHICKEN

Ingredients:
6 skinless and boneless chicken breasts
1 large can tomato sauce
1 small can tomato puree
1 can sliced mushrooms
1 can ripe olives, sliced or whole
1 tablespoon garlic
1 tablespoon lemon juice
1 teaspoon oregano
1 onion, chopped
1/2 cup wine or brandy (optional)
cooked rice
Salt to taste

Directions:
1. Wash and remove excess fat from chicken. Combine all ingredients in the slow cooker/Crock Pot, except the rice.
2. Cover and cook on low for 6 to 8 hours. Serve chicken and sauce over rice.

CROCK POT MEXICAN CHICKEN

Ingredients:
Chicken pieces
Taco seasoning

Directions:
1. Combine chicken and taco seasoning in the crock pot and cook all day on low or several hours on high.

CROCK POT ONE POT CHICKEN AND GRAVY

Ingredients:
Boneless, skinless chicken breasts
Potatoes, quartered, with jackets
About 6 stalks celery
1/2 pkg. baby carrots
1 can cream of chicken soup
1 pkg. dry onion soup mix

Directions:
1. Place vegetables on bottom of Crock Pot. Brown chicken breasts in PAM or vegetable spray. Place over vegetables.
2. Cover with the cream of chicken soup, undiluted. Sprinkle with dry onion soup mix. Do not add water.
3. Cover and cook all day on low, or 6 hours on high.

CROCK POT MUSHROOM CHICKEN

Ingredients:
1 pound boneless, skinless chicken breasts
1 package of chicken gravy mix
1 cup white wine
1 can of cream of mushroom (or chicken) soup
8 oz. cream cheese

Directions:
1. Put chicken in crock-pot. Sprinkle gravy mix on top. Pour soup over that, then pour wine over that.
2. Cook on low all day.
3. 30 minutes before serving, put cream cheese in. When ready to serve, remove chicken and whisk the sauce together. Serve over pasta or rice.

CROCK POT ORANGE BURGUNDY CHICKEN

Ingredients:
2 1/2 to 3 pounds frying chicken, cut up
1/2 cup orange marmalade
1/2 cup orange juice
1/2 cup dry red wine
2 Tablespoons cornstarch
2 Tablespoons brown sugar, packed
1 Tablespoon lemon juice
1 teaspoon salt

Directions:
1. Remove skin from chicken. Rinse and place in slow cooker. Combine remaining ingredients in a bowl and pour over chicken.
2. Cover and cook on low 6 to 8 hours. Serve with rice and spinach salad.

93

CROCK POT ORANGE CHICKEN

Ingredients:
6 Chicken breasts, boned and skinned
1/2 teaspoon Ginger
1 teaspoon Salt
Pepper
8 ounces Frozen concentrate orange juice
1 1/2 cups Shredded coconut
2 cups Orange segments or canned, mandarin oranges
2 Green onions, chopped

Directions:
1. Put chicken, ginger, salt, pepper and frozen orange juice in crock pot and cook on low 6 hours.
2. Serve chicken on hot cooked rice on platter. Top with coconut, orange segments and green onions.

CROCK POT ORANGE CINNAMON CHICKEN

Ingredients:
4 pounds Chicken pieces
1 cup Chicken broth
1 cup Raisins
1 Tablespoon Flour
1/4 pound Butter
2 cups Orange juice
1/4 teaspoon Cinnamon
Salt and pepper to taste

Directions:
1. Heat butter in a large skillet, and brown chicken. Remove chicken and place in crock pot as they brown.
2. Combine all other ingredients, except flour, in skillet. Mix well and pour over chicken.
3. Cover pot, turn on LOW and cook 4 6 hours, or until chicken is tender.
4. Remove one cup of sauce from pot and combine with flour, mixing well. Return sauce flour mixture to the pot.
5. Turn pot on HIGH and cook and additional half hour.

CROCK POT ORANGE CRANBERRY CHICKEN

Ingredients:
1 cup chopped fresh cranberries
2 Tablespoons brown sugar
5 slices cinnamon-raisin bread
2 Tablespoons melted margarine or butter
1/4 teaspoon grated orange peel
8 chicken breast halves, boned, skinned
1/4 cup orange juice
2 Tablespoons melted butter or margarine
1 orange, sliced

Directions:
1. In medium bowl, combine cranberries and brown sugar; set aside.
2. Toast bread, cut into 1/2-inch cubes. Combine bread cubes, 2 TBL melted butter, orange peel and cranberry mixture.
3. Place one chicken breast at a time in a small plastic bag or between sheets of waxed paper. Lightly pound with meat mallet. Repeat with all chicken breasts.
4. Spoon about 1/3 cup cranberry mixture on center of each. Roll up; skewer to close.
5. In shallow dish, combine orange juice and 2 TBL melted butter. Roll filled chicken breasts in orange-juice mixture.
6. Place in slow cooker. Cover and cook on LOWabout 5 hours. To serve, spoon drippings over chicken. Garnish with orange slices.

CROCK POT ORANGE GLAZED CHICKEN BREASTS

Ingredients:
1 (6-oz) frozen orange juice concentrate
1/2 teaspoon dried marjoram leaves
2 Tablespoons cornstarch
6 (6 ounce) chicken breast halves
1/4 cup water

Directions:
1. Combine thawed orange juice and marjoram in shallow dish. Dip each breast in orange juice mixture, put in the crock pot, pour remaining sauce over breasts.
2. Cover and cook on low 7-9 hours or on high for 4-5 hours.
3. Before serving, remove chicken breasts from crock pot. Mix water and cornstarch in the sauce mixture; cook covered on high for about 15-30 minutes. Serve over chicken.

CROCK POT ORANGE TERIYAKI CHICKEN

Ingredients:
1 pound skinless, boneless chicken breast halves or thighs
1 16 ounce package loose-pack frozen broccoli, baby carrots, and water chestnuts
2 Tablespoons quick-cooking tapioca

SAUCE:
1/2 cup chicken broth
2 Tablespoons brown sugar
2 Tablespoons teriyaki sauce
1 teaspoon dry mustard
1 teaspoon finely shredded orange peel
1/2 teaspoon ground ginger

Directions:
1. Cut chicken into 1" pieces. Place vegetables in crockpot. Sprinkle tapioca over veggies. Place chicken on top of that.
2. Combine sauce ingredients and pour over chicken.
3. Cover; cook on low-heat for 4-6 hours or on high for 2-3. Serve over rice.

CROCK POT PHILIPPINE CHICKEN

Ingredients:
1 chicken, cut up
1 cup water
1/2 cup vinegar
1/4 cup soy sauce
2 cloves garlic, sliced

Directions:
1. Put all in Crock Pot; cook for 6 to 8 hours on low. Serve over rice.

CROCK POT PROVENCALE CHICKEN SUPPER

Ingredients:
4 (6 oz.) chicken breasts, skinless & boneless
2 teaspoons dried basil
1/4 teaspoon salt, divided
1/4 teaspoon pepper, divided
1 cup diced yellow bell pepper
1 (16 oz.) can navy beans, rinsed and drained
1 (14 oz.) can pasta-style chunky tomatoes, undrained

Directions:
1. Place chicken in slow cooker and sprinkle with basil, 1/8 teaspoon salt and 1/8 teaspoonpepper.
2. Combine remaining salt, pepper, bell pepper, beans and tomatoes in bowl andstir well. Spoon over chicken.
3. Cover with lid and cook on high 1 hour and low 5 hours.
4. Spoon bean mixture into each of 4 shallow bowls. Top each with 1 breast and 3/4 cup bean mixture.

CROCK POT PIZZA CHICKEN

Ingredients:
4 skinless, boneless chicken breasts, cut into bite size pieces
1 onion, chopped
1 green bell pepper, chopped
2 stalks celery, sliced
1 (10.75 ounce) can condensed tomato soup
1 (10.75 ounce) can condensed cream of mushroom soup
2 Tablespoons tomato paste
1/2 cup water
1 Tablespoon dried parsley
1 Tablespoon dried oregano
1 Tablespoon dried basil
1 bay leaf
salt and pepper to taste

Directions:
1. Place chicken, onion, bell pepper and celery in a slow cooker.
2. In a medium bowl combine the tomato soup, cream of mushroom soup, tomato paste, water,parsley, oregano, basil, salt and pepper.
3. Mix well and pour mixture over chicken and vegetables in slow cooker. Stir to coat and add bay leaf.
4. Cook on Low setting for 8 hours, until chicken and vegetables are tender.

CROCK POT PROVINCIAL CHICKEN

Ingredients:
1 1/2 pounds chicken tenders, frozen
2 small zucchini, diced
1 can (4 oz) sliced black olives
1 Tablespoon sherry wine vinegar or balsamic vinegar
1 can diced tomatoes (about 15 ounces)
1 can (10 oz) cream of chicken soup with herbs
2 teaspoons dried parsley flakes
1 teaspoon dried basil
1 Tablespoon dried minced onion

1 cup shredded cheddar cheese
2 to 3 Tablespoons sour cream (optional)
hot noodles, rice or pasta

Directions:
1. Combine first 9 ingredients in 3 1/2-quart slow cooker/Crock Pot (or larger).
2. Cover and cook on low for 6 to 8 hours.
3. Add cheese and sour cream during the last 15 minutes. Serve over hot noodles, rice or pasta.

CROCK POT CHICKEN PARISIENNE

Ingredients:
6 medium chicken breasts
Salt, pepper and paprika
1/2 cup white wine
1 (10 1/2 oz.) can cream of mushroom soup
1 (4 oz.) can sliced mushrooms, drained or fresh
1 cup sour cream
1/4 cup flour

Directions:
1. Sprinkle chicken breasts with salt, pepper and paprika. Place in crock pot.
2. Mix wine, soup and mushrooms until well combined, mixing in sour cream now if cooking on low. Pour over chicken. Sprinkle with paprika.
3. Cover and cook on low for 6-8 hours. If cooking on high, cook for 2 1/2 to 3 1/2 hours adding cream during the last 30 minutes.

CROCK POT RUSSIAN CHICKEN

Ingredients:
1 bottle Russian dressing (16 oz.)
1 envelope onion soup mix
1 jar apricot preserves (10 oz.)
4 pieces chicken, (4 to 6 ounces each)
Seasoned salt and pepper to taste

Directions:
1. Combine dressing, preserves and onion soup mix in bowl and pour into a slow cooker/Crock Pot.
2. Sprinkle chicken with seasoned salt and pepper. Place chicken, skin side down, in slow cooker/Crock Pot.
3. Cook on LOW for 8 hours (HIGH 4 hours)

CROCK POT EASY SANTA FE CHICKEN

Ingredients:
1 (15 oz.) can black beans, rinsed and drained
2 (15.25 oz.) cans whole kernel corn, drained
1 cup bottled thick and chunky salsa
5 or 6 skinless boneless chicken breasts (4-6 ounces each)
1 8 oz. package cream cheese
1 cup shredded cheddar cheese

Directions:
1. In a 3.5 or 4 quart electric slow cooker, mix together the beans, corn, and 1/2 cup salsa. Top with the chicken breasts, then pour the remaining salsa over the chicken.
2. Cover and cook on the high heat setting 2.5 - 3 hours, or until the chicken is tender and white throughout; do not overcook or the chicken will toughen.
3. Remove the chicken and cut into bite sized pieces. Add back to the slow cooker.
4. Add the cream cheese (cut into cubes to melt faster), and turn slow cooker to high heat. Heat until cream cheese melts and blends into sauce. Serve over rice. Top with shredded cheese.

CROCK POT SPAGHETTI SAUCE WITH CHICKEN & SAUSAGE

Ingredients:
1 lb. Italian sausage
3-4 boneless chicken breasts, cut into 1-inch chunks
1 cup chopped green pepper
1 cup chopped onion
1-2 teaspoons Italian seasoning
2 (4 oz. each) cans mushroom stems and pieces, drained
2 jars spaghetti sauce
Hot cooked pasta

Directions:
1. In skillet, brown Italian sausage, piercing casings to allow excess fat to run out.
2. Remove to plate and cut into 1/2 to 1-inch chunks.
3. In same skillet, brown chicken pieces.
4. Place sausage and chicken in slow cooker. Add pepper and onion. Sprinkle with Italian seasoning. Add mushrooms.
5. Pour sauce over everything. Cover and cook on low for 6 to 8 hours. Stir before serving over spaghetti or other pasta.

CROCK POT SPANISH CHICKEN

Ingredients:
2 lb. boneless skinless chicken breast
Seasoned salt & pepper to taste
Black olives, pitted
Sliced mushrooms, drained
Stewed tomatoes
Liquid to cover (tomato soup or tomato sauce with equal amount of water or stock)

Directions:
1. Cut chicken into bite-sized pieces; season. Place with remaining ingredients in slow cooker.
2. Simmer all day on low. Serve over rice.

CROCK POT SPICY CHICKEN WINGS

Ingredients:
3 Tablespoons vinegar
24 chicken wings, drummettes
1/4 cup hot pepper sauce, or less to taste
1/2 cup melted butter
1 pkg. Hidden Valley Ranch original dry salad dressing mix

Directions:
1. Mix all ingredients together except chicken wings and salad dressing mix.
2. Place chicken wings in crock pot. Pour mixture over wings. Sprinkle with dry dressing mix.
3. Cook in Crock Pot on low 4 to 5 hours.

CROCK POT SWISS CHICKEN CASSEROLE

Ingredients:
6 chicken breasts, boneless and skinless
6 slices Swiss cheese
1 can cream of mushroom soup
1/4 cup milk
2 cups stuffing mix
1/2 cup butter or margarine, melted

Directions:
1. Lightly grease Crock Pot or spray with cooking spray. Place chicken breasts in pot. Top with cheese.
2. Combine soup and milk, stirring well. Spoon over cheese; sprinkle with stuffing mix. Drizzle melted butter over stuffing mix.
3. Cook on low 8 to 10 hours or high 4 to 6 hours.

CROCK POT TERIYAKI SAUCE WINGS

Ingredients:
3 pounds chicken wings
1 onion, chopped
1 cup soy sauce
1 cup brown sugar
2 teaspoons ground ginger
2 cloves garlic, crushed
1/4 cup dry sherry

Directions:
1. Rinse chicken, and pat dry. Cut off wing tips and discard. Cut each wing into 2 pieces, cutting at the joint.
2. Broil wings 4 inches from heat for about 10 minutes on each side, or until browned. Transfer to Crock Pot.
3. Mix all remaining ingredients together and pour over chicken wings.
4. Cook, covered, on low for 5 to 6 hours or on high for 2 to 3 hours. Stir once or twice to keep wings coated with sauce.

CROCK POT WHITE CHILI WITH CHICKEN

Ingredients:
1 lb. dry white northern beans
5 1/4 cups chicken broth
2 cloves garlic, minced
1 large white onion, chopped
1 Tablespoon ground white pepper
1 teaspoon salt
1 Tablespoon dried oregano
1 Tablespoon ground cumin
1/2 teaspoon ground cloves
1 (7 oz.) can diced green chilies
5 cups diced cooked chicken breast
1 3/4 cups chicken broth
1 Tablespoon diced jalapeno pepper (optional)
Flour tortillas

Condiments:
Shredded Monterey Jack cheese
Sliced black olives
Chunky salsa

Sour cream
Diced avocados
Directions:
1. Soak beans in water to cover for 24 hours then drain.
2. In slow cooker/Crock Pot or large kettle, combine beans, 5 1/4 cup chicken broth, garlic, onion, white pepper, salt, oregano, cumin, cloves.
3. Simmer on low, covered, for at least 5 hours until beans are tender. Stir occasionally.
4. Stir in green chiles, chicken and 1 3/4 chicken broth. For hotter taste, add jalapeno.
5. Cover and simmer for 1 more hour. Serve with flour tortillas and condiments.

CROCK POT EASY CHICKEN
Ingredients:
1 chicken, cut up
2 Tablespoons melted butter
Salt and pepper
2 Tablespoons dry Italian salad dressing
1 can mushroom soup
2 small pkg. cream cheese, cut in cubes
1/2 cup sherry
1 Tablespoon chopped onion
Directions:
1. Wash chicken and pat dry. Brush with butter, sprinkle with salt and pepper sparingly. Place in crock pot.
2. Sprinkle dry salad mix over chicken. Cover and cook on low 5-6 hours.
3. About 3/4 hour before serving, mix soup, cream cheese, wine and onion in saucepan. Cook until smooth.
4. Pour over chicken, cover and cook 30 minutes. Serve with sauce.

CROCK POT CHICKEN
Ingredients:
6 chicken breasts, skinned
2 cans cream of mushroom soup
1 (16 oz.) carton sour cream
Paprika
Directions:
1. Place chicken in crock pot. Cover with mushroom soup.
2. Cook on HIGH for 4 hours. The last 30 minutes add sour cream and paprika.

CROCK POT WINNING WINGS IN SWEET AND SOUR SAUCE
Ingredients:
16 chicken wings
4 Tablespoons wine or balsamic vinegar
1 cup apricot preserves
2 Tablespoons peanut butter (optional)
1 cup ketchup
4 Tablespoons horseradish
1 cup sweet onion, finely chopped
1 teaspoon hot sauce (optional)
Directions:
1. Pat the chicken wings dry and place then in the slow cooker/Crock Pot.
2. In a bowl, mix together remaining ingredients. Taste-check for a good balance of sweet and sour.
3. Pour the sauce over the wings. Cover the slow cooker/Crock Pot and cook on low until the chicken is tender, about 4 hours.

CROCK POT GOOEY CHICKEN BURRITOS

Ingredients:
2 large chicken breasts
12 oz. jar of salsa
1 can cream of chicken soup
1 can diced green chilies (mild)
1 1/2 cups of grated cheese
1 small onion
A handful of Spanish olives, sliced
2 Tablespoons cooking tapioca
Flour tortillas

Directions:
1. Combine all ingredients, except tortillas, in crockpot.
2. Cook on low, 8 hours. Spoon on to warmed tortillas and roll.

CROCK POT ITALIAN DINNER

Ingredients:
4 chicken breasts, cut in half
1 pkg. sweet Italian sausage, cut in half
1 large (16 oz.) container fresh mushrooms, cut in half
2 large onions, sliced thickly
2 large green peppers, sliced thickly
1 large (28 oz.) can stewed tomatoes
1 (8 oz.) can tomato sauce
1 Tablespoon Italian seasoning
Salt & Pepper

Directions:
1. Mix all ingredients together in crockpot; cook 6-8 hours on low.
2. Serve over pasta with lots of shredded mozarella cheese.

CROCK POT LEMONADE CHICKEN

Ingredients:
4 to 6 pieces chicken (breasts and legs)
1 (6 oz.) can frozen lemonade, thawed
2 Tablespoons brown sugar
3 Tablespoons ketchup
1 Tablespoon vinegar
2 Tablespoons cornstarch
2 Tablespoons cold water

Directions:
1. Arrange chicken pieces in crockpot. Combine lemonade, brown sugar, and ketchupand mix well. Pour over chicken.
2. Cover. Cook on high 3-4 hours or low 6-8 hours.
3. Remove chicken from pot, cover to keep hot. Transfer liquid to saucepan.
4. Skim fat; combine cornstarch and cold water and add slowly to liquid, while stirring over low heat. When thickened, serve with chicken over hot rice.

CROCK POT LACQUERED CHICKEN

Ingredients:
1 Tablespoon vegetable oil
2 lb. whole chicken
3 large onions, peeled and chopped
5 large tomatoes, chopped
1 medium orange, unpeeled, seeded, chopped
1 teaspoon sugar
1 teaspoon salt
1/8 teaspoon pepper
1/2 cup water
1 bouillon cube, crumbled
3 heaping Tablespoons red currant, raspberry or red grape jelly
1/4 cup sweet sherry

Directions:
1. In a medium skillet, over medium high heat, heat the oil and sauté the chicken, turning often, until well browned all over.
2. Remove the chicken to a plate. Sauté the onion in the skillet until well browned. Turn into the crockpot.
3. Place the tomatoes, orange, sugar, salt and pepper in the crock pot and set the chicken on top.
4. Rinse the skillet with the water and scrape into the cooker. Add the bouillon cube.

5. Cover and cook on Low for 5 to 7 hours.

6. Before serving, remove the chicken to a deep serving dish and keep warm.

7. Turn the pot contents into a skillet, set the heat to high and simmer until thick enough to mound on a spoon.

8. Stir in the jelly and the sherry and cook, stirring until the sauce boils. Do not overcook, lest the sauce lose its shiny quality. If sauce is not shinyenough, bring back to a very brisk boil and quickly stir in some jelly.

9. Pour sauce over the chicken and serve.

CROCK POT YUMMY CHICKEN WINGS

Ingredients:
12-18 chicken wings
1/3 cup soy sauce
1 teaspoon ginger
2 garlic cloves minced
2 green onions minced
1 Tablespoon honey
2 teaspoon oil

Directions:
1. Combine ingredients in Crock Pot.
2. Cook on low for 6-8 hours.

Crock Pot Chili

CROCK POT CHILI #1

Ingredients:
2 lbs. ground beef
1 large onion
1 large green pepper
1 large jalapeno pepper
Chili powder to taste
Garlic salt to taste
Salt to taste
Pepper to taste
Sugar to taste
2 cans crushed tomatoes
1 can tomato puree
1 can kidney beans
2 cans chili hot beans

Directions:
1. Brown beef. Saute chopped onion and green pepper in grease. Mix beef, onion and green pepper. Add spices; let stand 1 hour.
2. Add tomatoes, tomato puree, beans; cook in crock pot for 8-10 hours.

CROCK POT CHILI #2

Ingredients:
2 (8 oz.) cans tomato sauce
2 (16 oz.) cans dark red kidney beans, undrained
1 lb. hamburger meat
3 or 4 Tablespoons chili powder

Directions:
1. Cook the hamburger meat and drain well.
2. Mix all ingredients together in crock pot.
3. Cook on high for at least 1 to 2 hours. Stir occasionally.

CROCK POT CHILI #3

Ingredients:
1 lb. pork, cubed
1 (16 oz.) can stewed tomatoes
small can diced jalapenos
small can diced green chilies
2 to 4 garlic cloves, finely diced
Salt to taste
2 Tablespoons flour
1 cup water
2 Tablespoons oil

Directions:
1. Brown pork in oil. Add flour. Stir until pork is coated and flour is brown.
2. Put the pork and all remaining ingredients in the crock pot and simmer until pork is soft - 3 to 4 hours on high or 6 to 7 hours on low.

CROCK POT CHILI #4

Ingredients:
2 lb. hamburger or deerburger
2 cans Bush's chili hot beans
2 medium green peppers, chopped
2 medium onions, chopped
1 pkg. Williams chili seasoning
1 large can stewed tomatoes

Directions:
1. Brown meat, onions and green peppers. Add meat in and mix all remaining ingredients into crock pot.
2. Stir well and cook on low for 8 hours or on high for 4 hours. Salt and pepper to taste.

EASY CROCK POT CHILI

Ingredients:
4 cans lite kidney beans
2 lbs. hamburger
4 cans tomato soup
2 cans stewed tomatoes
2 medium onions
2 Tablespoons chili powder
2 teaspoons salt
1 teaspoon paprika
1/4 teaspoon garlic powder
2 or 3 bay leaves
1/4 teaspoon cayenne pepper (optional)

Directions:
1. Brown hamburger with chopped onions; drain and mix with all other ingredients in large crock pot.
2. Cook for 8 hours on low heat.

CROCK POT CHILI CON QUESO

Ingredients:
2 Tablespoons butter
1 medium onion, chopped
1 can jalapeno peppers, chopped
1 15 1/2 oz. tomatoes, chopped, undrained
1 jar pimiento, chopped, drained
3/4 cup cheddar cheese, grated
salt and pepper, to taste

Directions:
1. Saute onion in butter in medium saucepan. Combine next 3 ingredients with onion.
2. Transfer to crockpot and cook on low for 6 to 8 hours.
3. Add cheese, mixing thoroughly until melted.

CROCK POT CHILI DIP

Ingredients:
1 large jar (16 oz.) picante sauce, mild
2 cans refried beans
8 ounces sour cream
1/2 teaspoon chili powder
1 lb. ground beef
1 onion, chopped
Salt and pepper to taste
8 oz. Cheddar cheese, shredded
Jalapenos or mild chile, chopped, to taste

Directions:
1. Cook ground beef with onion; drain.
2. Mix everything together in slow cooker/Crock Pot and cook for 5-6 hours on low.

CROCK POT CHILI I

Ingredients:
2 onions, chopped
2 cloves garlic
1 lb. lean hamburger
2 Tablespoons chili powder
cumin to taste
2 cans (16 oz. ea.) tomatoes
2 cans tomato soup
2 cans kidney beans, drained salt and pepper to taste
optional: shredded cheese and/or sour cream for topping

Directions:
1. Cook onions and garlic in 2 Tablespoons oil till onions are yellow. Add hamburger and cook till browned. Stir in chili powder and cumin; cook 2 minutes more.
2. In crockpot, combine remaining ingredients. Stir in browned meat mixture. Cover and cook on Low setting for 8-10 hours.
3. To serve: ladle chili into bowls. Top with optional shredded cheese and/or sour cream, if desired.

CROCK POT CHILI II

Ingredients:

1 lb. ground beef, cooked and rinsed
60-70 ounces rinsed light or dark kidney beans
16 ounces tomato paste
16 ounces peeled chopped tomatoes (reserve liquid)
1/2 small onion, chooped
1 small green pepper, chopped
1 package chili seasonings
cayenne pepper to taste, if desired

Directions:

1. Combine all ingredients in the crockpot and cook on low at least 5 hours so the peppers and onions are cooked soft.
2. Use the reserved tomato liquid if it seems too thick for your taste.
3. Serve with tortillas, cheese, sour cream, and salsa.

CROCK POT CHILI III

Ingredients:

1 16 oz can kidney beans -- drained
2 14-1/2 oz can tomatoes
2 pounds ground chuck -- coarsely ground
2 medium onions -- coarsely chopped
1 green pepper -- coarsely chopped
2 cloves garlic -- crushed
3 Tablespoons chili powder
1 teaspoon pepper
1 teaspoon cumin
salt to taste

Directions:

1. Put all ingredients in crock pot in order listed. Stir once.
2. Cover and cook on Low 10-12 hours. (High 5-6 hours).
3. Serve with shredded cheddar cheese and tortilla chips.

CROCK POT CHILI CON CARNE

Ingredients:

4 pounds ground beef
3 Tablespoons shortening
2 cups chopped onion
2 garlic cloves -- crushed
4 Tablespoons chili powder
3 beef bouillon cubes -- crushed
1 1/2 teaspoons paprika
1 teaspoon oregano
1 teaspoon ground cumin
1/2 teaspoon cayenne pepper
1/2 cup beef stock
1 can tomatoes -- 28 ozs.
1 can tomato paste -- 8 oz.
4 cans red kidney beans -- 1 lb. cans

Directions:

1. Heat shortening in skillet and brown beef, discard fat. Combine all ingredients in removable liner, stirring well. Place liner in base.
2. Cover and cook on low 8-10 hours; high 4-5 hours or auto 6-7 hours.

CROCK POT CHILI WITH 4 KINDS OF BEANS

Ingredients:

1-2 pounds browned ground beef
2 cans chili hot beans
2 cans dark red kidney beans, drained
2 cans pinto beans, drained
2 cans kidney beans, drained
2 cans rotel tomatoes
1 package chili seasoning

Directions:

1. Put all ingredients in Crock Pot and cook on low all day (about 10 hours).

CROCK POT FAVORITE CHILI

Ingredients:
2 lbs. coarsely ground beef chuck
2 (16 oz.) cans red kidney beans, drained
2 (14 1/2 oz.) cans tomatoes, drained
2 medium onions, coarsely chopped
1 green pepper, seeded and coarsely chopped
2 cloves garlic, peel and crushed
2-3 Tablespoons chili powder
1 teaspoon black pepper
1 teaspoon cumin
Salt and pepper to taste

Directions:
1. In a large, preferably non-stick, saucepan brown the chuck and drain off the fat.
2. Put the ground beef and other ingredients in a 3 1/2 to 4 quart Crock Pot. Stir well.
3. Cover and cook on low for 10-12 hours.

CROCK POT HEARTY CHILI

Ingredients:
1 pound ground turkey
1/2 ground chuck
30 oz. tomato sauce
24 oz. V-8 (tomato- vegetable juice)
1/2 cup chopped onion
1/2 cup chopped celery
1 Tablespoon chili powder
1 cup chopped green pepper
1 cup chopped mushrooms
1 small jalapeno pepper (optional)
14 oz. stewed tomatoes
1/2 cup uncooked wild rice
2/3 cup brown sugar
14 oz. chili beans
1 oz. chili seasoning mix

Directions:
1. Brown ground turkey and ground beef. Drain well.
2. Place all other ingredients in a slow cooker and add the meat.

3. Cook on low for 6 to 9 hours. Serve with crackers or cornbread.

CROCK POT HOT CHILI CON QUESO

Ingredients:
1 1/2 cups half-and-half, scalded
1/2 pound grated Monterrey Jack cheese
1/2 pound grated sharp process cheese
1 Tablespoon butter
1/2 onion, minced
1 medium clove garlic, minced
1/4 cup dry white wine or low-sodium stock
1/4 cup flour
1/4 cup water
1 can chopped green chile peppers (4 oz)
1 to 2 Tablespoons chopped jalapeno (more or less depending on taste)
salt and pepper
dash cayenne pepper

Directions:
1. Pour scalded half-and-half into buttered Crock Pot.
2. Turn to high and stir in cheeses.
3. In small skillet, saute onion and garlic in butter until onion is tender. Add wine or stock and stir well.
4. Add to cheese mixture. Combine flour with water and stir in.
5. Cook covered on high for 30 minutes, or until cheese begins to melt.
6. Turn to low and cook about 4 to 6 hours, stirring 2 or 3 times during the first hour and occasionally after that.
If the mixture is too thin, mix 2 Tablespoons of flour with 2 Tablespoons of water and add.

CROCK POT MEXICAN CHILI

Ingredients:

2 (15 1/2 oz.) cans red kidney beans, drained
1 (28 oz.) can tomatoes, cut up
1 cup chopped celery
1 cup chopped onion
1 (6 oz.) can tomato paste
1/2 cup chopped green pepper
1 (4 oz.) can green chili peppers, drained and chopped
2 Tablespoons sugar
1 bay leaf
1/2 teaspoon garlic powder
1 teaspoon salt
1 teaspoon dried, crushed marjoram
Dash of pepper
1 lb. ground beef

Directions:

1. In skillet brown ground beef and drain. In crockpot combine all ingredients.
2. Cover, cook on low heat for 8 to 10 hours. Remove bay leaf and stir before serving.

CROCK POT NO-BEAN CHILI

Ingredients:

2 pounds ground beef, or cubed lean stew beef
1 (8 oz) can Tomato sauce
1 (6 oz) can Tomato paste
1 (16 oz) can Stewed tomatoes , optional
2 Tablespoons Chili powder
1 1/2 teaspoons Salt
1 teaspoon Hot pepper sauce, or more

Directions:

1. Combine all ingredients in slow cooker.
2. Cover and cook on low for 8-10 hours.

CROCK POT SOUR CREAM CHILI BAKE

Ingredients:

1 pound Ground beef
1 can Pinto beans, drained (15 oz)
1 can Enchilada sauce (10 oz)
1 can Tomato sauce (8 oz)
1 cup Shredded process American cheese
1 Tablespoon Instant minced onion
1 cup Water
4 cups Corn chips
1 cup Sour cream
1/2 cup Shredded process American cheese

Directions:

1. Brown ground beef; drain. Transfer meat to Crock Pot.
2. Stir in beans, enchilada sauce, tomato sauce, 1 cup of cheese, onion and 1 cup of water.
2. Reserve 1 cup of corn chips; crush the remaining chips and add to the meat mixture.
4. Cover and cook on low heat for 8 to 10 hours. To serve, top with sour cream, remaining cheese, and reserved corn chips.

CROCK POT TACO CHILI

Ingredients:

1 1/2 to 2 pounds lean ground beef
1 medium onion, chopped
1 pkg. (1 1/4oz) taco seasoning mix
2 cans (14 1/2oz ea.) diced tomatoes
1 can (10oz.) diced tomatoes with green chilies
1 can (16oz) pinto beans, rinsed and drained
1 15oz. can chili beans in sauce
1 cup frozen whole kernel corn
Shredded cheese (mozzarella, Monterey Jack or cheddar)
Slightly crushed tortilla chips

Directions:

1. In a large skillet, cook ground beef and onion, one-half at a time, till meat is browned and onion is tender. Drain off fat.
2. Transfer to a 3 1/2- to 5-quart crock pot. Stir in dry taco seasoning mix, diced tomatoes, diced tomatoes with green

chilies, pinto beans, chili beans in chili sauce, and corn.

3. Cover; cook on low for 8 to 10 hours or on high for 4 to 5 hours. Sprinkle each serving with some cheese and chips.

CROCK POT TEXAS CHILI
Ingredients:
6 strips bacon
2 lbs. boneless beef cubes
2 cans (15 oz.) kidney beans, drained
1 can (28 oz.) tomatoes, cut up
1 can (8 oz.) tomato sauce
1 cup finely chopped onion
1/2 cup thinly sliced carrots
1/2 cup finely chopped green pepper
1/2 cup finely chopped celery
2 Tablespoons minced parsley
2 cloves garlic minced
1 bay leaf
2 Tablespoons chili powder
1 teaspoon salt
1/8 teaspoon pepper
Directions:
1. Fry bacon until crisp. Remove bacon and drain on paper towel.
2. Brown half the beef cubes in pan with bacon drippings five minutes. Place in slow cooker. Repeat with remaining meat.
3. Stir bacon and remaining ingredients into 3 1/2 quart slow cooker.
4. Cover and cook on low setting about 10 hours or until beef is tender. Stir occasionally.

CROCK POT TEX MEX CHILI
Ingredients:
1 pound ground beef or pork sausage
2 cloves garlic -- minced
3 teaspoons chili powder
1/2 teaspoon ground cumin
1 (15 1/2 oz.) red kidney beans drained
1 cup chopped celery
1 cup chopped onion
1/2 cup chopped green pepper

1 (16 oz.) can tomatoes -- cut up
1 Rotel tomatoes and chilies
1 cup V8 juice or tomato juice
1 (6 oz.) can tomato paste
1/4 teaspoon salt
Shredded Cheddar cheese
Sour cream
Directions:
1. In skillet brown meat and garlicup Drain. Stir in chili powder and cumin; cook 2 minutes more.
2. In crock pot combine beans,celery, onions, green pepper. Add undrained tomatoes, tomatoes and chilies,vegetable juice, tomato paste and salt. Stir in cooked meat.
3. Cover cook over low heat setting for 10-12 hours or on high 4-5 hours

CROCK POT VEGETABLE CHILI
Ingredients:
2 medium zucchini -- chopped
1 medium red bell pepper -- chopped
1 medium green bell pepper -- chopped
3 carrots -- peeled and chopped
3 celery ribs -- chopped
2 medium onions -- chopped
2 large tomatoes -- chopped OR 1 can Italian tomatoes -- drained and chopped
1 can whole kernel corn -- (15.25 oz) well drained
1 can garbanzo beans (chick-peas) -- (15.25 oz) rinsed and drained
2 teaspoons chili powder
2 teaspoons ground cumin
1 can mild salsa -- (15 oz)
1/3 cup tomato paste
salt and pepper
Directions:
1. In a 4-quart electric slow cooker, mix together the zucchini, bell peppers, carrots,celery, onions, tomatoes, corn, garbanzo beans, chili powder, cumin and salsa.

2. Cover an cook on the low heat setting about 8 hours or until the vegetables are almost tender.
3. Stir in the tomato paste. Season with salt and pepper to taste

CROCK POT VEGGIE CHILI 2
Ingredients:
Olive oil
1-2 large yellow onions, diced
2 cloves garlic, minced
1 red pepper, diced fairly large
1 green pepper, diced fairly large
2 28-oz. cans crushed tomatoes
1 Tablespoon cumin
1 teaspoon cayenne (or to your taste)
1 package frozen corn
2 cans black beans
1-1.5 cup picante sauce
Salt to taste
Grated cheddar, if desired
Cashew nuts, if desired
Directions:
1. Sauté onions in the olive oil. Add garlic.
2. After onion and garlic are haveturned golden brown, add cumin, and cayenne. Fry for a couple of minutes.
3. Add the peppers, sauté them for a few minutes.
4. Put the crushed tomatoes, corn, beans and picante sauce into the crock pot, and add the onion mixture.
5. Cook on low about 10 hours

CROCK POT BLACK BEAN CHILI
Ingredients:
1 lb. dry black beans
2 Tablespoons oil
6 garlic cloves, minced or pressed
2 onions, chopped
1/4 teaspoon crushed red pepper flakes (more if you like hot food)
1 Tablespoon chili powder
1 Tablespoon ground cumin

1 teaspoon dried oregano
1 bay leaf
1 28 oz. can chopped tomatoes in juice
1 Tablespoon soy sauce
2 cup water
6 oz. can tomato paste
1 Tablespoon red wine vinegar
2 cans contrasting beans (pinto, garbanzo, great northern, etc.)-- drained and rinsed
garnishes: grated cheese, sour cream, chopped parsley, onion, etc.
Directions:
1. Rinse and sort the beans and place in the slow cooker/Crock Pot with a generous amount of water.
2. Cook on low overnight (no presoaking necessary). In the morning drain the cooking water.
3. Heat the oil in a skillet and saute the onions, garlic and red pepper flakes. Cook 1 minute, then add chili powder and cumin and cook 2 minutes, stirring.
4. Add this mixture to the slow cooker/Crock Pot along with all remaining ingredients except canned beans and garnishes. Stir well and cook on low all day.
5. Stir in canned beans an hour or so before serving. Serve with garnishes.

EASIEST CROCK POT CHILI
Ingredients:
1 1/2 lb. ground beef
1/2 cup chopped onion
1 clove garlic, minced
1 (16 oz.) can tomatoes
1 (6 oz.) can tomato paste
1 (16 oz.) can kidney beans
1-2 Tablespoons chili powder
Salt and pepper to taste
Directions:
1. Brown beef with onion and garlic in skillet, drain.
2. Mix with remaining ingredients in crock pot on low for 6 hours

CROCK POT BEST CHILI

Ingredients:
1 lb. ground beef
2 large onions, chopped
1 large green bell pepper, chopped
2 Tablespoons chili powder
2 teaspoons salt
1/8 teaspoon paprika
1/8 teaspoon red pepper, crushed
1 (28 oz.) can tomatoes
1 (20 oz.) can kidney beans, drained
1 large bay leaf

Directions:
1. Brown ground beef in skillet for 10 minutes, drain.
2. Add onions, green pepper, chili powder, salt, paprika and red pepper. Simmer for 10 minutes.
3. Add tomatoes, beans and bay leaf.
4. Pour into crock pot and cook on medium for 6 to 8 hours. Add a small amount of water if necessary.
5. Remove bay leaf before serving.

CROCK POT BLACK BEAN CHILI

Ingredients:
3/4 cup cooked black beans
1 lb. stew beef, cubed
3 Tablespoons oil
1/4 cup chopped onion
1/4 cup chopped green peppers
1/2 cup diced green chilies
3 Tablespoons tomato paste
3 to 4 beef bouillon cubes, or beef base
1/4 teaspoon ground cumin
1 teaspoon minced garlic
1/2 teaspoon salt and pepper
1 cup shredded Monterey Jack or cheddar cheese

Directions:
1. Brown stew beef in oil with onion and green pepper.
2. Combine all ingredients except cheese and cook 6 to 8 hours on low.

3. Sprinkle cheese over individual servings.

CROCK POT POTATO CHILI

Ingredients:
1 lb. hamburger
1/4 cup chopped onion
2 teaspoons salt
3 cloves garlic
5 small to medium potatoes
beef bouillon
14.5oz can tomatoes
1/2 teaspoon onion powder
1/2 teaspoon garlic salt
1/2 teaspoon cumin
1 Tablespoon paprika
1 Tablespoon chili powder
Worcestershire sauce
pepper to taste
1/2 cup water

Directions:
1. Brown 1 lb. hamburger , salt, chopped onion and cloves of garlic in a frying pan; drain oil.
2. Cut up potatoes in 1/4" slices. Put potatoes in crock pot, add hamburger.
3. Mix beef bouillon with a little hot water to dissolve, add to crock pot.
4. Blend tomatoes in blender (the kind w/added seasonings is fine), add to crock pot.
5. Add the 1/2 teaspoon each onion, garlic salt, cumin, paprika , chili powder, a couple of shakes of Worcestershire sauce, black pepper, and 1/2 c water.
6. Cook on high 3 to 4 hours, or low 6 or 7 hours.

CROCK POT WHITE CHILI #1

Ingredients:
3 15-oz cans great northern, pinto, or cannellini beans, drained
2 1/2 cups chopped, cooked chicken
1 cup chopped onion
1 1/2 cup chopped red, green, and/or yellow pepper
2 jalapeno chili peppers, stemmed and chopped
2 cloves garlic, minced
2 teaspoons ground cumin
1/2 teaspoon salt
1/2 teaspoon dried oregano, crushed
3 1/2 cups chicken broth
Shredded Monterey Jack cheese (optional)
Broken tortilla chips (optional)

Directions:
1. In a Crock Pot combine the drained beans, chicken, onion, sweet pepper, jalapeno peppers, garlic, cumin, salt, and oregano.
2. Stir in chicken broth.
3. Cover; cook on low-heat setting for 8 to 10 hours or on high-heat setting for 4 to 5 hours.
4. Ladle soup into bowls. Top each serving with some cheese and tortilla chips, if desired.

CROCK POT WHITE CHILI

Ingredients:
1 1/4 lb. ground turkey
1 cup chopped onion
1/2 cup diced green pepper
1 teaspoon minced garlic
1 teaspoon Oregano
2 teaspoons Cumin
3 cans (15 oz or so) Cannelloni Beans (or any white bean)
1 cup chicken broth
1 teaspoon chili powder
1/2 teaspoon salt
1/4 teaspoon pepper

Directions:
1. Brown the ground turkey with onion, green pepper, garlic, and oregano and put it in the crockpot.
2. Add 2 cans beans along with broth, cumin, chili powder, salt andpepper. Let it cook a bit on low.
3. In the blender, blend the remaining can of beans and add it to the chili.
4. Cook on low until done.

Crock Pot Fish and Seafood

CROCK POT CITRUS FISH
Ingredients:
1 1/2 lb. fish filets
Salt and pepper to taste
1 medium onion, chopped
5 Tablespoons chopped parsley
4 teaspoons oil
2 teaspoons grated lemon rind
2 teaspoons grated orange rind
Orange and lemon slices
Directions:
1. Butter slow cooker/Crock Pot and put salt and pepper on fish to taste.
2. Place fish in pot. Put onion, parsley and grated rinds and oil over fish.
3. Cover and cook on low for 1 1/2 hours. Serve garnished with orange and lemon slices.

CROCK POT COCONUT THAI SHRIMP AND RICE
Ingredients:
2 (10 oz.) cans chicken broth
1 cup water
1 teaspoon coriander
1/2 teaspoon cumin
1 teaspoon salt
1/2 teaspoon cayenne pepper
zest and juice of 2 limes (1/3 cup of juice)
7 cloves minced garlic
1 Tablespoon minced fresh ginger
1 medium onion chopped
1 red bell pepper chopped
1 carrot peeled and shredded
1/4 cup flaked coconut
1/2 cup golden raisins
2 cups converted rice
1 lb. peeled and deveined jumbo cooking shrimp (thawed if frozen)
2 oz. fresh snow peas cut into strips
toasted coconut for garnish (optional)

Directions:
1. In a 5 quart crock pot, combine chicken broth, water, coriander, cumin, salt, cayenne pepper, lime zest, lime juice, garlic and ginger.
2. Stir in onion, pepper, carrot, coconut, raisins and rice.
3. Cover and cook on low 3 1/2 hours, or until rice is tender. Check after 3 hours and if liquid is absorbed, but rice is not tender, add 1 more cup water.
4. When rice is tender, stir in shrimp and snow peas. Cook 30 minutes longer. Sprinkle with toasted coconut and serve.

CROCK POT SALMON BAKE
Ingredients:
3 cans salmon, 1 lb. each
4 cups bread crumbs, soft 10 slices
1 can tomatoes in puree, 1 lb.
1 green pepper, chopped
3 teaspoons lemon juice
1 can cream of onion soup, condensed
2 chicken bouillon cubes, crushed
6 eggs, well beaten
1 can cream of celery soup, condensed
1/2 cup milk
Directions:
1. Grease removable liner well. Combine all ingredients, except celery soup and milk, in removable liner. Place liner in base.
2. Cover and cook on low 4-6 hours or auto for 3 hours.
3. Combine cream of celery soup with 1/2 cup of milk and heat in saucepan. Use as sauce for salmon bake.

CROCK POT SHRIMP MARINARA

Ingredients:

1 (16 oz.) can of tomatoes, cut up
2 Tablespoons minced parsley
1 clove of garlic, minced
1/2 teaspoon dried basil
1 teaspoon salt
1/4 teaspoon pepper
1 teaspoon dried oregano
1 (6 oz.) can tomato paste
1/2 teaspoon seasoned salt
1 lb. cooked shelled shrimp
Grated Parmesan cheese
Cooked spaghetti

Directions:

1. In a Crock Pot, combine tomatoes with parsley, garlic, basil, salt, pepper, oregano, tomato paste and seasoned salt.
2. Cover and cook on low for 6 to 7 hours.
3. Turn control to high, stir in shrimp, cover and cook on high for 10 to 15 minutes more.
4. Serve over cooked spaghetti. Top with Parmesan cheese.

CROCK POT SHRIMP CREOLE

Ingredients:

1 1/2 cup diced celery
1 1/4 cup chopped onion
3/4 c. chopped bell pepper
1 (8 oz.) can tomato sauce
1 (28 oz.) can whole tomatoes
1 clove garlic
1 teaspoon salt
1/4 teaspoon pepper
6 drops Tabasco (optional)
1 lb. shrimp, deveined & shelled

Directions:

1. Combine all ingredients except shrimp.
2. Cook 3 to 4 hours on high or 6 to 8 hours on low. Add shrimp last hour of cooking. Serve over hot rice.

CROCK POT SWEET AND SOUR SHRIMP

Ingredients:

1 package (6 ox.) frozen Chinese pea pods, partially thawed
1 can (13 oz.) juice-pack pineapple chunks or tidbits (drain and reserve juice)
2 Tablespoons cornstarch
3 Tablespoons sugar
1 chicken bouillon cube
1 cup boiling water
1/2 cup reserved pineapple juice
2 teaspoons soy sauce
1/2 teaspoon ground ginger
2 cans (4 1/2 oz. each) shrimp, rinsed & drained
2 Tablespoons cider vinegar
Fluffy rice

Directions:

1. Place pea pods and drained pineapple in Crock-Pot.
2. In a small saucepan, stir together cornstarch and sugar.
3. Dissolve bouillon cube in boiling water and add with juice, soy sauce and ginger to saucepan. Bring to a boil, stirring, and cook sauce for about 1 minute or until thickened and transparent.
4. Gently blend sauce into pea pods and pineapple.
5. Cover and cook on Low setting for 4 to 6 hours.
6. Before serving, add shrimp and vinegar, stirring carefully to avoid breaking up shrimp. Serve over hot rice.

CROCK POT TUNA NOODLE CASSEROLE

Ingredients:

2 cans cream of celery soup
1/3 cup dry sherry
2/3 cup milk
2 Tablespoons parsley flakes
10 ounces frozen peas
2 cans tuna, drained
10 ounces egg noodles, cooked
2 Tablespoons butter or margarine
dash curry powder (optional)

Directions:

1. In a large bowl, thoroughly combine soup, sherry, milk, parsley flakes, vegetables, and tuna. Fold in noodles.
2. Pour into greased Crock Pot. Dot with butter or margarine.
3. Cover and cook on Low 7 to 9 hours. (Cook noodles just until tender.)

CROCK POT TUNA SALAD CASSEROLE

Ingredients:

2 cans tuna, drained and flaked
1 can cream of celery soup
4 hard-cooked eggs, chopped
1 cup diced celery
1/2 cup mayonnaise
1/4 teaspoon pepper
1 1/2 cups crushed potato chips

Directions:

1. Combine all ingredients except 1/4 cup of the crushed potato chips; stir well.
2. Pour into greased Crock Pot. Top with remaining potato chips.
3. Cover and cook on Low setting for 5-8 hours.

CROCK POT SHERRIED CRAB MEAT

Ingredients:

2 13-ounce cans crab meat
2 10 -ounce cans golden mushroom or cream of mushroom soup

6 Tablespoons butter
1/4 cup dry sherry
1/2 teaspoon Worcestershire
1/2 cup light cream sauce
Salt and pepper
3 green onions with tops, finely chopped
2 eggs, beaten

Directions:

1. Remove any cartilage or shell from crab meat; break into pieces and place inCROCK-POT.
2. Add all remaining ingredients except eggs. Stir gently.
3. Cover and cook on high 1 hour, then on Low 2 to 3 hours. Stir in eggs during last hour.Serve over hot toast or in patty shells.

CROCK POT SALMON AND POTATO CASSEROLE

Ingredients:

4 potatoes, peeled and thinly sliced
3 Tablespoons flour
salt and pepper
1 can (16 ounces) salmon, drained and flaked
1 medium onion, chopped
1 can (10 3/4 ounces) cream of mushroom soup
1/4 cup water
nutmeg

Directions:

1. Place half of the potatoes in greased Crock Pot. Sprinkle with half of the flour, salt and pepper. Cover with half the salmon; sprinkle with half the onion. Repeat layers in order.
2. Combine soup and water. Pour over potato-salmon mixture. Dust with nutmeg.
3. Cover and cook on Low for 7-10 hours.

Crock Pot Pasta and Macaroni

CROCK POT SPAGHETTI

Ingredients:
1 1/2 lbs. ground beefs
1 1/2 teaspoons Italian seasoning
2 Tablespoons dry onions
1/2 teaspoon garlic powder
1 teaspoon salt
1 (4 oz.) can mushrooms
3 cups tomato juice
2 (8 oz.) cans tomato sauce
1 (4 oz.) pkg. spaghetti, broken in   pieces

Directions:
1. Brown ground beef in skillet. Place in crock pot.
2. Add all remaining ingredients (except dry spaghetti) and stir together.
3. Cook on high 4 to 5 hours. Add dry spaghetti and stir in. Cook on high for 1 hour more.

CROCK POT LASAGNA

Ingredients:
1 pkg. pepperoni slices
1 lb. hamburger
1 onion, diced
1 green pepper, diced
1 can mushrooms
1 pkg. kluski noodles
1 large jar pizza sauce
1 large jar spaghetti sauce
1 pkg. each shredded Colby & Mozzarella cheese

Directions:
1. Cook together hamburger, onion, green pepper and mushrooms. Layer this with the rest of the ingredients in the crock pot.
2. Cook on high for 2 to 3 hours.

CROCK POT RAVIOLI CASSEROLE

Ingredients:
1.5 lbs. lean ground beef
1 medium onion, chopped
2 garlic cloves, minced
1 28 oz. can peeled tomatoes, in thick tomato puree
1 15 oz. can tomato sauce
2 teaspoons Italian seasoning
1/4 teaspoon pepper
1 lb. bow-tie pasta or fettuccine, freshly cooked
1 10 oz. pkg froz.en chopped spinach, defrosted and squeezed to remove excess moisture
2 cups ricotta cheese
1/2 cup freshly grated Parmesan cheese

Directions:
1. In a large skillet over medium-high heat, cook the ground beef, onion and garlic,stirring often to break up lumps, until the meat loses its pink color, about 5 minutes.
2. Tilt the pan to drain off excess fat, then transfer the beef mixture to a3.5-qt slow cooker.
3. Add the tomatoes with their puree, the tomato sauce, Italian seasoning, and pepper, stirring to break up the tomatoes with the side of a spoon.
4. Cover and slow cook for 7 to 8 hours on low.
5. Skim the fat from the surface of the meat sauce. Stir in the cooked pasta, spinach, and ricotta and Parmesan cheeses, and slow cook for 5 more minutes.

CROCK POT STUFFED PASTA SHELLS

Ingredients:
18 jumbo pasta shells
1 lb. lean ground beef
1 onion, chopped
1 clove garlic, minced
2 cups Mozzarella cheese, shredded
½ cup seasoned bread crumbs
1 Tablespoon parsley flakes
1 egg, beaten
2 jars meatless spaghetti sauce (15½ oz. each)
½ cup grated Parmesan cheese

Directions:
1. Cook pasta shells according to directions, just until tender and drain.
2. Brown beef, onion and garlic on stove top, drain. Add Moz.zarella, bread crumbs,parsley and egg.
3. Stuff shells, set aside.
4. Pour 1 jar of sauce into crock pot. Arrange stuffed shells in sauce. Top with other jar of sauce and Parmesan cheese.
5. Cover and cook on low 5 to 7 hours.

CROCK POT BEEFY PASTA SAUCE

Ingredients:
1.5 pounds ground round
2 (15 oz.) cans tomato sauce
2 (14.5) oz. cans diced tomatoes, undrained
2 (6oz.) cans tomato paste
1 (8oz.) package sliced fresh mushrooms, or omit1.5 cups chopped onions
1 cup water
¾ cup chopped green pepper
2 Tablespoons brown sugar
2 teaspoon dried basil
1 teaspoon dried oregano
¼ teaspoon salt
¼ teaspoon pepper
1/8 teaspoon ground red pepper
2 minced cloves garlic
1 beef bouillon cube

Directions:
1. Cook meat in large skillet on medium-high until brown. Stir to crumble.
2. Drain well and place in crock pot. Add tomato sauce and next 14 ingredients.
3. Cover with lid and cook on high for 1 hour and low for 6-7 hours.

CROCK POT MACARONI AND CHEESE

Ingredients:
1 (16 oz.) pkg. macaroni, cooked & drained
1 Tablespoon salad oil
1 (13 oz.) can evaporated milk
1 1/2 cups milk
1 teaspoon salt
3 cups shredded sharp cheddar cheese
1/2 cup melted butter

Directions:
1. Lightly grease Crock Pot. Toss macaroni and oil. Add all remaining ingredients.
2. Stir, cover and cook on low 3 to 4 hours, stirring occasionally.

CROCK POT MACARONI AND CHEESE 2

Ingredients:
1 large box macaroni, cooked and drained
2 Tablespoons oil
2 sticks butter
1 large can evaporated milk
1 1/2 cups milk
1 large onion, chopped fine
3 cups Cheddar cheese, grated (12 oz.)
1 can Cheddar cheese soup

Directions:
1. Oil crock pot, mix all ingredients, using only 1/2 of grated cheese. Put mixture in crock pot and put remaining cheese on top.
2. Let simmer in crock pot on low for 4 or more hours.

CROCK POT MACARONI & CHEESE 3

Ingredients:
2 cups dry macaroni
2 lb. box Velveeta cheese
1 stick butter
3 cups milk

Directions:
1. Cook macaroni until almost done.
2. In crock pot on high, mix butter and cheese cut in small pieces until melted.
3. Add macaroni, milk and stir well. Set crock pot on low until meal time, stirring occasionally.

CROCK POT MACARONI

Ingredients:
1 (8 oz.) pkg. macaroni
1 large can evaporated milk
1 1/2 cups milk
2 eggs, beaten
1/4 cup melted butter
1 teaspoon salt
3 cups sharp cheese
Pepper to taste

Directions:
1. Cook and drain macaroni. Grate cheese. Grease crock pot.
2. Mix all ingredients in crock pot. Reserve some of the cheese to put on top. Sprinkle with paprika.
3. Cook on low for 3 1/4 hours.

CROCK POT FARMHOUSE MACARONI AND CHEESE

Ingredients:
3 cups cooked elbow macaroni, rinsed and drained
2 Tablespoons Hormel bacon bits
1/4 cup chopped onion
1-3/4 cups (one 14-1/4 ounce can) stewed tomatoes, undrained
1 - 1/2 cups (6 oz.) shredded cheddar cheese
1 (10-3/4 oz.) can cream of mushroom soup

Directions:
1. In a slow cooker, combine macaroni, bacon bits, onion, undrained stewed tomatoes and cheddar cheese.
2. Pour mushroom soup over top. Mix well to combine.
3. Cover and cook on LOW for 6 to 8 hours. Mix well before serving.

CROCK POT LASAGNA

Ingredients:
1 lb. ground beef
1 large onion, chopped
2 garlic gloves, minced
1 can (29 oz.) tomato sauce
1 cup water
1 can (6 oz.) tomato paste
1 teaspoon salt
1 teaspoon dried oregano
1 package (8oz.) no-cook lasagna noodles
4 cups (16 oz.) shredded mozzarella cheese
1 1/2 cups (12 oz.) small-curd cottage cheese
1/2 cup grated Parmesan cheese

Directions:
1. In a skillet, cook beef, onion and garlic over med. heat until meat is no longer pink; drain.
2. Add the tomato sauce, water, tomato paste, salt and oregano; mix well.
3. Spread a fourth of the meat sauce in an ungreased 5-qt slow cooker.
4. Arrange a third of the noodles over sauce (break the noodles if necessary).
5. Combine the cheeses; spoon a third of the mixture over noodles. Repeat layers twice. Top with remaining meat sauce.
6. Cover and cook on low for 4-5 hours or until noodles are tender.

CROCK POT SPAGHETTI SAUCE

Ingredients:
4 Tablespoons cooking oil
1 small onion, finely chopped
1 (15 1/2 oz.) can tomato sauce
1 ½ cup water
½ teaspoon pepper
½ teaspoon red pepper, optional
1 lb. ground beef
1 (29 oz.) can tomato puree
1 (6 oz.) can tomato paste
1 teaspoon salt
½ teaspoon oregano
2 lbs. sausage (Italian links or country style)

Directions:
1. Brown ground beef in 2 tablespoon hot oil in frying pan. When almost browned, add onion and continue browning until onion is tender.
2. Pour meat and onion into 3 1/2 quart crockpot. Add puree, sauce, paste, water, salt, pepper and oregano and set dial on low setting.
3. Cut 2 lbs. sausage into pieces and brown in remaining 2 tablespoons oil. When brown, place sausages in sauce in crockpot.
4. Continue cooking for 12 hours. (If you like your sauce sweeter, you could add 1/4 to 1/2 cup sugar to this.)

CROCK POT MACARONI PIE

Ingredients:
8 oz. box (cooked) macaroni
3 cup grated cheese
1 (16 oz.) can of evaporated milk
1 1/2 cup sweet milk
2 eggs
1/4 cup margarine
1 teaspoon sugar
Salt and pepper to taste

Directions:
1. Combine cooked macaroni with other ingredients and pour into a greased crockpot.
2. Cook 3 1/2 hours on medium heat.

CROCK POT PASTA AND BROCCOLI

Ingredients:
1 medium onion
1 can cream of mushroom soup
1 lb. Velveeta
1 pkg. frozen broccoli & cauliflower
1 pkg. shell noodles

Directions:
1. Mix onion, cream of mushroom soup and Velveeta in a slow cooker/Crock Pot on high until melted.
2. Add broccoli and cauliflower until hot. Add cooked shells right before serving.

CROCK POT SPAGHETTI SAUCE WITH CHICKEN & SAUSAGE

Ingredients:
1 lb. Italian sausage
3-4 boneless chicken breasts cut into 1-inch chunks
1 cup chopped green pepper
1 cup chopped onion
1-2 teaspoon Italian seasoning
2 (4 oz. each) cans mushroom stems and pieces, drained
2 jars spaghetti sauce
Hot cooked pasta

Directions:
1. In skillet, brown Italian sausage, piercing casings to allow excess fat to run out.
2. Remove to plate and cut into 1/2 to 1-inch chunks.
3. In same skillet, brown chicken pieces. Place sausage and chicken in slow cooker. Add pepper and onion.

4. Sprinkle with Italian seasoning. Add mushrooms. Pour sauce over everything.
5. Cover and cook on low for 6 to 8 hours. Stir before serving over spaghetti or other pasta.

CROCK POT SUN-DRIED TOMATO SPAGHETTI SAUCE
Ingredients:
1 1/2 cups chopped sun-dried tomatoes
1 medium onion, chopped
1 cup celery, chopped
2 cloves garlic, minced
36 oz. whole or chopped tomatoes, undrained
2/3 cup chablis or other dry white wine1
1 teaspoon dried fennel seed
1 1/2 teaspoon basil
1/2 teaspoon oregano
1/2 teaspoon pepper
Salt to taste
Directions:
1. Place all ingredients in slow cooker/Crock Pot and cook on low for 6-8 hours.

CROCK POT VEGETABLE PASTA
Ingredients:
2 Tablespoons butter or margarine
1 zucchini, 1/4" slice
1 yellow squash, 1/4" slice
2 carrots, thinly sliced
1 1/2 cups mushrooms, fresh, sliced
1 package broccoli, frozen, cuts
4 green onions, sliced
2 to 3 cloves garlic, minced
1/2 teaspoon basil, dried
1/4 teaspoon salt
1/2 teaspoon pepper
1 cup parmesan cheese, grated
12 ounces fettuccine
1 cup mozzarella cheese, shredded
1 cup cream
2 egg yolks

Directions:
1. Rub crock pot sides with butter.
2. Put zucchini, yellow squash, carrots, mushrooms, broccoli, onions, garlic, seasonings and parmesan in the Crock Pot.
3. Cover; cook on High 2 hours.
4. Cook fettuccine according to package directions; drain.
5. Add cooked fettuccine, mozzarella, cream and egg yolks. Stir to blend well.
6. Allow to heat for 15 to 30 minutes. For serving turn to Low for up to 30 minutes.

CROCK POT SPAGHETTI
Ingredients:
1 lb. ground beef, browned (put into crockpot)
1 envelope spaghetti sauce mix
2 Tablespoons instant minced onion
8 oz. can tomato sauce
4 1/2 cup tomato juice or V-8
4 oz. can mushrooms, drained
4 oz. dry spaghetti broken into thirds (about 1 1/2 cup)
Directions:
1. Combine all but spaghetti noodles in crockpot and stir.
2. Cover and cook on low 6-8 hours. Turn to high for last hour and add spaghetti. Stir often.

CROCK POT SPAGHETTI SAUCE #1

Ingredients:
1 pound ground beef
chopped onion -- to taste
2 cans tomatoes -- (1 lb.) cut up
1 can tomato sauce -- (8 oz.)
1 can tomato paste -- (12 oz.)
1 cup beef broth (bouillon)
2 Tablespoons parsley
1 Tablespoon brown sugar
1 teaspoon dried oregano leaves
1 teaspoon dried basil leaves
1 teaspoon salt
1/4 teaspoon pepper

Directions:
1. Brown meat and onion in fry pan, drain off fat; transfer to crock pot.
2. Add remaining ingredients. Cover and cook on low for 6-8 hours. Serve over hot spaghetti.

CROCK POT SPAGHETTI SAUCE #2

Ingredients:
3- 15 oz. cans tomato sauce
1- 12 oz. can tomato paste
2 Tablespoons minced onions
1 teaspoon chili powder
1-1/2 teaspoons garlic powder
1-1/2 teaspoons Italian seasoning

Directions:
1. Cook on low in crockpot for 4-1/2 hrs.

CROCK POT SPAGHETTI SAUCE #3

Ingredients:
1-6 pound can crushed tomatoes
2-15 ounce cans diced tomatoes
1-12 ounce can tomato paste
1 pound Italian sausage or ground beef, cooked and broken up
1 large green pepper, diced
1 medium onion, chopped
3-4 cloves of garlic, minced

Italian seasoning, oregano, celery salt, celery seed-to taste.

Directions:
1. Sauté the peppers, onions, and garlic in a bit of oil, and put it in the crockpot.
2. Add all other ingredients to the pot and cook on low all day.

CROCK POT SPAGHETTI SAUCE #4

Ingredients:
1 1/2 lbs. ground chuck, browned
1 1/2 cups chopped onion
2 cloves garlic
1 15oz. can tomato sauce
2 6oz. cans tomato paste
1 Tablespoon salt
2 teaspoons dried oregano
1/4 teaspoon thyme
1 bay leaf

Directions:
1. In crock pot combine all ingredients. Stir well, and cook on high 4-5 hours.

CROCK POT EASY SPAGHETTI

Ingredients:
1 lb. ground chuck
1/2 cup chopped onion
2 cloves garlic, minced
2 (8 oz. each) cans tomato sauce
1 to 1 1/2 teaspoons Italian seasoning
1 (4 oz.) can sliced mushrooms, drained
3 cups tomato juice
6 oz. dry spaghetti, broken into 4 to 5 inch pieces

Directions:
1. Brown ground chuck in skillet, drain and put in Crock Pot. Add all remainingingredients except dry spaghetti; stir well.
2. Cover; cook on Low 6 to 8 hours (High:3 to 5 hours). Turn to high last hour and stir in dry spaghetti.

CROCK POT VEGGIE AND HAM MACARONI AND CHEESE

Ingredients:

1-1/2 cups (one 12 fluid oz. can) Carnation Evaporated Skim Milk
3 Tablespoons all-purpose flour
1-1/2 cups (6 oz.) shredded Cheddar cheese
2 teaspoon prepared mustard
1/4 teaspoon black pepper
2-1/2 cups hot cooked elbow macaroni
1 cup extra-lean ham
1 cup (one 8 oz. can) cut green beans, rinsed and drained
1 cup (one 8 oz. can) sliced carrots, rinsed and drained

Directions:

1. In a covered jar, combine evaporated skim milk and flour. Shake well to blend.
2. Pour milk mixture into a large skillet sprayed with butter flavored cooking spray.
3. Cover over medium heat for 3 minutes or until mixture starts to thicken, stirring often.
4. Stir in Cheddar cheese, mustard and black pepper. Pour mixture into a crock pot.
5. Add macaroni, ham, green beans and carrots. Mix well to combine.
6. Cover and cook on LOW for 4 to 6 hours. Mix well before serving

CROCK POT PASTA WITH EGGPLANT SAUCE

Ingredients:

1 medium eggplant
1 medium onion -- chopped
1 can Italian-style tomatoes -- (28 ounce) cut up
1 can tomato paste -- (6 ounce) Italian-style
4 oz. mushrooms sliced and lightly sautéed
2 cloves garlic -- minced
1/4 cup dry red wine
1/4 cup water
5 1/2 teaspoon dried oregano -- crushed
1/2 cup kalamata olives -- pitted & sliced (or pitted ripe olives)
2 Tablespoons fresh parsley -- snipped
4 cups cooked pasta -- hot cooked penne pasta
1/3 cup Parmesan cheese -- grated or shredded
2 Tablespoons toasted pine nuts -- optional

Directions:

1. Peel eggplant, if desired; cut eggplant into 1-inch cubes.
2. In a 3 1/2 to 5 1/2 quart slow cooker combine eggplant, onion, undrained tomatoes, tomato paste, mushrooms, garlic, wine, water, and oregano.
3. Cover and cook on low-heat setting for 7 to 8 hours or on high-heat setting for 3 1/2 to 4 hours.
4. Stir in olives and parsley. Season to taste with salt and pepper.
5. Serve over pasta with Parmesan cheese.

Crock Pot Pork

CROCK POT PORK

Ingredients:

3-5 lb. pork (may use smoked pork shoulder)
1 large onion, sliced
2 apples, peel & cut up in pieces
2 Tablespoons chutney or 1 cup dried fruit (mixed)
1 cup apple cider or apple juice
1/2 cup water
1 or 2 garlic cloves
1 bay leaf
salt & pepper to taste

Directions:

1. Cook all ingredients together in crock pot 4 or 5 hours on high temperature.
2. Thicken gravy. Remove bay leaf. Slice meat and serve.

CROCK POT PORK BARBECUE

Ingredients:

1 (5-7 lb.) fresh pork shoulder
1 Tablespoon salt
2 Tablespoons sugar
pepper to taste
1 1/4 cups vinegar
1/2 cup ketchup
1/2 cup barbecue sauce
1 1/2 Tablespoons crushed red pepper
Dash of hot sauce

Directions:

1. Put pork in crock pot. Sprinkle salt and pepper over shoulder and add vinegar.
2. Cover and simmer 12 hours.
3. Remove from pot and pick meat from bones. Strain liquid and keep approximately 2 cups.
3. Add remaining ingredients. Mix with minced meat and return to crock pot.
4. Cook on low until juice is cooked down (or cook on a high setting for shorter time).

CROCK POT PORK AND GRAVY

Ingredients:

4-5 pork shoulder chops
1 pkg. Lipton onion soup mix
1 can cream of chicken soup
10 oz. water

Directions:

1. Trim pork chops of excess fat and cut into "stew size" pieces. Lightly brown and place in bottom of crock pot.
2. Combine remaining ingredients and pour over pork. Cook 4-6 hours on low until tender.
3. Serve over rice or with mashed potatoes.

CROCK POT PORK BARBECUE

Ingredients:

1 (3-4 lb.) pork loin roast
salt and freshly ground black pepper to taste
crushed red pepper flakes or ground red pepper to taste
2 Tablespoons sugar
2 cups white vinegar
12 to 16 hamburger buns

Directions:

1. Trim fat from roast and place in 5 quart electric slow cooker.
2. Sprinkle roast with salt, pepper and crushed red pepper. Add sugar and vinegar.
3. Cook on low 12 to 14 hours.
3. When done, remove roast from cooker and place in a large skillet, reserving cooking juices.
4. Flake or shred roast, removing any fat. Mix meat, some of cooking juices and ketchup.
5. Simmer mixture over medium heat until juices evaporate. Serve on lightly toasted hamburger buns.

CROCK POT PORK CHOPS

Ingredients:
4-6 pork chops
1 can chicken with rice soup
3/4 cup flour
1 teaspoon garlic powder

Directions:
1. Mix flour and garlic powder in plastic bag. Shake pork chops in bag until well coated.
2. Fry until light brown. Place pork chops in bottom of crock pot. Cover with can of soup.
3. Cook on high for 4 hours or simmer on low several hours.

CROCK POT PIZZA PORK CHOPS

Ingredients:
6 pork loin chops, 1 inch thick (about 2 1/4 pounds)
1/2 teaspoon salt
1/4 teaspoon pepper
1 Tablespoon vegetable oil
1 medium onion chopped (1/2 cup)
2 cups tomato pasta sauce
4 cups cooked orzo
1 cup shredded mozzarella cheese (4 oz.)

Directions:
1. Remove excess fat from pork. Sprinkle pork with salt and pepper.
2. Heat oil in 12" skillet over medium-high heat. Cook pork in oil about 5 minutes, turning once, until brown.
3. Place pork in 3 1/2 to 6 quart slow cooker.
4. Sprinkle onion over pork. Add pasta sauce.
5. Cover and cook on low heat setting 4 to 6 hours or until pork is very tender.
6. Place orzo on platter. Top with pork and sauce. Sprinkle with cheese.

CROCK POT PORK CHOP DINNER #1

Ingredients:
1 1/2 cups diced carrot
2 1/2 cups diced potato
1 cup diced onion
1 cup diced parsnip
6 pork loin chops, trimmed of fat
1 teaspoon liquid gravy browner
10 oz. can Condensed cream of mushroom soup
1/2 cup water

Directions:
1. Put carrot in 5 qt slow cooker. Layer potato, onion and parsnip over top.
2. Brush both sides of pork chops with gravy browner. Lay over parsnip. Stir soup with water together in bowl. Pour over all.
3. Cover. Cook on Low for 9 to10 hours or High for 4 1/2 to 5 hours.

CROCK POT PORK CHOP DINNER #2

Ingredients:
4 pork chops
red potatoes, quarted, no set amount
1 onion, sliced into rings
2 cans cream of mushroom soup
salt and pepper, to taste

Directions:
1. Place the pork chops on the bottom of crock pot. Season chops with salt and pepper.
2. Layer the potatoes on top and season. Last layer will be the onions. Pour the soup over all of this.
3. Cook in crockpot 6-8 hours on low

CROCK POT PORK CHOPS A LA ORANGE

Ingredients:

3 pounds pork chops
2 cups orange juice
2 cans mandarin oranges drained, (11 oz.)
1 can pineapple tidbits drained, (8 oz.)
Salt and pepper

Directions:

1. Salt and pepper pork chops and put in a crockpot; cover with orange juice.
2. Cook on high 3 to 4 hours or on low 6 to 8 hours.
3. About 30 minutes before serving add the oranges and pineapple just to warm. Serve with rice or noodles.

CROCK POT PORK CHOPS AND APPLE SLICES

Ingredients:

4 pork loin chops (1" thick) well trimmed
2 medium apples peeled, cored and sliced
1 teaspoon butter
1/4 teaspoon nutmeg (optional)
salt and pepper

Directions:

1. In skillet, brown pork chops quickly; drain well.
2. Arrange a layer of sliced apples in crockpot, then a layer of pork chops; repeat. Dot with butter; sprinkle with nutmeg. Add salt and pepper.
3. Cover and cook on low setting 6 to 8 hours.

CROCK POT PORK HOCKS AND BLACK EYED PEAS

Ingredients:

1 1/2 cups dry black-eyed peas
4 small smoked pork hocks (1 1/2 lb.)
4 cups reduced-sodium chicken broth
1 medium green sweet pepper, chopped
1 medium onion, chopped
1 stalk celery, chopped
2 bay leaves
1/4 teaspoon ground red pepper
2 cups sliced okras or one 10 oz. pkg. frozen whole okra, thawed and cut into 1/2"slices

Directions:

1. Rinse black-eyed peas; place in a large saucepan. Add enough water to cover peas by 2".
2. Bring to boiling; reduce heat. Simmer, uncovered, for 10 minutes. Remove from heat. Cover and let stand for 1 hour.
3. Drain and rinse peas. In a 3 1/2, 4-, or 5- quart crock pot combine the black-eyed peas, pork hocks, broth, sweet pepper, onion, celery, bay leaves, and red pepper.
4. Cover; cook on low-heat setting for 8-10 hours or on high-heat setting for 4-5 hours.
5. Add okra. Cover; let stand for 10 minutes or until okra is tender.
6. Remove pork hocks. When cool enough to handle, cut meat off bones; cut meat into bite-size pieces. Discard bones and bay leaves.
7. To serve, stir meat into black-eyed pea mixture.

CROCK POT PORK ROAST WITH SWEET POTATOES

Ingredients:

1 (3 lb.) boneless pork roast (or cubed lean pork)
2 to 3 large sweet potatoes
1 green bell peppers
1/2 cup apple cider
3 Tablespoons brown sugar
1 teaspoon cinnamon
salt and pepper to taste

Directions:

1. Put roast or cubed pork in the crock pot. Cut sweet potatoes and green peppers in large pieces and add them.
2. Mix the remaining ingredients and pour over all; cook all day on low or about 4 hours on high. Serve with rice.

CROCK POT RED PORK CHOPS

Ingredients:
4-6 pork chops
1 12-oz bottle hunts chili sauce
ketchup
water
1/2 cup brown sugar
2 teaspoons dry mustard

Directions:
1. Pour Chili Sauce into crockpot, refill bottle with ketchup and pour into crockpot. Refill bottle with water and pour into crockpot.
2. Add sugar and mustard. Arrange pork chops in pot. Cook on high until done.

CROCK POT SAUSAGE IN TOMATO GRAVY

Ingredients:
1 finely chopped onion
4 cans tomato sauce, equal parts water
1 can tomato paste
1 can rotel smoked sausage (four links)
cooked meatballs (optional)

Directions:
1. Chop up sausage and make sure meatballs are cooked.
2. Place all ingredients in crockpot and season to taste.
3. Cook on low for 7-8 hours. Serve over rice.

CROCK POT SAUSAGE KRAUT

Ingredients:
1 (32 oz) bag sauerkraut (from deli or meat section)
1/2 cup dark brown sugar, packed
1 large onion, chopped coarsely
1 pound Polish sausage
1 teaspoon caraway seeds, optional

Directions:
1. Place sauerkraut in colander, and rinse well with cold water. Squeeze dry. Put into a large bowl.

2. Add brown sugar, onion, and seeds, if desired. Mix well until kraut is a delicate caramel color.
3. Place kraut mixture in a greased crock pot. Slice the sausage into large chunks, and place on top of the kraut.
4. Cook on low heat for about 6 hours. If feasible, stir about half way throughcooking time.
5. Serve hot with mashed potatoes

CROCK POT SOUTHWESTERN STYLE CHALUPAS

Ingredients:
1 (4 pound) pork roast
1 pound dried pinto beans
1 (4 ounce) can chopped green chile peppers
2 Tablespoons chili powder
2 teaspoons cumin
1 teaspoon oregano
salt and pepper to taste
1 quart water
1 (16 ounce) package corn chips

Directions:
1. In a slow cooker, combine pork roast, pinto beans, chile peppers, chili powder, cumin seed, oregano, salt, pepper and water.
2. Simmer on low for 4 hours.
3. Remove roast and pull meat apart; remove any bones or fat. Return pork to slow cooker and continue cooking for 2 to 4 more hours.
4. Add more water if necessary. Place corn chips on a serving plate. Spoon pork mixture over chips and serve with desired toppings.

CROCK POT SPICED APPLE PORK ROAST

Ingredients:
1 3 lb. pork roast (any type)
1 24 oz. jar 'spiced' applesauce

Directions:
1. Place the roast into the crock pot. Pour the jar of apple sauce over the roast.
2. Cover and cook on low for 6-8 hours.
3. Remove roast, slice and serve over mashed potatoes.

CROCK POT TAMALE PIE

Ingredients:
2 cups chicken broth or bouillon
1 cup yellow cornmeal
1 Tablespoon chopped fresh cilantro
1/2 lb. pork sausage
1 lb. stew meat cut into cubes
1 onion, chopped
1/2 cup finely chopped celery
1 mild green chile pepper, seeded and chopped
1/2 cup chopped sun-dried tomatoes
1 can (8 oz) drained whole kernel corn
1 can (2 1/2 oz) sliced ripe olives drained
1/2 teaspoon salt
1/8 teaspoon pepper

Directions:
1. Bring broth or bouillon to boil in medium saucepan. Stirring constantly, slowly add cornmeal. Simmer mixture 5 minutes, stirring often. Stir in cilantro.
2. Using a greased spatula, spread cornmeal mixture on bottom and about 2 inches up sides of slow- cooker.
3. In large bowl, combine sausage, stew meat, onion, celery, chile pepper, sun-dried tomatoes, corn, sliced olives, salt and pepper.
4. Carefully spoon into center of cornmeal-lined pot.
5. Cover and cook on LOW 7 to 8 hours. Garnish with ripe olives, if desired.

CROCK POT TANGY PORK CHOPS

Ingredients:
4 boneless pork chops (thick cut)
1/2 teaspoon salt
1/8 teaspoon pepper
2 medium onions, chopped
1 large green pepper, sliced
1 can (14 1/2 oz) stewed tomatoes
1/2 cup ketchup
2 Tablespoons cider vinegar
2 Tablespoons brown sugar
2 Tablespoons Worcestershire sauce
1 Tablespoon lemon juice
1 beef bouillon cube
2 Tablespoons cornstarch
2 Tablespoons water

Directions:
1. Place chops in crockpot. Sprinkle with salt and pepper.
2. Add the onions, green pepper, and tomatoes. Mix ketchup, vinegar, sugar, Worcestershire, lemon juice, and bouillon.
3. Pour over veggies. Cook on low for 6-8 hours.
4. Mix cornstarch and water and stir into liquid, turn on high and cook another 30 minutes. Serve over rice.

CROCK POT TERIYAKI CHOPS

Ingredients:
4 boneless pork chops
1 large can pineapple slices (including juice)
1 bottle teriyaki sauce
2 Tablespoons brown sugar
salt and pepper

Directions:
1. Season the chops with salt and pepper. Place in crockpot then pour the teriyaki sauce, pineapple w/juice, and brown sugar on top.
2. Cook on low 6 hours and serve over rice.

CROCK POT TEX MEX PORK

Ingredients:
3 pounds pork shoulder
2 (1 ounce) packages taco seasoning mix
chili powder to taste
crushed red pepper to taste

Directions:
1. Place pork shoulder in a slow cooker with taco seasoning. If desired, add chili powder and/or red pepper flakes.
2. Add water until meat is covered. Place lid on pot and cook on low for 8 hours.
3. Remove pork shoulder from pot and shred.
4. Serve with warm tortillas and your choice of garnishes, such as: lettuce, grated cheese, chopped onions, guacamole, salsa, sour cream, and olives.

CROCK POT TEX MEX PORK LOIN ROAST

Ingredients:
1 (8 ounce) can tomato sauce
1 cup barbeque sauce
1 onion, chopped
2 (4 ounce) cans diced green chili peppers
1/4 cup chili powder
1 teaspoon ground cumin
1 teaspoon oregano
1/4 teaspoon ground cinnamon
2 1/2 pounds boneless pork loin roast, trimmed
1/2 cup chopped fresh cilantro

Directions:
1. In a 3 quart or larger slow cooker, mix tomato sauce, barbeque sauce, onion,green chilies, chili powder, cumin, oregano and cinnamon.
2. Add pork and spoon sauce over to cover. Cover and cook on low 8 to 10 hours or until pork is tender.
3. Remove pork to a cutting board. Using 2 forks, pull meat into shreds.

4. Pour sauce into a serving dish, stir in cilantro and shredded pork.
5. Serve rolled up in tortillas, taco shells or on burger buns with shredded lettuce, diced red onion and sour cream.

CROCK POT APPLE GLAZED PORK ROAST

Ingredients:
3-4 lb. port lion roast, well trimmed
salt & pepper
4 to 6 apples, quartered
1/4 cup apple juice
3 Tablespoons brown sugar
1 teaspoon ground ginger

Directions:
1. Place apple quarters on bottom of crock pot. Place roast on top. Sprinkle w/salt &pepper.
2. Combine apple juice, sugar & ginger. Spoon over roast, covering entire top.
3. Cover & cook on LOW 10-12 hrs.

CROCK POT APPLE GLAZED PORK ROAST #2

Ingredients:
4 lb. pork loin roast
6 apples
1/4 cup apple juice
3 Tablespoons brown sugar
1 teaspoon ginger, ground

Directions:
1. Rub roast with salt and pepper. Brown pork roast under broiler to remove excess fat; drain well.
2. Core and quarter apples. Place apple quarters in bottom of crock pot. Place roast on top of apples.
3. Combine apple juice, brown sugar, and ginger. Spoon over top surface of roast, moistening well.
4. Cover and cook on Low for 10-12 hours.

CROCK POT BAKED HAM IN FOIL

Directions:
1. Pour 1/2 cup water in Crock-Pot.
2. Wrap precooked 3 to 4 pound ham in foil, place in Crock-Pot.
3. Cover and cook on high 1 hour, then low 6 to 7 hours or until ham is hot. If cooking larger ham, cook 1 hour on high then low 8 to 10 hours.

CROCK POT BARBECUE PORK SANDWICHES

Ingredients:
1 pork roast
1 bottle barbecue sauce
About 1/2 to 1 cup water

Directions:
1. Place everything in crockpot on high for 6 hrs. on high or low for about 10 hrs.
2. When done, remove meat from bone and serve on hamburger buns or rolls with more bar-b-que sauce or ketchup.

CROCK POT BARBECUED PORK ROAST #2

Ingredients:
1 pork roast
Juice of 1 lemon
1 small onion, cut up
1 teaspoon sugar
1 bottle barbecue sauce

Directions:
1. Cook roast covered in water (start with hot water) in crock pot overnight on low 10-12 hours.
2. Pour off water and pull meat into shredded pieces.
3. Sauté onion in a little butter.
4. Combine barbecue sauce, onions, sugar and juice of lemon with meat in crock pot and cook on high for 1 1/2 to 2 1/2 hours, or on low for 3 to 6 hours.

CROCK POT BIGOS

Ingredients:
1 onion, chopped
1 clove garlic, minced
2 Tablespoons butter
1 pound cabbage
1 quart sauerkraut, rinsed and drained
1/2 pound mushrooms, sliced
1 pound boneless pork butt, cut in 1" cubes
1 pound boneless veal, cut in 1" cubes
1/2 pound Polish sausage, sliced 1/2" thick
1/2 cup beef stock
1 cup chopped tomatoes
2 tart apples, diced
1/2 cup pitted prunes
1 bay leaf
1 teaspoon salt
1/2 teaspoon pepper
1/2 cup red wine

Directions:
1. Combine all ingredients in crock pot and cook on low 8 to 10 hours.

CROCK POT BARBECUE SAUCE

Ingredients:
1 cup chopped celery
1 medium onion chopped
1 Tablespoon butter
2 Tablespoons vinegar
1 Tablespoon brown sugar
3 Tablespoons Worcestershire sauce
1 Tablespoon lemon juice
1 teaspoon salt (optional)
1 teaspoon mustard
1 cup ketchup
1 cup water
2 lb. ground beef

Directions:
1. Sauté the celery and onion in the butter until golden brown.< p/>
2. Combine all ingredients in a crock pot. Cook slowly for 2 - 2 1/2 hours.

CROCK POT BARBECUED PORK STRIPS

Ingredients:
1/2 cup soy sauce
1/4 cup dry sherry
1/2 cup brown sugar
2 cloves garlic, crushed
1/8 teaspoon pepper
1/2 cup barbecue sauce
1 8-ounce can pineapple chunks (do not drain)
3 pounds lean pork, cut into strips, browned, and drained

Directions:
1. Combine all ingredients except pork strips in Crock Pot and stir well. Add pork and stir to coat.
2. Cook on low, covered, for 8 to 10 hours. Serve with sauce.

CROCK POT BAYOU GUMBO

Ingredients:
3 Tablespoons all purpose flour
3 Tablespoons oil
1/2 pound smoked sausage, cut into 1/2 inch slices
2 cups frozen cut okra
1 large onion, chopped
1 large green bell pepper, chopped
3 garlic cloves, minced
1/4 teaspoon ground red pepper (cayenne)
1/4 teaspoon pepper
1 (14.5 ounce) can diced tomatoes, undrained
1 (12-ounce) package frozen shelled deveined cooked medium shrimp, rinsed
1 1/2 cups uncooked regular long-grain white rice
3 cups water

Directions:
1. In small saucepan, combine flour and oil; mix well.
2. Cook, stirring constantly, over medium-high heat for 5 minutes. Reduce heat to medium; cook, stirring constantly, about 10 minutes or until mixture turns reddish brown.
3. Place flour-oil mixture in 3 1/2 to 4 quart Slow Cooker. Stir in all remaining ingredients except shrimp, rice and water.
4. Cover; cook on low setting for 7-9 hours. When ready to serve, cook rice in water as directed on package.
5. Add shrimp to gumbo mixture in slow cooker/Crock Pot; mix well. Cover; cook on low setting for additional 20 minutes.
6. Serve gumbo over rice.

CROCK POT CAJUN BREW PORK N BEANS

Ingredients:
5 cans (14 oz.) pork-n-beans
2 8 oz. cans tomatoe sauce
2 onions (chopped)
6 hot links (sliced)
1/4 bottle barbeque sauce (average size)
the following are "to taste"
Worcestershire sauce
hot sauce
cajun seasonings
liquid smoke
mustard
brown sugar

Directions:
1. Mix all ingredients in a crockpot and set to high. Let it cook all day, stirring occasionally.

CROCK POT CANNELLINI ALLA CATANIA

Ingredients:
1 lb. dried canellini beans (white kidney beans)
6 cups water
2 hot italian sausages, sliced
1 large onion, chopped
1 large garlic clove, minced
2 large tomatoes, ripe, peeled and coarsley chopped

128

1 bay leaf, crumbled
1/2 teaspoon thyme, crumbled
1/2 teaspoon basil, crumbled
3 strips of orange rind (1 in.)
1 teaspoon salt
1/4 teaspoon pepper
1 teaspoon instant beef broth
Directions:
1. Pick over beans and rinse. Cover beans with water in a large kettle; bring to boiling; cover; cook 2 minutes; remove from heat; let stand 1 hour.
2. Pour into slow cooker.
3. Brown sausages in a small skillet; push to one side; sauté onion and garlic in same pan until soft.
4. Stir in tomato, bay leaf, thyme, basil, orange strips, salt and pepper and instant beef broth.
5. Bring to boiling; stir into beans; cover.
6. Cook on low for 10 hours or on high for 5 hours or until beans are tender.

CROCK POT CHOPS IN A CROCK

Ingredients:
6 pork chops, browned
1 onion, chopped
3 Tablespoons catsup
10.5 oz can cream of mushroom soup
2 teaspoons Worcestershire sauce
Directions:
1. Place into crockpot and simmer about 4-5 hours. Serve with rice, noodles or potatoes.

CROCK POT CROCKED KIELBASA

Ingredients:
1/2 pound lean ground beef
1 pound kielbasa sausage, sliced
1 can whole tomatoes, (28 ounces) undrained
9 ounces frozen french-cut green beans
1 can pitted black olives, (6

ounces)(drained and left whole)
1/2 cup red wine
3 garlic cloves, minced
1 medium onion, sliced
1 medium green pepper, chopped
1 teaspoon basil, crushed
1 teaspoon oregano, crushed
1/2 teaspoon thyme, crushed
1/4 teaspoon pepper
1 pound pasta of your choice
4 ounces parmesan, freshly grated
Directions:
1. In a medium skillet, saute ground beef. When browned, transfer to crockpot.
2. Add all other ingredients except pasta and parmesan Simmer on low for 6-8 hours.
3. Cook pasta according to directions. Ladle Crocked Kielb.asa over pasta in large bowls. Use the Parmesan cheese to garnish.

CROCK POT AUTUMN PORK CHOPS

Ingredients:
6 pork chops
2 medium acorn squash, unpeeled
3/4 teaspoon salt
2 Tablespoons melted butter
3/4 cup brown sugar, packed
3/4 teaspoon brown bouquet sauce
1 Tablespoon orange juice
1/2 teaspoon orange peel, grated
Directions:
1. Trim excess fat from chops. Cut each squash into 4 to 5 crosswise slices; remove seeds.
2. Arrange 3 chops on bottom of slow-cooking pot.
3. Place all squash slices on top; then another layer of remaining 3 chops.
4. Combine salt, butter, sugar, bouquet sauce, orange juice, and orange peel. Spoon over chops.

5. Cover and cook on low for 4 to 6 hours or until done.

6. Serve one or two slices of squash with each pork chop.

CROCK POT AUTUMN PORK ROAST

Ingredients:
3 to 4 lb. pork roast
salt & pepper
1 cup cranberries, finely chopped
1/4 cup honey
1 teaspoon grated orange peel
1/8 teaspoon ground cloves
1/8 teaspoon ground nutmeg

Directions:
1. Sprinkle roast with salt and pepper. Place in crock pot.
2. Combine remaining ingredients. Pour over roast.
3. Cover. Cook on low for 8 to 10 hours or on High for 4-5 hours.

CROCK POT BEST PORK ROAST

Ingredients:
4-5 pound pork roast
6-8 cloves garlic
pepper
basil
1 cup dry white wine
onion

Directions:
1. Cut 6-8 holes into the roast just big enough to fit a clove of garlic.
2. Put a garlic clove (peeled) into each hole. Rub outside with cracked pepper and basil.
3. Pour dry white wine in the bottom of the Crock Pot. Place roast in the Crock Pot, put slices or wedges of onion on top and around the roast.
4. Cover and cook on low all day or until done.

CROCK POT BLACK BEAN CHILI WITH PORK

Ingredients:
1 lb. boneless pork, cut into cubes
2 (16 oz.) cans black beans, drained
1 red or yellow bell pepper, chopped
1 medium tomato, peeled, seeded and chopped
1 small red onion, thinly sliced
1 clove garlic, crushed
1/2 teaspoon ground cumin
2 teaspoons chili powder
1/2 teaspoon salt
1 can tomato sauce
1/2 cup sour cream
2 Tablespoons chopped cilantro

Directions:
1. In a crockpot, stir together pork, beans, bell pepper, tomato, onion, garlic, cumin, chili powder, salt, and tomato sauce.
2. Cover and cook on low 8 to 9 hours. Spoon into bowls and top with sour cream and cilantro.

CROCK POT BONELESS TWICE COOKED BBQ RIBS

Directions:
1. Place about 1 1/2 lb. of boneless ribs in the CP on low with enough water to cover, about 3 TBS of BBQ sauce, fresh chopped garlic, 1/3 CUP brown sugar and a couple dashes of ketchup.
2. Cook on low about 5 hours until done. Cook on the BBQ to crisp them up and baste with more BBQ sauce.

CROCK POT CANTONESE DINNER

Ingredients:
1 1/2 lb. pork steak 1/2" thick cut into strips
2 Tablespoons oil
1 onion large, sliced
1 green pepper small cut into strips
1 4 oz. can mushrooms, drained
1 8 oz. can tomato sauce
3 Tablespoons brown sugar
1 1/2 Tablespoons vinegar
1 1/2 teaspoons salt
2 teaspoons worcestershire sauce

Directions:
1. Brown pork in oil in skillet. Drain on double paper towel.
2. Place pork strips and all remaining ingredients into crock pot.
3. Cover and cook on low for 6 to 8 Hr (high 4 hr) Serve over hot fluffy rice.

CROCK POT FARMER'S PORK CHOPS

Ingredients:
4 pork chops
1 clove garlic, chopped
salt & pepper to taste
4 medium potatoes, sliced
2 onions, sliced
1-1/2 cup sour cream
1-1/2 teaspoons salt
1/2 teaspoon dry mustard

Directions:
1. Trim excess fat from chops and roll in flour. Brown chops and garlic in hot fat. Season.
2. Layer in crock pot potatoes, browned chops, and onions.
3. Blend sour cream, salt, and mustard. Pour over top.
4. Cook on Low 4 - 6 hours.

CROCK POT CATALINA RIBS

Ingredients:
1 1/2-2 lb. boneless pork ribs
1 onion chopped
2 cloves garlic, minced
1 (8 oz) bottle of Catalina salad dressing

Directions:
1. Place ribs in crock pot.
2. Add in rest of ingredients and cook low for 5-7 hours.

CROCKPOT CHICKEN FRIED CHOPS

Ingredients:
1/2 cups all purpose flour
2 teaspoons salt
1 1/2 teaspoons ground mustard
1/2 teaspoon garlic powder
6 pork chops, trimmed
2 Tablespoons vegetable oil
1 can condensed cream of chicken soup, undiluted
1/3 cup water

Directions:
1. In a shallow bowl, combine flour, salt, mustard and garlic powder; dredge pork chops.
2. In a skillet, brown the chops on both sides in oil.
3. Place in a slow cooker or crockpot.
4. Combine soup and water; pour over chops.
5. Cover and cook on low for 6-8 hours or until meat is tender. If desired, thicken pan juices and serve with the pork chops.

CROCK POT CHOPS OR RIBS

Ingredients:
6 or 8 chops or ribs to fill crock pot
1/4 cup chopped onion
1/2 cup chopped celery
1 cup catsup
1/2 cup water
1/4 cup lemon juice
2 Tablespoons brown sugar

3 Tablespoons Worcestershire sauce
2 Tablespoons vinegar
1 Tablespoon mustard
1/2 teaspoon salt
1/4 teaspoon pepper
Directions:
1. Mix ingredients together & pour over meat in pot. Cook until tender.

CROCK POT COLA HAM
Ingredients:
1/2 cup brown sugar
1 teaspoon dry mustard
1/4 cup cola
3 to 4 pound pre-cooked ham
Directions:
1. Combine brown sugar and mustard. Moisten with cola to make a smooth paste. Reserve remaining cola.
2. Score the ham with shallow slashes in a diamond pattern. Rub ham with mixture.
3. Place ham in crockpot and add remaining cola.
4. Cover and cook on high for 1 hour, then turn to low and cook for 6 to 7 hours.

CROCK POT CORNY HAM AND POTATO SCALLOP
Ingredients:
5 potatoes, peeled and cubed
1 1/2 cups cubed cooked ham
1 (15 ounce) can whole kernel corn, drained
1/4 cup chopped green bell pepper
2 teaspoons instant minced onion
1 (11 ounce) can condensed cheddar cheese soup
1/2 cup milk
3 Tablespoons all-purpose flour
Directions:
1. In a 3 1/2 to 4 quart slow cooker, combine potatoes, ham, corn, green pepper and onion; mix well.
2. In a small bowl, combine soup, milk and flour; beat with wire whisk until smooth.

3. Pour soup mixture over potato mixture and stir gently to mix.
4. Cover and cook on low setting for about 8 hours or until potatoes are tender.

CROCK POT COUNTRY STYLE RIBS AND KRAUT
Ingredients:
12 oz. sauerkraut
brown sugar to taste
1-2 lb. country style ribs
Directions:
1. Place the ribs in a crockpot. Sweeten the sauerkraut to taste with the brown sugar.
2. Cook on low heat 8-10 hours.

CROCK POT CRANBERRY PORK
Ingredients:
1 (16 ounce) can cranberry sauce
1/3 cup French salad dressing
1 onion, sliced
3 pounds pork roast
Directions:
1. In a medium bowl, combine the cranberry sauce, salad dressing and onions.
2. Place pork in a slow cooker and pour the sauce over the pork.
3. Cook on high setting for 4 hours OR on low setting for 8 hours.

CROCK POT CRANBERRY PORK ROAST

Ingredients:

4 medium potatoes, peeled and cut into 1" chunks
One 3-pound boneless center-cut pork loin roast, rolled and tied
1 can (16 ounces) whole-berry cranberry sauce
1 can (5.5 ounces) apricot nectar
1 medium onion, coarsely chopped
1/2 cup coarsely chopped dried apricots
1/2 cup sugar
1 teaspoon dry mustard
1/4 teaspoon crushed red pepper

Directions:

1. Place the potatoes in a 3 1/2-quart (or larger) slow cooker, then place the roast over the potatoes.
2. In a large bowl, combine the remaining ingredients; mix well and pour over the roast.
3. Cover and cook on the low setting for 5 to 6 hours. Remove the roast to a cutting board and thinly slice.

CROCK POT CRAZY STANDING UP PORK CHOPS

Ingredients:

4 loin pork chops, lean
2 medium onions, sliced
1 teaspoon butter
salt & pepper, to taste
spices of your choice

Directions:

1. Stand chops in crockpot, thin side down. Sprinkle with salt, pepper and spices of your choice.
2. Cover with the onion slices, which have been separated into rings.
3. Place butter on top, and cook on LOW heat for 6 to 8 hours, or until chops are tender and onions are done.

CROCK POT CREOLE BLACK BEANS

Ingredients:

1 to 2 pounds smoked sausage, cut into 1" slices
3 15 oz. cans black beans, drained
1 1/2 cups onions, chopped
1 1/2 cups green pepper, chopped
1 1/2 cups celery, chopped
3 cloves garlic, minced
2 teaspoons leaf thyme
1 1/2 teaspoons leaf oregano
1 1/2 teaspoons white pepper
1/4 teaspoon black pepper
1/4 teaspoon cayenne pepper
1 chicken bouillon cube
5 bay leaves
1 can 8-oz. tomato sauce
1 cup water
hot boiled rice

Directions:

1. Brown sausage in a skillet over medium heat. Drain fat and transfer to crockpot.
2. Combine remaining ingredients in crockpot. Cover and cook on low 8 hrs. or on high 4 hrs. Remove bay leaves. Serve over cooked rice. Serves 6 to 8.

CROCK POT JAMBALAYA

Ingredients:

1 pound chicken breasts, boneless, cut in 1" cubes
1 pound smoked sausage, sliced
1 pound shrimp, cooked
28 ounces crushed tomatoes
1 medium onion, chopped
1 green pepper, chopped
1 cup chicken broth
1/2 cup white wine
2 teaspoons oregano
2 teaspoons parsley
2 teaspoons cajun seasoning
1 teaspoon cayenne pepper
2 cups rice, cooked

Directions:
1. Cut chicken and slice sausage. Chop onion and green pepper. Put all in slow cooker/Crock Pot.
2. Add remaining ingredients, except shrimp and rice. Cook in slow cooker/Crock Pot on low for 6-8 hours or on high for 3-4 hours.
3. 30 minutes before eating, add cooked shrimp and cooked rice; allow to heat.

CROCK POT FRANKS IN SPICY TOMATO SAUCE

Ingredients:
1 cup ketchup
1/2 cup firmly packed brown sugar
1 Tablespoon red wine vinegar
2 teaspoons soy sauce
1 teaspoon Dijon mustard
1 clove garlic, minced
1 pound beef or chicken frankfurters, cut into 1" pieces

Directions:
1. Place ketchup, brown sugar, vinegar, soy sauce, mustard, and garlic in the crock pot.
2. Cover and cook on High until blended. Stir occasionally.
3. Add frankfurters and stir to coat. Cook until thoroughly blended.

CROCK POT SPARERIBS

Ingredients:
2 to 3 lb. country style spareribs (pork), fresh or frozen
1 cup ketchup
1 cup cola (coke, diet coke, etcup)

Directions:
1. Combine ketchup and cola. Place ribs in crock pot. Pour mixture over ribs.
2. Cook 2 hours on high and at least 2 hours on low. May cook for several hours on low.

CROCK POT GARLIC PORK ROAST AND SWEET POTATOES

Ingredients:
3 1/2-pound pork boneless loin roast
1 Tablespoon vegetable oil
1 teaspoon salt
1/2 teaspoon pepper
3 cups 1-inch pieces peeled sweet potatoes
1 medium onion, sliced
4 cloves garlic, peeled
1 cup chicken broth

Directions:
1. Remove fat from pork. Heat oil in 10-inch skillet over medium-high heat. Sprinkle pork with salt and pepper.
2. Cook pork in oil about 10 minutes, turning occasionally, until brown on all sides.
3. Place sweet potatoes, onion and garlic in 3 1/2- to 6 quart slow cooker. Place pork on vegetables.
4. Use small amount of the chicken broth to deglaze skillet. Pour drippings and remaining broth over pork.
5. Cover and cook on low heat setting 8 to 10 hours or until pork and vegetables are tender.

CROCK POT GLAZED COCKTAIL SAUSAGES

Ingredients:
3/4 cup apricot preserves
1/4 cup prepared yellow mustard
2 scallions chopped
1/2 pound precooked mini smoked sausages

Directions:
1. In a 1-quart mini electric slow cooker; mix together the preserves and mustard.
2. Stir in scallions and sausages. Cover, plug in the cooker and cook for 3 hours or until very hot.
3. Remove the cover, stir to mix and serve immediately with toothpicks.

CROCK POT HAM AND POTATOES #1

Ingredients:
5 or 6 potatoes, sliced thin
1 to 2 cups ham, cubed
1 medium onion, sliced
1 can cream of mushroom soup
1 cup shredded cheddar cheese

Directions:
1. Layer one half of the potatoes, ham, and onions in crockpot. Season with salt and pepper then half of the cheese.
2. Add remaining potatoes, ham, onions and cheese. Spread undiluted soup evenly over top so air doesn't reach the potatoes.
3. Sprinkle with paprika. Cover and cook on Low for 8 hours

CROCK POT HAM AND POTATOES #2

Ingredients:
6-8 slices ham
8-10 medium potatoes, peeled and thinly sliced
1 medium onion, peeled and thinly sliced
Salt and pepper
1 cup grated Cheddar cheese
2 cans cream of celery or mushroom soup
Paprika

Directions:
1. Put half of ham, potatoes and onions in crock pot. Sprinkle with salt and pepper,then grated cheese. Repeat with remaining half.
2. Spoon undiluted soup over top.Sprinkle with paprika.
3. Cover and cook on low 8-10 hours or on high 4 hours

CROCK POT HAM AND SCALLOPED POTATOES

Ingredients:
1 cup water
1/2 teaspoon cream of tartar
5 medium potatoes
1 cup chopped onion
salt & pepper to taste
SAUCE
1/4 cup all purpose flour
1 teaspoon salt
1/8 teaspoon pepper
2 cups milk
1 cup grated cheddar cheese
2 cups cubed boneless smoked ham

Directions:
1. Combine water and cream of tartar in large bowl. Stir and add potatoes. Stir well, drain.
2. Layer potatoes and onion in a crock pot (5 quart) and sprinkle with salt and pepper.
Sauce:
1. Stir flour, salt, and pepper together in a saucepan. Wisk in milk gradually until no lumps remain.
2. Heat and stir until boiling. Pour 1/2 of sauce over potatoes. Sprinkle cheese and ham over top, then top that with remaining sauce.
3. Cover and cook on low for 9-10 hours or high for 4 1/2 - 5 hours.

CROCK POT HONEY MUSTARD BBQ SHORT RIBS

Ingredients:
3 to 3.5 lb. beef short ribs
1 Tablespoon Dijon-style mustard
1 garlic clove, crushed
2 Tablespoons honey
1/2 teaspoon salt
1/8 teaspoon pepper
1 cup bottled hickory smoked barbecue sauce
2 Tablespoons cornstarch

2 Tablespoons cold water
cooked noodles
Directions:
1. Place short ribs in slow-cooker. In medium bowl, combine mustard, garlic, honey, salt, pepper, and barbecue sauce. Pour over ribs.
2. Cover and cook on LOW 6 to 7 hours or until tender. Refrigerate several hours or overnight.
3. Skim any solidified fat from top. Remove ribs; heat in microwave or conventional oven.
4. Dissolve cornstarch in cold water. Add to sauce from ribs.
5. Cook and stir in microwave or on stovetop until hot and slightly thickened. Pour hot sauce over warm ribs. Serve on cooked noodles.

CROCK POT HONEY RIBS AND RICE
Ingredients:
2 lb. lean spare ribs
1 can condensed beef bouillon
1/2 cup water
2 Tablespoons maple syrup
2 Tablespoons honey
3 Tablespoons soy sauce
2 Tablespoons barbecue sauce
1/2 teaspoon dry mustard
Directions:
1. Bake ribs at 350°F for 1 hour (1/2 hour per side) or broil for 15 to 20 minutes to remove fat.
2. Cut into single servings. Combine ingredients in crackpot, stir to mix. Add ribs.
3. Cover and cook overnight or on low for 8 hours. Serve over rice.

CROCK POT HOT DOG AND BACON ROLLUPS
Ingredients:
2 pkg. hot dogs, cut in half
brown sugar
1 lb. bacon, cut into in the middle
Directions:
1. Take a piece of hot dog and piece of bacon, wrap bacon around hot dog. Stick a toothpick through bacon to hold.
2. Place one layer in bottom of Crock Pot and cover with brown sugar. Repeat until all the hot dogs have been used.
3. Cook 3 to 4 hours.

CROCK POT KALUA PORK
Ingredients:
4 to 5 pound pork butt
1 Tablespoon liquid smoke
2 1/2 Tablespoons sea salt
Directions:
1. Preheat oven to 325°F. Rub pork with liquid smoke and 1 1/2 Tablespoons of the salt. Wrap pork in foil and seal completely.
2. Place pork in roasting pan and bake for 5 hours.
3. After baking, shred pork, sprinkle with the remaining salt.

CROCK POT KIELBASA #1
Ingredients:
3 pounds of kielbasa
3 jars of peach preserves
Directions:
1. Slice the kielbasa in coins and pour the preserves on top, no need to stir.
2. Put crockpot on LOW for 4 or 5 hours.

CROCK POT KIELBASA #2

Ingredients:

3 pounds of kielbasa
1 - 2 pound box of dark brown sugar

Directions:

1. Cut up kielbasa into 1/2" chunks, put into crock pot.
2. Add whole box of brown sugar. No need to stir until brown sugar starts to liquefy.
3. Cook on low for 5 hours.

CROCK POT CREAMY SCALLOPED POTATOES AND HAM

Ingredients:

3 lb. medium size potatoes peeled and sliced
1 onion chopped
1 cup shredded cheddar cheese
1 cup cooked ham
1 can (10 3/4 oz) reduced fat cream of mushroom soup
1/2 cup water

Directions:

1. Combine potatoes, onion, cheese and ham in slow cooker/Crock Pot.
2. In small bowl, stir together soup & water. Pour over potato mixture.
3. Cover pot. Cook on High for 4 hours or until potatoes are tender. Stir mixture just before serving.

CROCK POT SWEET AND SOUR FRANKS

Ingredients:

1 cup chili sauce
1 cup currant jelly
3 Tablespoons lemon juice
1 Tablespoon prepared mustard
2 pounds cocktail franks or hot dogs cut into bite-sized pieces
2 cans pineapple chunks, 27 ounces each

Directions:

1. Combine first four ingredients in Crock Pot; mix well to break up jelly chunks.
2. Cover and cook on high 15 to 20 minutes to soften jelly and blend sauce ingredients.
3. Add cut-up hot dogs or cocktail franks. Add pineapple. Cover and cook on high for 2 hours; or low for 4 hours. Keep on low while serving.

CROCK POT SWEET AND SOUR KIELBASA

Ingredients:

1 pound kielbasa
1 (10 oz.) jar red currant jelly
1/2 (5 oz.) jar golden spicy mustard (add whole jar for more spicy)

Directions:

1. Cut kielbasa to bite-size pieces. Add to boiling water. Boil 8 to 10 minutes; poke with fork to release grease from meat.
2. In slow cooker/Crock Pot, melt jelly on low heat. Add mustard.
3. When kielbasa is done boiling, rinse, then add to slow cooker/Crock Pot mixture. Coat all of the meat.
4. Simmer for 1 hour or more on low.

CROCK POT MAPLE COUNTRY STYLE RIBS

Ingredients:

1 1/2 pounds country style ribs
1 Tablespoon maple syrup
1 Tablespoon soy sauce
2 Tablespoons dried minced onion
1/4 teaspoon ground cinnamon
1/4 teaspoon ground ginger
1/4 teaspoon ground allspice
1/2 teaspoon garlic powder
1 dash ground black pepper

Directions:
1. Combine ribs, maple syrup, soy sauce, minced onion, cinnamon, ginger, allspice, garlic powder and pepper in a slow cooker.
2. Cover and cook on Low for 7 to 9hours

CROCK POT MAPLE COUNTRY RIBS

Ingredients:
3 pounds country-style pork ribs
1 cup pure maple syrup
1/2 cup applesauce
1/4 cup ketchup
3 Tablespoons lemon juice
1/4 teaspoon of each: salt, pepper, paprika, garlic powder and ground cinnamon

Directions:
1. Mix and cook 4-6 hours on LOW.

SWEET AND SOUR RIBS BROWN SUGAR SAUCE

Ingredients:
2 cups brown sugar
1/4 cup all-purpose flour
1/3 cup water
1/2 cup white vinegar
2 Tablespoons soy sauce
2 Tablespoons ketchup
1/4 teaspoon ground ginger
1/4 teaspoon garlic powder
3 lb.s meaty spare ribs, cut into 2 or 3 rib sections

Directions:
1. Mix brown sugar and flour in a saucepan. Add water. Stir.
2. Add next 5 ingredients. Heat and stir until boiling and thickened.
3. Layer ribs in a 5 quart crock pot, spooning sauce over each layer.
4. Cover. Cook on low for 10 hours or on High for 5 to 6 hours until ribs are very tender.

CROCK POT SWEET AND SOUR SAUSAGE BALLS

Ingredients:
1/2 cup brown sugar
2 lb. sausage
1 1/4 cups ketchup
1 Tablespoon soy sauce
1 Tablespoon lemon juice
1 can chunk pineapple

Directions:
1. Roll sausage in balls, brown and add other ingredients.
2. Cook until done in slow cooker.

CROCK POT SWEET AND SOUR PORK

Ingredients:
4-6 pork shoulder steaks
1 Tablespoon cooking oil
1 can (15 oz.) crushed pineapple
1/2 cup chopped green pepper
1/2 cup water
1/3 cup brown sugar
2 Tablespoons ketchup
1 Tablespoon quick-cooking tapioca
3 teaspoons soy sauce
1/2 teaspoon dry mustard

Directions:
1. In skillet, brown pork steaks on both sides in hot oil. Drain fat. Transfer to crock pot.
2. In a bowl, combine pineapple, green pepper, water, brown sugar, ketchup, tapioca, soy sauce and dry mustard. Pour over pork steaks.
3. Cover and cook on low for 8-10 hours or on high for 4-5 hours. Serve over rice.

CROCK POT SQUASH AND PORK CHOPS

Ingredients:
6 thick pork chops
2 medium acorn squash
3/4 teaspoon salt
2 Tablespoons margarine, melted
3/4 cup brown sugar
3/4 teaspoon Kitchen Bouquet or browning sauce
1 Tablespoon orange juice
1/2 teaspoon orange peel, grated

Directions:
1. Trim excess fat from pork chops. Cut each squash into 4 or 5 crossways slices; remove seeds.
2. Arrange 3 chops on bottom of crock pot. Place all squash slices on top; then another layer of three remaining chops.
3. Combine salt, butter, sugar,bouquet sauce, orange juice and orange peel. Spoon over chops.
4. Cover and cook on low 6-8 hours or until done. Serve one or two slices of squash with each pork chop

CROCK POT CIDER MILL HAM

Ingredients:
1 to 1 1/2 lb. canned ham
1 cup apple juice
1/3 cup brown sugar
1 teaspoon prepared mustard

Directions:
1. Slice ham into 4 slices and place in crockpot.
2. Combine apple juice, brown sugar and mustard. Pour over ham slices.
3. Cover and cook 7 to 10 hours.

CROCK POT PORK CHOPS & STEW

Ingredients:
6 pork loin chops
4 Tablespoons flour
2 Tablespoons oil
6 medium potatoes, cubed
1 medium onion, chopped
1 small cabbage, cut in thin wedges
4 carrots, diced
1/4 teaspoon salt
1/2 teaspoon pepper
2 teaspoons beef bouillon granules
1/4 cup water
1 can (14 1/2 oz.) sliced stewed tomatoes
1/2 cup sour cream
2 Tablespoons cornstarch

Directions:
1. Trim fat from chops. Coat with 2 Tablespoons flour. Brown chips in oil over medium heat.
2. Place potatoes, onion and carrots in slow cooker. Sprinkle remaining flour over and toss to coat.
3. Layer over potato mixture, in order, cabbage, salt, pepper, chops, bouillon, 1/4 cup water and stewed tomatoes with juice. Do Not Stir.
4. Cover and cook on high 3 1/2-4 hours or on low for 7-8 hours.
5. Optional: In small saucepan, stir sour cream and cornstarch until smooth. Measure cooking liquid and add enough water or milk to equal 1 1/2 cups. Stir into saucepan. Cook and stir over medium heat until thick and mixture comes to a boil. Serve with chops.

CROCK POT ITALIAN SAUSAGES

Ingredients:

3-4 lb. Italian sausages (sweet or hot)
2 medium green peppers, sliced
1 large onion, sliced
28-30 oz jar spaghetti sauce

Directions:

1. Cook sausage whole in covered frying pan. Drain and slice.
2. Put all ingredients in crockpot and cook 2-3 hours on high. Turn to low to keep warm.

CROCK POT SAUERKRAUT

Ingredients:

2 bags sauerkraut, drained
1 (32 oz.) can stewed tomatoes
1 large onion, chopped
1/2 green pepper, chopped
pepper to taste
garlic powder to taste
1 pkg. smoked sausage, sliced
1 pkg. spicy hot sausage, sliced

Directions:

1. Mix first 6 ingredients together in a crock pot.
2. Cook on slow for 4 hours.
3. Spoon out 3/4 of liquid. Add sausage and cook for 2 more hours.

CROCK POT SAUSAGE & POTATOES

Ingredients:

1 1/2 lb. Polish sausage, sliced
1 large pkg. frozen hash brown potatoes
1 can Cheddar cheese soup
1/2 (15 oz.) can evaporated milk
1 bunch green onions, diced
pepper
garlic powder
1 can of diced chilies (optional)

Directions:

1. Grease crock pot.
2. Combine sausage, potatoes, onions and spices in crock pot.
3. Mix together soup and milk; pour over ingredients in crock pot. Stir together.
4. Simmer in pot about 6 hours, stirring occasionally.

CHINESE STYLE COUNTRY RIBS

Ingredients:

1/4 cup soy sauce
1 clove garlic, crushed
1/4 cup orange marmalade
4 lb. country style spareribs
2 Tablespoons catsup

Directions:

1. Combine soy sauce, marmalade, catsup, and garlicup
2. Brush on both sides of the ribs. Place in a crockpot.
3. Pour remaining sauce over all.
4. Cover and cook on low for 8 to 10 hours.

CROCK POT NORTH CAROLINA STYLE PORK

Ingredients:

Part 1
1 3-6 lb. pork shoulder or Boston butt roast
1 Tablespoon paprika
2 Tablespoons brown sugar
1/2 teaspoon each salt and pepper

Part 2
8 oz. cider vinegar
4 teaspoons of Worcestershire sauce
1/2 teaspoon dry mustard
1/2 teaspoon garlic salt
1/2 teaspoon sugar
1/4 to 1/2 teaspoon of cayenne red pepper

Directions:

1. Set pork aside, mix all other ingredients in part 1 together and rub over entire pork roast.
2. Place in crock pot on high for 6-7 hours time.
3. Mix part 2 ingredients together in medium size bowl, before pork roast is done cooking.
4. When Pork roast is very tender, with a fork, remove roast from crock pot.
5. Chop roast into a very fine degree. Take a Tablespoon and ingredients from Part 2 (BBQ sauceingredients) and spoon over the chopped roast.

CROCK POT CAJUN SAUSAGE & RICE

Ingredients:

8 oz. kielbasa sausage, cut in 1/4" slices
1 (14 1/2oz) can diced tomatoes with liquid
1 medium onion, diced
1 medium green pepper, diced
2 celery stalks, thinly sliced
1 Tablespoon chicken bouillon granules
1 Tablespoon steak sauce
3 bay leaves or 1 teaspoon dried thyme
1 teaspoon sugar
1/4 to 1/2 teaspoon hot pepper sauce
1 cup uncooked instant rice
1/2 cup chopped parsley (optional)

Directions:

1. Combine sausage, tomatoes, onion, green pepper, celery bouillon, steak sauce,bay leaves, sugar and hot pepper sauce in crockpot.
2. Cover and cook on LOW for 8 hours.Remove bay leaves; stir in rice and 1/2 cup of water. Cook an additional 25minutes.
3. Stir in parsley if desired.

Crock Pot Soups

CROCK POT 16 BEAN SOUP

Ingredients:
1 package 16 Bean Soup
3 bay leaves
1 Tablespoon crushed oregano
2 cans no-fat chicken stock
Additional water to cover
3 stalks celery chopped
3 carrots diced
1 large onion chopped
3 cloves garlic sliced
1 pound turkey Italian sausage sliced
2 cans stewed (or diced) tomatoes

Directions:
1. Combine first 5 ingredients (liquid should cover mixture by 1"-2") in Crock Pot.
2. Cook on high for 2 hours.
3. Add remaining ingredients and turn cooker to low and cook for additional 3 hours.

CROCK POT BARBECUED BEAN SOUP

Ingredients:
1 lb. great northern beans, soaked
2 teaspoons salt
1 medium onion, chopped
1/8 teaspoon ground pepper
2 lb. beef short ribs
6 cups water
3/4 cup barbecue sauce

Directions:
1. Place all ingredients in Slow Cooker except barbecue sauce.
2. Cover and cook on Low 10 to 16 hours.
3. Before serving, remove short ribs and cut meat from bones.
4. Return meat to Slow Cooker. Stir in barbecue sauce before serving.

CROCK POT CARAMELIZED FRENCH ONION SOUP

Ingredients:
1 (10.5 oz.) can beef consommé, undiluted
1 (10.5 oz.) can beef broth, undiluted
2 cups water
1/2 teaspoon dried thyme
1/4 cup dry white wine
6 cup large croutons
1 cup (4 oz.) shredded Swiss cheese

Directions:
1. Combine first 5 ingredients in a 3 1/2-quart crock pot.
2. Cook, covered, at HIGH 2 1/2 hours or until thoroughly heated. Stir in wine.
3. Ladle soup into 6 ovenproof bowls, and top evenly with croutons and cheese. Place bowls on a jellyroll pan.
4. Broil 3" from heat (with electric oven door partially open) 5 minutes or until cheese is melted. Serve immediately.

CROCK POT CHICKEN SOUP

Ingredients:
2 onions, chopped
3 carrots, sliced
2 stalks celery, sliced
2 teaspoons salt
1/4 teaspoon pepper 1/2 teaspoon basil
1/4 teaspoon leaf thyme
3 Tablespoons dry parsley flakes
1 package frozen peas (10 oz.)
1 2-1/2 to 3 lb. whole fryer
4 cups water or chicken stock
1 cup noodles

Directions:
1. Place all ingredients in slow cooker/Crock Pot, except noodles, in order listed.

2. Cover and cook on LOW 8 to 10 hours, or HIGH 4 to 6 hours.
3. One hour before serving, remove chicken and cool slightly.
4. Remove meat from bones and return meat to slow cooker/Crock Pot. Add noodles.
5. Turn to HIGH. Cover and cook 1 hour.

CROCK POT CONGRESSIONAL BEAN SOUP

Ingredients:
1 lb. small white beans
8 cups water
2 cups ham, diced
1 cup onion, diced
1 cup celery, chopped
2 Tablespoon parsley, chopped
1 teaspoon salt
1/4 teaspoon pepper
1 bay leaf

Directions:
1. Assemble ingredients in Slow Cooker.
2. Cover and cook on low 8-10 hours or until beans are tender.

CROCK POT BEEF N BREW VEGETABLE SOUP

Ingredients:
3 medium onions, sliced
1 lb. carrots, cut into 1/2" slices
4 parsnips, cut into 1/2" slices
2 bay leaves
4 cloves garlic, minced
1 Tablespoon snipped fresh thyme or 1 teaspoon dried thyme, crushed
1/2 teaspoon pepper
2 Tablespoons quick cooking tapioca
1 1/2 lb. beef stew meat, cut into 1" cubes
1 14-1/2 oz. can beef broth
1 12 oz. can beer

Directions:
1. In a 5 or 6 quart crockpot, place onions, carrots, parsnips, garlic, bay leaves, dried thyme, and pepper. Sprinkle with tapioca.

2. Place meat on top of vegetables. Add beef broth and beer.
3. Cover; cook on low-heat setting for 10 to 12 hours or on high-heat setting for 5 to 6 hours.
4. To serve, remove bay leaves; if using fresh thyme, stir in now.

CROCK POT BEEF TACO BEAN SOUP

Ingredients:
2 lb. rump roast
1 pk taco seasoning
1 can Mexican style diced tomatoes (15 oz.)
1 small can green chiles
1 can tomato sauce (8 oz.)
1 onion - chopped
2 beef bouillon cubes
2 cans red kidney beans, (15 oz. each), rinsed, drained
Shredded cheddar cheese

Directions:
1. Cut roast into bite sized chunks. Roll in taco seasoning and add to crock pot.
2. Add the tomatoes, chiles, tomato sauce, onion, and bouillon cubes.
3. Cover and cook on LOW 6 hours or until meat is tender.
4. Add the drained beans and cook until the beans are heated through; around 30 minutes. Serve topped with cheese, and/or the toppings that you like.

CROCK POT BLACK BEAN SOUP

Ingredients:
2 cans, 15 oz. each, black beans, drained and rinsed
2 cans, 4.5 oz., each, chopped green chiles
1 can, 14.5 oz., Mexican Stewed tomatoes, undrained
1 can, 14.5 oz., diced tomatoes, undrained
1 can, 11 oz., whole kernel corn, drained

4 green onions, sliced
2 to 3 Tablespoons chili powder
1 teaspoon ground cumin
1/2 teaspoon dried minced garlic
Directions:
1. Combine all ingredients in a crock pot.
2. Cover and cook on high 5 to 6 hours.

CROCK POT BROCCOLI SOUP
Ingredients:
4 cups water
4 chicken bouillon cubes
1/4 cup chopped onion
2 cups diced potatoes
1 bag frozen, chopped broccoli
2 cans cream of chicken soup
1/2-1 lb. Velveeta cheese, cubed
Directions:
1. Mix water, bouillon cubes, onions, potatoes and broccoli in a crock pot. Cook on high until broccoli is thawed.
2. Add cream of chicken soup and cheese, to taste, to mixture.
3. Turn crock pot on low and cook for 2 hours.

CROCK POT CABBAGE CHILI SOUP
Ingredients:
3 cups coarsely chopped cabbage
1 cup chopped onions
3 cups Healthy Choice tomato juice
1 (10-1/2 oz.) can Healthy Request Tomato Soup
10 oz. kidney beans, rinsed and drained
2 teaspoons chili seasoning mix
Directions:
1. In a slow cooker, combine cabbage, onion, tomato juice and tomato soup. Add kidney beans and chili seasoning mix.
2. Mix well to combine. Cover and cook on LOW for 6-8 hours. Mix well before serving.

CROCK POT CHEESE AND MEATBALL SOUP
Ingredients:
2 cups water
1 cup corn -- whole kernel
1 cup potato -- chopped
1 cup celery -- chopped
1/2 cup carrot -- sliced
1/2 cup onion -- chopped
2 cubes beef bouillon
1 jar Cheez whiz -- (16 oz.)
1 pound ground beef
1/4 cup bread crumbs
1 large egg
1/2 teaspoon salt
1/2 teaspoon tabasco sauce
Directions:
1. Mix ground beef, bread crumbs, egg, salt and tabasco sauce together thoroughly. Shape into medium size meatballs.
2. Place uncooked meatballs and all other ingredients, except Cheez Whiz, in crock pot. Stir gently.
3. Cover and cook on low for 8 to 10 hours. Before serving add Cheez Whiz, stirring gently until well blended.

CROCK POT CHEESE SOUP
Ingredients:
1/2 stick butter
3 green onions -- chopped
3 stalks celery with leaves -- chopped
2 carrots -- grated
2 cans chicken broth
2 cans cheese soup
1 can cream of potato soup parsley flakes
Tabasco sauce -- to taste salt and pepper -- to taste
8 ounces sour cream/or plain nonfat yogurt
3 Tablespoons cooking sherry
Directions:
1. Melt butter over low heat and sauté onions, celery and carrots.

144

2. Place in crock pot with chicken broth; other soups, parsley, Tabasco, salt & pepper. Stir in sour cream.
3. Cook on low 4 to 6 hours. Add sherry and stir before serving.

CROCK POT CHEESE SOUP

Ingredients:
2 cans cream of celery soup
1 soup can of milk
1 lb. cheddar, cubed
1 teaspoon Worcestershire sauce
1 teaspoon paprika

Directions:
1. Put all ingredients into crock pot on low for 4 to 6 hours. Serve with croutons.

CROCK POT LENTIL SOUP

Ingredients:
1 cup dry lentils
1 cup chopped carrot
1 cup chopped celery
1 cup chopped onion
2 cloves garlic, minced
1/2 teaspoon dried basil, crushed
1/2 teaspoon dried oregano, crushed
1/4 teaspoon dried thyme, crushed
1 bay leaf
3 1/2 cup chicken broth
1 1/2 cup water
1 (14 1/2 oz.) can Italian-style stewed tomatoes
1/4 cup snipped fresh parsley
2 Tablespoons cider vinegar

Directions:
1. Rinse lentils. In CP place lentils, carrot, celery, onion, garlic, basil, oregano,thyme, and bay leaf.
2. Stir in broth, water and undrained tomatoes.
3. Cover; cook on low for 12 hours or on high-heat setting for 5 to 6 hours.
5. Discard bay leaf. Stir in parsley and vinegar (if desired). .

CROCK POT CHICKEN NOODLE SOUP

Ingredients:
3 carrots, peeled and cut into chunks
3 stalks celery, cut into chunks
1 large onion, quartered
3 boneless skinless chicken breast halves
2 cans chicken broth
2 to 3 soup cans of water
a generous shake of dried dill and a generous shake of dried parsley
8 oz. eggnoodles

Directions:
1. Put vegetables in crock pot. Add chicken. Pour in broth and water. Add dill and parsley.
2. Cover and cook on low 8 hours.
3. Remove veggies and chicken from crock pot. Add noodles, turn to high and heat while you shred the chicken and mince the veggies.
4. Return chicken and veggies to crock pot and heat through. It takes the noodles about 20 minute to cook.

CROCK POT CHICKEN SOUP

Ingredients:
2 carrots
2 celery stalks
2 onions
3 boneless, skinless chicken breast
2 teaspoon salt
1/2 teaspoon pepper
4 cups chicken broth
4 to 5 cups water
1 Tablespoon dried parsley
1 Tablespoon dried dill
6 oz. noodles

Directions:
1. Slice carrots, celery and onion. Place in crock pot. Add chicken, broth,water, and spices.
2. Cover and cook on low 8 to 10 hours.
3. One hour before serving, remove chicken and vegetables from pot.

4. Add 6oz noodles to pot, cover and turn to high. While noodles are cooking, shred the chicken and mince the vegetables.
5. Return chicken and veggies to the pot. Cook til noodles are done.

CROCK POT CHICKEN SOUP
Ingredients:
1 pkg. boneless, skinless chicken breasts
1 pkg. chicken soup starter
1 large can chicken broth
2 cups each carrots & celery
1 cup slivered onions
Seasonings according to taste(parsley flakes, garlic, salt, pepper)
Directions:
1. Place all ingredients in crock pot and fill crock pot with water to the top.
2. Cover,turn on medium-high, approximately 8 hours.
3. Remove chicken breasts from crock pot with tongs. Cut meat on plate and return meat to soup mixture.
4. Make rice or noodles for thicker soup.

CROCK POT CHICKEN NOODLE SOUP
Ingredients:
1 whole chicken (2 1/2-3 1/2 lb.)
3-4 cans Swanson chicken broth
1 (8 oz.) pkg. frozen mixed vegetables (corn, zucchini, carrots)
1 (8 oz.) pkg. large egg noodles, cooked
salt and pepper to taste
Directions:
1. Turn crock pot to high position. Wash whole chicken and clean out insides. (No need to keep inards).
2. Place whole chicken in crock pot, cover and cook on high for 3-4 hours or until chicken falls off bones.
3. Remove chicken, let it cool.
4. While chicken is cooling, put 3-4 cans of chicken broth into the crock pot and change temperature to low.

5. De-bone entire chicken and put into crock pot with broth.
6. Add frozen vegetables and spices and cook on low for 1 hour.
7. During that time, cook egg noodles according to package directions. When the noodles are done, add them to the crock pot and season to taste.
8. Cook 1/2 hour longer.

CROCK POT CHUNKY VEGETABLE CLAM CHOWDER
Ingredients:
2 (6 1/2 oz.) cans minced clams
2 cup peeled potatoes, cut into 1/2" cubes
1 cup finely chopped onion
1 cup chopped celery
1 teaspoon sugar
1/4 teaspoon salt
1/4 teaspoon pepper
2 (10 3/4 oz.) cans condensed cream of potato soup
2 cups water
1 cup nonfat dry milk powder
1/3 cup flour
1 cup cold water
4 slices bacon, crisp-cooked, drained, and crumbled
paprika
Directions:
1. Drain clams, reserving liquid. Cover clams; chill.
2. In crock pot combine reserved clam liquid, potatoes, onion, celery, carrot, sugar, salt, and papper.
3. Stir in potato sour and 2 cups water.
4. Cover; cook on low heat for 8 to 10 hours or on high heat for 4 to 5 hours.
5. After time is up, if using low heat setting, turn to high.
6. In a medium bowl combine nonfat dry milk powder and flour. Gradually whisk in 1 cup cold water; stir into soup.

7. Cover; cook on high 10 to 15 minutes or till thickened. Stir in clams. Cover; cook 5 minutes more.

CROCK POT CLAM CHOWDER I
Ingredients:
4 cans of cream of potato soup
4 cans of New England clam chowder
2 cans minced clams with juice
1 onion, chopped and sauteed in 1 stick butter
1 quart half and half
Directions:
1. Sauté onions in butter, then add all ingredients in crockpot for 4 hours.

CROCK POT CLAM CHOWDER II
Ingredients:
4 (6 1/2 oz.) cans clams
1/2 lb. salt pork or bacon, diced
1 large onion, chopped
6 to 8 large potatoes, pared and cubed
3 cups water
3 1/2 teaspoons salt
1/4 teaspoon pepper
4 cups half and half cream or milk
3 to 4 Tablespoons cornstarch
Directions:
1. Cut clams into bite sized pieces if necessary. In skillet, sauté salt pork or bacon and onion until golden brown; drain.
2. Put into Crock Pot with clams. Add all remaining ingredients, except milk.
3. Cover; cook on high 3 to 4 hours or until potatoes are tender.
4. During the last hour of cooking, combine 1 cup of milk with the cornstarch. Add that and the remaining milk and stir well; heat through.

CROCK POT CORN CHOWDER
Ingredients:
6 slices bacon, diced
1/2 cup chopped onion
2 cups diced peeled potatoes
2 pkgs. (10 oz. each) frozen whole-kernel corn, broken apart
1 can (16 oz.) cream-style corn
1 Tablespoon sugar
1 teaspoon Worcestershire sauce
1 teaspoon seasoned salt
1/4 teaspoon pepper
1 cup water
Directions:
1. In skillet, fry bacon until crisp; remove and reserve. Add onion and potatoes to bacon drippings and saute for about 5 minutes; drain well.
2. Combine all ingredients in crock pot; stir well. Cover and cook on Low setting for 4 to 7 hours.

CROCK POT CORN CHOWDER 2
Ingredients:
3 (16 oz.) cans of corn, drained
2 large potatoes, cut into 1" chunks
1 & 1/2 can chicken broth
1 large onion, diced
1 teaspoon salt
pepper to taste
2 pints half and half
1/2 stick butter
Directions:
1. Put everything except the dairy products in the crockpot and cook on low for 7-8 hours.
2. Remove to a blender, and puree. Return to crockpot, add half & half and butter; stir.
3. Cook on high for one hour. Stir and serve.

CROCK POT DUMPLING SOUP

Ingredients:

1 lb. lean steak, cut into 1" cubes
1 pkg. onion soup mix
6 cup water (hot)
2 carrots, peeled & shredded
1 stalk finely chopped celery
1 tomato, peeled & chopped
1 cup packaged biscuit mix
6 Tablespoons milk
1 Tablespoon finely chopped parsley

Directions:

1. With pot on low, sprinkle steak with dry onion soup mix. Pour hot water over steak. Stir in carrots, celery and tomato.
2. Cover and cook on low 4-6 hours or until meat is tender.
3. Turn pot control to HIGH.
4. In separate small bowl, combine biscuit mix with parsley. Stir in milk with fork until mixture is moistened.
5. Drop dumpling mixture into crock pot with a teaspoon. Cover and cook on high for about 30 minutes.

CROCK POT OYSTER STEW

Ingredients:

2quarts whole milk
1/2 cup butter
2 pints fresh oysters
1 1/2 teaspoons salt
2 teaspoons Worcestershire sauce

Directions:

1. In crock pot heat milk on high for 1 1/2 hours.
2. In saucepan, melt butter and add oysters with liquid. Simmer on low until edges of oysters curl.
3. Add seasonings. Combine with the hot milk in crock pot and cook on low for 2-3 hours, stirring occasionally.

CROCK POT SOUP

Ingredients:

3 cups water
2 small onions, chopped
2 stalks celery, chopped
2 carrots, sliced thin
1 lb. can tomatoes
1 teaspoon pepper
1 Tablespoon all seasoning
1 (10 oz.) pkg. frozen mixed vegetables
1 lb. ground beef, browned and drained
2-4 Tablespoons or 2 cubes beef bouillon
1/2 cup margarine
1/2 cup flour

Directions:

1. Put all ingredients in crock pot. Cover. Cook low 8-10 hours.
2. One hour before done, turn to high.
3. Make roux (paste) of flour and butter. Add some of hot soup to it, stirring until smooth. Return to soup. Mix.
4. Cook on high 1 hour until thickened.

CROCK POT HAM-BEAN SOUP

Ingredients:

1 ham bone (with small amount of ham still on)
2 cup Navy beans or mixed beans
8 cup water
1 clove garlic, minced (or 1/2 teaspoon garlic powder)
1 Tablespoon lemon juice
1 Tablespoon honey
1 bay leaf
1 large onion, chopped
salt & pepper, to taste

Directions:

1. Wash beans. Put everything in crock pot along with ham bone.
2. Start cooking at high, turn to low once it starts cooking. Cook on low for 8 hours.

CROCK POT HAM BROCCOLI CHOWDER

Ingredients:
2 Tablespoons flour
1 small can evaporated milk
2 cup ham, diced
1 pkg. frozen chopped broccoli
1/4 cup onion, minced
1 cup Swiss cheese, grated
2 cups water
1 cup light cream

Directions:
1. Mix flour and evaporated milk in cooker. Add other ingredients except cream.
2. Cook on low 7 hours, or on automatic for 4 hours.
3. Before serving, stir in cream and heat.

CROCK POT MEXICAN POTATO CORN CHOWDER

Ingredients:
14 small potatoes, peeled and diced
1 can (17 oz.) cream style corn
1 can (12 oz.) whole kernel corn-do not drain
2 Tablespoons chicken bouillon powder
1 can (4 oz.) diced green chilies
1 Tablespoon + margarine
1 large onion (brown), diced fine
1 green pepper, diced fine
garlic powder
seasoned salt
dash of Worchesteshire sauce
2 cups medium Cheddar cheese, shredded
1 1/2 cups Monterey Jack cheese, shredded

Directions:
1. Cover potatoes with water and boil gently, uncovered until you can pierce them easily with a fork.
2. Add sautéed onion and green pepper. Stir in corns, chilies and seasonings (season salt, garlic powder, dash of Worchesteshire sauce). Heat until bubbly.

3. Place in large (5-6 qt.) crockpot on high until it bubbles again and then turn to low.
4. Stir in shredded cheese. Simmer on low for at least 1 hour

CROCK POT MEXICAN SOUP

Ingredients:
1 lb. lean ground beef
8 cup chicken stock
4 Tablespoon flour
1 egg
1 red chili pepper
4 medium carrots, grated
5 1/2 Tablespoon Minute rice
1/2 lb. spinach fresh or frozen chopped
1/2 teaspoon oregano
1/4 lb. ham chopped
2 1/2 Tablespoon parsley

Directions:
1. Mix beef, 1/2 cup stock, flour and egg. Form into small balls. Set aside.
2. Put remaining stock, chili pepper, carrots and rice in crockpot on high to simmer. When simmering add meat balls, cover and cook 1/2 hour.
3. Turn heat on low and cook 3 hours.
4. Add other ingredients and cover and cook for 20 more minutes.

CROCK POT TURKEY SOUP

Ingredients:
1 lb. ground turkey
1/4 teaspoon pepper
1/4 teaspoon oregano
1/4 teaspoon basil
3 teaspoons beef bouillon
3 cup boiling water
1 cup (8 oz.) tomato sauce
1 Tablespoon soy sauce
1 cup diced celery
1 cup diced carrots
1 large diced onion
1 cup fresh mushrooms
1 cup diced green pepper (optional)

Directions:

1. Add all ingredients except sliced mushrooms. Cover and cook on low for 6 to 8 hours.
2. Add mushrooms and turn up to high for 10 to 15 minutes.

CROCK POT ITALIAN VEGETABLE SOUP

Ingredients:
1 can corn
1 can Italian zucchini squash
1 (16 oz.) can tomatoes
1 (8 oz.) can tomato sauce
2-3 diced potatoes
1-2 lb. hamburger
2 Tablespoons oregano leaves
A pinch basil leaves
¼ teaspoon garlic salt
3 bay leaves

Directions:
1. Brown hamburger. Drain well. Add all ingredients in crock pot.
2. Cook on low 6- 8 hours.

CROCK POT MINESTRONE SOUP #1

Ingredients:
3 cups water
1 1/2 lb. beef shank
1 medium onion, diced
2 carrots, diced
2 stalks celery with tops, sliced
1/2 cup vermicelli
1 16-ounce can tomatoes
2 teaspoons salt
1 zucchini, sliced
1 10-ounce package (frozen mixed vegetables)
1/2 cup shredded cabbage
1 Tablespoon dried basil
1 clove garlic, minced
1 pound can garbanzo beans
1 teaspoon oregano

Directions:
1. Place all ingredients in crock pot except zucchini. Stir to mix thoroughly.
2. Cover and cook on Low 10 to 12 hours (High: 4 to 5 hours).
3. During last hour, remove meat and bones. Cut meat from bones and return to soup with zucchini.
4. Turn crock pot to High and cook one hour. Ladle into bowls and sprinkle with Parmesan cheese.

CROCK POT MINESTRONE SOUP #2

Ingredients:
1/2-3/4 lb. browned ground meat
2 16 oz. cans diced tomatoes
1 16 oz. can tomato sauce
7 cups water
4 beef bouillon cubes
1/2 onion, chopped
1 clove garlic
1 1/2 teaspoons Italian seasoning
1 small pkg frozen vegetables
1 15 oz. can white beans
1 cup pasta

Directions:
1. Place everything except the pasta in the crockpot and simmer on low all day (6-8 hrs).
2. Turn up to high and add the pasta.
3. Simmer on high about 1 hour until pasta is cooked through. Top with parmesan cheese.

CROCK POT MINESTRONE SOUP #3

Ingredients:
16 oz. tomatoes, stewed -- canned, cut in pieces
2 medium onions -- chopped
2 cloves garlic -- crushed
1 cup carrots -- diced
1 cup celery -- diced
1 large zucchini -- thinly sliced
16 oz. kidney beans -- canned
6 oz. tomato paste -- canned
1 Tablespoon parsley, freeze-dried flakes
2 teaspoons salt
1/8 teaspoon black pepper -- finely ground
6 cups "beef style" vegetarian broth
1/4 pound spaghetti -- cut in 2" pieces
1/2 teaspoon ground sage
1 teaspoon dried basil -- crushed
2 cups shredded cabbage -- optional

Directions:
1. Place all ingredients except spaghetti in slow cooker; stir, Cover.
2. Turn heat control to LOW; cook 10 to 12 hours.
3. Add spaghetti. Cover and cook 1 hour longer.

CROCK POT COSTA RICAN BEEF & VEGETABLE SOUP WITH YELLOW RICE

Soup Ingredients:
2 lb. lean, boneless beef chuck in 1 1/2 inch cubes
1 large onion, thinly sliced
1 cup celery, thinly sliced
3 cloves garlic, minced
1 dry bay leaf
1 large red bell pepper, seeded and cut into thin, bite-size strips
1 1/2 cups water
2 cans (about 14 1/2 oz.) beef broth
yellow rice (recipe below)
1 large ear corn, cut into 3/4 inch thick slices
4 cups coarsely shredded cabbage
1/3 cup lightly packed cilantro leaves
salt and pepper

Directions:
THE SOUP:
1. Arrange beef cubes slightly apart in a single layer in a shallow baking pan.
2. Bake in a 500 oven until well browned (about 20 minutes).
3. In a 3 1/2 quart or larger crockpot, combine onion, celery, garlic, bay leaf and bell pepper. Transfer browned beef to crockpot.
4. Pour a little of the water into baking pan, stirring to dissolve drippings and pour into crockpot. Add broth and remaining water.
5. Cover and cook on low about 8 hours.
6. About 15 minutes before beef is done, prepare Yellow Rice. While rice is cooking, increase cooker setting to high; add corn.
7. Cover; cook for 5 minutes. Add cabbage; cover and cook until cabbage is bright green, 8 to 10 more minutes.
8. Stir in cilantro; season with salt and pepper. Ladle soup into wide, shallow bowls; add a scoop of rice to each.

THE RICE:
Ingredients:
1 Tablespoon salad oil
1 small onion, finely chopped
1 cup long-grain white rice
1/4 teaspoon ground turmeric
1 3/4 cups water

Directions:
1. Heat oil in 2-quart pan over medium heat. Add the onion; cook, stirring until onion is soft but not browned, (3 to 5 minutes).
2. Stir in the rice and turmeric; cook, stirring occasionally, for about 1 minute.
3. Pour in the water and reduce heat to low and cook until rice is tender, about 20 minutes.

CROCK POT CREAM OF SWEET POTATO SOUP

Ingredients:
3 Sweet potatoes, peeled and sliced
2 c Chicken bouillon
1 ts Sugar
1/8 ts Each ground cloves and nutmeg
Salt to taste
1 1/2 c Light cream, half-and-half, or milk

Directions:
1. Put sweet potatoes and bouillon in cooker.
2. Cover and cook on high 2 to 3 hours or until potatoes are tender.
3. Force potatoes and liquid through food mill or puree in blender. Put back in cooker with remaining ingredients.
4. Cover and cook on high 1 to 2 hours.

CROCK POT SPLIT PEA SOUP

Ingredients:
1 (16 oz.) pkg. dried green split peas, rinsed
1 hambone, or 2 meaty ham hocks, or 2 cup diced ham
3 carrots, peeled & sliced
1 medium onion, chopped
2 stalks of celery plus leaves, chopped
1 or 2 cloves of garlic, minced
1 bay leaf
1/4 cup fresh parsley, chopped (optional)
1 Tablespoon seasoned salt (or to taste)
1/2 teaspoon fresh pepper
1 1/2 quarts hot water

Directions:
1. Layer ingredients in slow cooker, pour in water. DO NOT STIR.
2. Cover and cook on high 4 to 5 hours or on low 8 to 10 hours until peas are very soft and ham falls off bone.
3. Remove bones and bay leaf. Serve garnished with croutons.

CROCK POT SEAFOOD CHOWDER

Ingredients:
2 lb. frozen fish filets
1/4 lb. bacon or salt pork, diced
1 medium onion, chopped
4 medium potatoes, peeled and cubed
2 cups water
1 1/2 teaspoons salt (unless you are using fresh salt-water fish)
1/4 teaspoon pepper
1 can evaporated milk

Directions:
1. Thaw frozen fish in refrigerator. Cut into bite-sized pieces.
2. In skillet, saute bacon or salt pork and onion until meat is cooked and onion is golden. Drain and put into Crock Pot with the fish pieces.
3. Add potatoes, water, salt and pepper. Cover and cook on low for 6 - 9 hours.
4. Add evaporated milk during last hour.

CROCK POT HAM AND BEAN SOUP WITH VEGETABLES

Ingredients:
1 pound dried navy beans soaked overnight
1 hot pepper
1 carrot, sliced
salt and pepper
4 cups water
1 ham butt (2 to 3 pounds)
1 onion, sliced
1 package frozen peas
2 garlic cloves
1 green pepper diced
1/2 small head cabbage, shredded

Directions:
1. Drain beans. Place all ingredients except frozen vegetables and cabbage in crock pot.
2. Cover and cook on Low 10 to 12 (or more) hours.

3. Turn to high and remove ham. Add peas, limas and cabbage.
4. Cook for 1 to 2 hours on High or until vegetables are tender.

CROCK POT HAM AND LENTIL SOUP

Ingredients:
2 cups lentils
/2 pound ham -- diced
1 onion -- chopped
1 bay leaf
2 ribs celery -- chopped
1 clove garlic -- minced
salt and pepper -- to taste
Directions:
1. Combine all ingredients with 2 quarts water in the crock pot.
2. Cook on low, covered, 8 to 10 hours.

CROCK POT VEGETABLE BEEF SOUP

Ingredients:
1 pound ground chuck 1 cup chopped onion
1 large (28 oz.) can whole tomatoes (chopped)
3 cup diced potatoes
1 (16 oz.) can cut green beans
2 teaspoon chili powder
2-3 dashes cayenne pepper sauce
2 (10 1/2 oz.) cans condensed beef bouillon
1 cup chopped celery 1 cup sliced carrots
1 teaspoon salt
1 teaspoon Worcestershire sauce
Directions:
1. Brown meat with onion and celery; drain off fat. Place into crock pot.
2. Stir in remaining ingredients and add 1 or 2 cups water.
2. Cover and cook on low for 8-10 hours.

CROCK POT ZESTY BEEF AND VEGETABLE SOUP

Ingredients:
1 lb. ground beef
1/2 cup chopped onion
2 cloves garlic, minced
2cup pre-shredded coleslaw mix
1(10 oz.) package frozen whole kernel corn
1(9 oz.) package frozen cut green beans
4 cups hot-style vegetable juice (like V-8)
1 (14 1/2 oz.) can Italian-style stewed tomatoes
2 Tablespoons Worcestershire sauce
1 teaspoon dried basil
1/4 teaspoon pepper
Directions:
1. In a large skillet cook ground beef, onion, and garlic till meat is brown and onion is tender. Drain off fat.
2. In crock pot combine meat mixture, coleslaw mix, frozen corn,frozen beans, vegetable juice, undrained tomatoes, Worcestershire sauce, basil,and pepper.
3. Cover; cook on low-heat setting for 8 to 10 hours or on high-heat setting for 4 to 5 hours.

CROCK POT CHOWDER

Ingredients:
6 slices of crisp bacon, crumbled
4 medium potatoes, peeled and diced
1/2 cup minced onions, chopped
1 (16 oz.) can cream corn
2 cans (13 3/4 oz.) chicken broth
1 teaspoon salt
1/4 teaspoon pepper
1 can evaporated milk
Directions:
1. Place all ingredients, except milk in a crock pot.
2. Cover and cook on low for 10 to 12 hours.
3. Add milk and cook covered for 1 hour.

CROCK POT POTATO SOUP
Ingredients:
8 potatoes (peeled or not) chopped
1 onion, chopped
2 celery ribs chopped
2 carrots, peeled and chopped small
1 can chicken broth
2 Tablespoons dried parsley
1 1/2 teaspoons salt
1/4 teaspoon pepper
1 cup milk
1/2 cup flour
sliced green onions, grated cheese, and chopped bacon for toppings
Directions:
1. Put all ingredients down to and including the pepper into the crockpot. Add water to within 1" of the top of the crockpot (this recipe is for a 5 qt, so adjustaccordingly).
2. Cook on high for 8 hours.
3. 1 hour before serving, put milk into a small container with a lid, add flour and shake until well mixed. Add to the soup.

CROCK POT POTATO SOUP 2
Ingredients:
6 potatoes
2 leeks
2 onions
1 carrot
1 stalk celery
4 cup water
1 1/2 teaspoon salt
4 chicken bouillon cubes
1 can cream of mushroom soup
1 can cream of celery soup
1 Tablespoon parsley flakes
2 Tablespoons butter
13 oz. can evaporated milk
Chopped chives

Directions:
1. Cut all vegetables to bite-size. Put all ingredients except milk and chives, in the crock pot.
2. Cover and cook on low for 10 to 12 hours or high for 3-4 hours. Stir in evaporated milk during the last hour.

CROCKPOT POTATO SOUP 3
Ingredients:
6 potatoes, peeled and sliced
1 carrot, sliced
1 stalk celery, sliced
4 chicken bouillon cubes
1 Tablespoon parsley flakes
5 cups water
1 Tablespoon salt
pepper
1/3 cup margarine
1 (13 oz.) can evaporated milk
Directions:
1. Put all ingredients in crockpot, except milk. Cook on low 10-12 hours.
2. Stir in evaporated milk during last hour.

CROCK POT FISHERMAN CATCH CHOWDER
Ingredients:
1 lb. - 1 1/2 lb. fish (use any combination of the following: flounder, ocean perch, pike, rainbow trout, haddock or halibut)
1/2 cup onion; chopped
1/2 cup celery; chopped
1/2 cup pared carrots; chopped
1/4 cup parsley; snipped
1 teaspoon leaf rosemary
1 can (16 oz.) whole tomatoes; mashed
1/2 cup dry white wine
1 bottle (8 oz.) clam juice
1 teaspoon salt
3 Tablespoons flour
3 Tablespoons butter, melted
1/3 cup light cream

Directions:
1. Cut cleaned fish into 1-inch pieces. Combine all ingredients except flour, butter and cream in crockpot; stir well.
2. Cover and cook on LOW setting for 7-8 hours, on HIGH setting for 3-4 hours.
3. One hour before serving, combine flour, butter and cream. Stir into fish mixture.
4. Continue to cook until mixture is slightly thickened.

CROCK POT FRENCH ONION SOUP #1

Ingredients:
2 quarts bouillon, beef -- blended
6 cups onions -- thinly sliced
1/4 cup margarine
1 1/2 teaspoons salt
1/4 cup sugar
2 Tablespoons flour
1/4 cup cooking sherry -- optional

Directions:
1. Pour bouillon in crockpot; cover and set on high.
2. Cook onions slowly in large skillet in margarine; cover and let cook for about 15 minutes.
3. Uncover and add salt, sugar and flour. Stir well. Add to stock in craokpot.
3. Cover and cook on low for 6-8 hours.
4. Add sherry anytime during the last 2-3 hours of cooking.
5. Place a slice of french bread in each serving dish. Place a slice of mozzarella cheese over the bread. Pour hot soup over this combination.

CROCK POT FRENCH ONION SOUP #2

Ingredients:
2 pounds onions -- sliced thin
1 Tablespoon sugar
1 teaspoon salt
1/4 cup margarine
Tablespoons olive oil
2 Tablespoons flour
2 cans condensed beef broth
2 cans condensed beef consommé
1/2 cup dry white wine
1 teaspoon Worcestershire sauce
3 soup cans water
Topping:1 loaf French bread -- sliced
olive oil
parmesan cheese -- freshly grated
Swiss cheese -- freshly grated

Directions:
1. Melt margarine and olive oil together in large skillet. Add sliced onions, sugar and salt to skillet, sauté approximately 20 minutes or until golden.
2. Sprinkle onions with flour and cook an additional 2 - 3 minutes.
3. To crockpot, add the remaining ingredients and the onion mixture.
4. Cook at least 8 hours.
5. Brush 1" slices of French bread on both sides with olive oil. Sprinkle one side with parmesan cheese and broil.
6. Put broiled side down in hot soup, sprinkle top side of bread with parmesan and top with grated Swiss cheese. Broil until bubbly

CROCK POT FRENCH ONION SOUP #3

Ingredients:

4 large yellow onions -- thinly sliced
1/4 cup butter
3 cups rich beef stock
1 cup dry white wine
1/4 cup medium dry sherry
1 teaspoon Worcestershire sauce
1 clove garlic -- minced
6 slices French bread -- buttered
1/4 cup Romano or parmesan cheese

Directions:

1. Using a large frying pan, slowly sauté the onions in butter until limp and glazed. Transfer to crock pot.
2. Add beef stock, white wine, sherry, Worcestershire and garlicup
3. Cover. Cook on low 6 to 8 hours.
4. Place French bread on a baking sheet. Sprinkle with cheese. Place under preheated broiler until lightly toasted.
5. To serve, ladle soup into bowl. Float a slice of toasted French bread on top.

CROCK POT FRESH TOMATO SOUP

Ingredients:

8 medium tomatoes
1medium onion -- chopped
2carrots -- peeled and thinly sliced
1garlic clove -- crushed
1Tablespoon brown sugar
1 Tablespoon chopped fresh basil
1 Tablespoon chopped parsley
2 teaspoons Worcestershire sauce
1/2 teaspoon salt
1/8 teaspoon pepper
3 cups chicken broth or bouillon

Directions:

1. Drop tomatoes in a pan of boiling water for 15 to 20 seconds; immediately rinse with cold water.
2. Remove skins. Cut in half crosswise; squeeze out and discard seeds.

3. Combine in slow-cooker with onions, carrots, garlic, brown sugar, basil, parsley,Worcestershire sauce, salt, pepper and broth (or bouillon).
3. Cover and cook onLOW 5 to 6 hours or until vegetables are very soft.
4. Puree in blender or food processor fitted with metal blade. Serve in individual bowls.

CROCK POT HAMBURGER VEGETABLE SOUP

Ingredients:

tomato soup
stewed tomatoes (Italian style)
hamburger (browned)
corn
carrots
green beans
parmesan cheese
Use 1 can of soup for each person, 1/4 lb. hamburger for each person, and ¼ can vegetables for each person.

Directions:

1. Brown meat, then add everything into CrockPot and leave it on low for about 3 hours (stir occasionally).
2. Top each bowl with parmesan cheese.

CROCK POT HAMBURGER SOUP

Ingredients:

1 lb. lean ground beef
1/4 teaspoon pepper
1/4 teaspoon oregano
1/4 teaspoon basil
1/4 teaspoon seasoned salt
1 envelope onion soup mix
1 (8 oz.) can tomato sauce
1 Tablespoon soy sauce
1 cup celery, chopped
1 cup carrots, sliced
1/2 cup macaroni, cooked
1/4 cup Parmesan cheese, grated

Directions:
1. Crumble beef into crock pot. Add pepper, oregano, basil, seasoned salt and dry onion soup mix.
2. Stir in 3 cups boiling water, tomato sauce and soy sauce, then add celery and carrots.
3. Cover and cook on low for 6 to 8 hours.
4. Turn control on high. Add cooked macaroni and Parmesan cheese.
5. Cover and cook on high for 10-15 minutes.

CROCK POT HEARTY BEAN SOUP

Ingredients:
3 cups chopped parsnips
2 cups chopped carrots
1 cup chopped onion
1-1/2 cups dry great northern beans
5 cups water
1-1/2 lb. smoked ham hocks
2 garlic gloves, minced
2 teaspoons salt
1/2 teaspoon pepper
1/8 to 1/4 teaspoon hot pepper sauce

Directions:
1. Soak beans overnight. In a 5 qt. cooker, place parsnips, carrots, and onion. Top with beans.
2. Add water, ham, garlic, salt, pepper and hot sauce.
3. Cook on high 6-8 hours until beans are tender.

CROCK POT HEARTY POTATO SOUP

Ingredients:
6 potatoes -- peeled and cut into 1/2" cubes
2 medium onions -- diced
2 carrots -- thinly sliced
ribs celery -- thinly sliced
2 cans (14 1/2 oz. each) chicken broth
1 teaspoon dried basil

1 teaspoon salt
1/2 teaspoon pepper
1/4 cup all-purpose flour
1 1/2 cups half-and-half

Directions:
1. Combine first 8 ingredients in a slow cooker.
2. Cook, covered, at High 3 hours or until vegetables are tender.
3. Stir together flour and half-and-half; stir into soup.
4. Cover and cook 30 minutes or until thoroughly heated.

CROCK POT HERBED VEGETABLE SOUP

Ingredients:
1 10 oz. package frozen green beans
1 10 oz. package frozen corn
1 cup chopped onion
1 cup finely chopped carrots
1 cup coarsely chopped zucchini
2 cloves garlic, minced
6 cups veg. broth
1 6 oz. can tomato paste
2 Tbs parsley
1 teaspoon dried marjoram
1/2 teaspoon dried basil
1 bay leaf
1 4 oz. package small pasta (1 1/2 cups)

Directions:
1. Put all ingredients except pasta into crackpot. Stir. Cover and cook on low for 7-9 hours or high for 3-4 hours.
2. Add pasta and cook on low or high for an hour more. Discard bay leaf and serve.

CROCK POT LAZY DAY BEEF AND VEGETABLE SOUP

Ingredients:

2 1/2 pounds beef for stew, cut into 3/4" pieces
2 cans (14 to 14 1/2 ounces each) ready-to-serve beef broth
1 can (15 ounces) chickpeas, drained
1 can (15 ounces) diced tomatoes with garlic and onions, undrained
1 cup water
1 teaspoon salt
1 teaspoon dried Italian seasoning, crushed
1/2 teaspoon pepper
2 cups frozen mixed vegetables
1 cup uncooked Ditalini or other small pasta
shredded Romano cheese (optional)

Directions:

1. Combine beef, broth, chickpeas, tomatoes, water, salt, Italian seasoning and pepper in 4 1/2 to 5 1/2-quart slow cooker; mix well. Cover and cook on HIGH 5hours or on LOW 8 hours. (No stirring is necessary during cooking)
2. Stir in mixed vegetables and pasta. Continue cooking, covered, 1 hour or untilb.eef and pasta are tender. Stir well before serving. Serve with cheese, if desired.

CROCK POT MEDITERRANEAN BEEF SOUP

Ingredients:

2 medium zucchini cut into bite sized pieces
1 large chopped onion
1 (2 inch) cinnamon stick
3/4 pound stew meat cut into bite sized pieces
2 (14.5oz) cans diced tomatoes with oregano, basil and garlic, undrained
1/2 teaspoon pepper
Cooking Spray

3.5 cups hot cooked orzo (about 1 3/4 cups uncooked rice shaped pasta), cooked without salt or fat

Directions:

1. Place first 6 ingredients in slow cooker coated with spray. Stir well.
2. Cover and cook on high 1 hour and low 7-9 hours.
3. Discard cinnamon stick. Serve over cooked orzo.

CROCK POT OLD FASHIONED VEGETABLE SOUP

Ingredients:

2 lb. soup bones or 1 lb. beef short ribs
2 quarts water
1 teaspoon salt
1 teaspoon celery salt
1 small onion, chopped
1 cup carrots, diced
1/2 cup celery, diced
2 cups potatoes, diced
1 lb. can whole kernel corn, undrained
1 lb. can tomatoes or home canned,cut up
2 turnips, peeled and finely chopped

Directions:

1. Place the meat, water, salts, onions, carrots and celery in crock pot.
2. Cover and cook on low for 4-6 hours. Remove bones, chop meat and return to pot.
3. Add potatoes, corn, tomatoes and turnips. Cover and cook on high for 2-3 hours more.

CROCK POT PESTO SOUP

Ingredients:

1 lb. white beans, soaked overnight
1 potato, diced
2 carrots, diced
2 leeks, diced
2 tomatoes, diced
1/4 lb. green beans, diced
2 zucchini, diced
2 sage leaves, minced or 1/4 teaspoon powdered sage
1 teaspoon salt
1/2 teaspoon pepper
2 oz. vermicelli
Pesto Sauce
3 cloves garlic, minced
6 basil leaves, minced
1/2 cup grated Parmesan cheese
1/2 cup olive oil

Directions:

1. Combine all ingredients except vermicelli and sauce in a slow cooker with 2 quarts water.
2. Cover and cook on high 2 hours.
3. Turn heat to low and cook, covered for 8 hours.
4. Add vermicelli, turn on high and cook, covered for 30 minutes.
5. Combine sauce ingredients, stir into soup and serve.

CROCK POT SEAFOOD CHOWDER

Ingredients:

1 1/2 pounds fish fillets
1/4 pound bacon -- diced
1 medium onion -- chopped
3/4 cup green onion (with tops) -- chopped
2 medium potatoes -- pared and cubed
1 1/2 cups water
1/2 teaspoon salt
1/4 teaspoon pepper
1 (13 ounce) can evaporated milk

Directions:

1. Cut fish into bite-sized pieces. In small skillet, sauté bacon and onion until golden. Drain and put into Crockpot with fish.
2. Add all remaining ingredients except evaporated milk. Cover and cook on low 6-9 hours or until potatoes are tender (High 3 1/2 hours).
3. Add evaporated milk during last hour.

CROCK POT SOUTHWESTERN VEGETABLE SOUP

Ingredients:

2 lb. ground beef
1 cup onion (diced)
1 cup bell pepper (diced)
1 cup celery (diced)
2 cans Hunt's diced tomatoes
1 pkg. frozen French-style green beans
1 pkg. frozen whole kernel corn
2 cans kidney beans
1 teaspoon cumin
3 Tablespoons chili powder
1/2 teaspoon garlic powder
1/2 teaspoon oregano
1/4 teaspoon red cayenne pepper
2 cups cooked rice

Directions:

1. Brown ground beef with onion, peppers, and celery. Drain well and rinse with HOT water.
2. Combine with all other ingredients EXCEPT rice in a large crockpot.
3. Simmer on low 4 hours. Add rice about 30 minutes before serving.

CROCK POT TACO SOUP

Ingredients:
1 pound lean ground beef -- browned and drained
2 packages taco seasoning mix
1 16 oz. can tomatoes with green chilies -- undrained
1 16 oz. can black beans -- undrained
1 16 oz. can corn -- undrained
1 can black olives -- chopped or sliced
1 medium onion -- chopped
1/2 bell pepper -- chopped
4 tomatillos (optional) -- chopped

Directions:
1. Place everything in a large crockpot, add water, if necessary, to fill.
2. Cook on low for 5 or more hours until flavors are blended.
3. Top each bowl with a handful ofshredded cheddar cheese. Serve with sour cream, taco chips and salsa on the side.

CROCK POT TORTILLA SOUP

Ingredients:
1 onion chopped
2 cloves minced garlic
2 ribs chopped celery
1/4 to 1/2 cup chopped bell pepper
1 thinly sliced zucchini
1 thinly sliced yellow squash
1 16oz bag frozen corn
2 cans chicken broth
1 can diced tomatoes
1 small can tomato sauce
1/2 cup chopped cilantro
1/2 teaspoon cumin
1/2 teaspoon chili powder
shredded cheese (Monterey jack or cheddar)
tortilla chips

Directions:
1. Sauté first four ingredients.
2. Place all ingredients into the crock pot (except the cheese and chips) and cook on low about 6hours

CROCK POT KANSAS CITY STEAK SOUP

Ingredients:
3 cup water
2 small chopped onions
3 stalks chopped celery
2 sliced carrots
1 lb. canned tomatoes
1 teaspoon pepper
Salt as desired
1 (10 oz.) pkg. frozen mixed vegetables
1 lb. diced chuck roast or top round, browned and drained
2-4 Tablespoons beef base, granules or paste
1/2 cup butter or margarine
1/2 cup flour

Directions:
1. Put all ingredients except butter and flour in crock pot.
2. Cover and cook on low 8-10 hours. One hour before serving, turn to high.
3. Make a roux of 1 stick melted butter or margarine and 1/2 cup flour. Stir until smooth.
4. Pour into crock pot and stir until thickened.

CROCK POT COUNTRY CHICKEN SOUP

Ingredients:
2 small onions (chopped)
2 stalks celery, diced
2 carrots, sliced
1 teaspoon salt
1/4 teaspoon pepper
1/2 teaspoon basil
1/4 teaspoon thyme
1/4 teaspoon sage
2 Tablespoons dry parsley flakes
1 (10 oz.) pkg. frozen peas
1 (2 1/2 to 3 lb.) whole broiler/fryer chicken
2 1/2 cups water
1/3 cup raw converted rice

Directions:
1. Place all ingredients in crock pot EXCEPT RICE in order listed.
2. Cover and cook on low 8 to 10 hours (high 4 to 6 hours).
3. Give hour before serving, remove chicken and cool slightly. Remove meat from bones and return to crock pot.
4. Add rice. Cover and cook the additional hour on high.

CROCK POT BEEF BARLEY SOUP

Ingredients:
2 lb. beef shanks
2 cups thinly sliced carrots
1 cup sliced celery
3/4 cup chopped green pepper
1 large onion, sliced
1 (16 oz.) can cut up tomatoes
1/4 cup snipped parsley
1 Tablespoon instant beef bouillon granules
2 teaspoons salt
3/4 teaspoon dried basil, crushed
5 cups water

Directions:
1. Cut beef into cubes, brown on all sides, and drain well.
2. In crock pot place carrot, celery, green pepper and onion. Place beef on top.
3. Combine undrained tomatoes, barley, parsley, bouillon, salt and basil. DO NOT STIR.
4. Cover and cook on low heat 10 to 12 hours. Remove bones if used and skim any fat. Season with salt and pepper to taste.

CROCK POT SOUP

Ingredients:
Chuck roast about 2-3 1/2 lb., cut into small chunks
5 medium potatoes, diced
5 carrots, diced
1 large onion, diced
4-5 sticks celery, chopped
1 can Rotel tomatoes
1 small can corn
1 small can green beans
salt and pepper

Directions:
1. Put all ingredients into the crock pot and turn on high until the mixture starts to boil. Turn on low and cook all day.

CROCK POT BEEF BARLEY SOUP

Ingredients:
1 pound stew beef
2 cup carrots, sliced thin
1 cup celery, thin sliced
3/4 cup chopped green pepper
1 cup chopped onion
1/2 cup barley
1/4 chopped parsley
3 beef bouillon cubes or equivalent beef base
2 teaspoon salt
3/4 teaspoon dried basil
2 Tablespoon catsup

161

Directions:
1. Layer in crock pot: Vegetables and meat then barley and remaining ingredients.Cover with 5 cups water. Do not stir.
2. Cook on low for 9 to 11 hours.

Crock Pot Turkey

CROCK POT SUPPERTIME STEW

Ingredients:
16 oz. ground 90% lean turkey
3 cups (15 oz.) sliced raw potatoes
1 1/2 cup chopped celery
2 cups sliced carrots
1 cup chopped onion
1 1/2 cup frozen peas
1 3/4 cups (one 15 oz. can) Hunt's chunky Tomato Sauce
2 teaspoons Italian seasoning

Directions:
1. In a large skillet sprayed with butter-flavored cooking spray, brown meat.
2. Combine potatoes, celery, carrots, onion and peas in crock pot. Spoon browned meat over vegetables.
3. In a small bowl, combine tomato sauce andItalian seasoning. Evenly pour sauce over meat.
4. Cover and cook on LOW for 6 to 8hours. Mix well before serving.

CROCK POT CRANBERRY-APPLE TURKEY BREAST

Ingredients:
2 teaspoons melted butter or margarine
1/2 cup chicken broth
1 large apple, cored and chopped
1/2 cup chopped onion
1 stalk celery, chopped
1 cup whole berry cranberry sauce
3/4 teaspoon poultry seasoning
2 cups seasoned crumb-style stuffing
2 to 3 pounds turkey breast cutlets

Directions:
1. Combine butter, chicken broth, apple, onion, celery, cranberry sauce, poultry seasoning and stuffing.

2. Place 3 tablespoons stuffing mix on each turkey cutlet. Roll up and tie.
3. Place turkey in crock pot. Cover; cook on LOW 8 hours (HIGH 4 hours).

CROCK POT TURKEY MEATBALLS

Ingredients:
1 1/2 cups barbecue sauce (your favorite)
10 ounces Apple jelly
2 Tablespoons Tapioca (for thick sauce if desired)
1 Tablespoon Vinegar
1 Egg, beaten
1/4 cup Seasoned bread crumbs, fine
2 Tablespoons Milk
1/4 teaspoon Garlic powder
1/4 teaspoon salt
1/4 teaspoon onion powder
1 pound Ground turkey
Non-stick vegetable spray

Directions:
1. In 3 1/2 or 4 quart crockpot, stir together barbecue sauce, jelly, tapioca (if used), and vinegar.
2. Cover; cook on high-heat setting while preparing meatballs.
3. For meatballs, in large bowl combine egg, bread crumbs, milk, garlic powder, salt, and onion powder. Add ground turkey and mix well.
4. Shape into 1/2 to 3/4-inch meatballs. Spray a 12-inch non-stick skillet; add meatballs and brown on all sides over medium heat.
5. Drain meatballs. Add meatballs to crock pot; stir gently.
6. Cover; cook on high heat setting for 1 1/2 to 2 hours.

CROCK POT TURKEY SANDWICHES

Ingredients:
6 cups diced turkey
3 cups diced cheese (American or Velveeta)
1 can cream of mushroom soup
1 can cream of chicken soup
1 onion, chopped
1/2 cups Miracle Whip

Directions:
1. Mix all ingredients and put in Crock Pot for 3-4 hours. Stir occasionally.

CROCK POT BBQ TURKEY SANDWICHES

Ingredients:
1/2 onion
1 clove garlic
1cup catsup
1/3 cup Brown sugar
1/4 teaspoon chili powder
1/4 teaspoon salt pepper to taste
2 cups diced (cooked) turkey

Directions:
1. Sautéed onion and garlic, put in crock pot.
2. Add catsup, brown sugar, chili powder, salt, pepper, and turkey.
3. Let cook all day on low heat. Serve on bread for sandwiches.

CROCK POT TURKEY AND RICE CASSEROLE

Ingredients:
2 cans cream of mushroom soup
3 cups water
3 cups converted long-grain white rice (uncooked)
1 cup thinly sliced celery
1 to 2 cups cubed cooked turkey
2 cups frozen mixed vegetables (peas & carrots, oriental mix, etc.) 1 teaspoon poultry seasoning
1 Tablespoon dried minced onion

Directions:
1. Pour soup and water into Crock Pot and stir to combine. Add remaining ingredients and mix well.
2. Cover and cook 6 to 8 hours on low or 3 to 4 hours on high.

CROCK POT TURKEY BARBECUE

Ingredients:
2 to 3 lb. turkey fillets
2 green peppers, chopped
1 teaspoon. celery salt
Dash of pepper
2 teaspoons chopped onion
18 ounce thick barbecue sauce

Directions:
1. Prepare turkey fillets with dash of pepper across tops. Bake in 350 degree oven for 1 hour covered.
2. Mix barbecue sauce, celery salt, (thin with water if needed) in 5 quart slow cooker/Crock Pot, set on high.
3. Add green peppers and onions. Allow to heat while turkey is baking.
4. Chop turkey in small to medium chunks and add to slow cooker/Crock Pot.
5. Simmer on high for 2 to 3 hours, or turn to low and cook for 4 to 6 hours.

CROCK POT TURKEY MADEIRA

Ingredients:
1 1/2 lb turkey breast tenders
2 ounce porcini mushrooms (dried)
3/4 cup chicken broth
3 Tablespoons Madeira wine
1 Tablespoon lemon juice
salt and pepper to taste

Directions:
1. Combine all ingredients in crock pot.
2. Cover and cook on low for 6 to 8 hours. Thicken juices with cornstarch if desired, and serve with rice.

ROCK POT LOW FAT TURKEY

Ingredients:

1 and 1/2 pounds Turkey Breast (boneless)
1 package of dry gravy mix
1 cup of Dry White Wine
1 Onion (Cut into four slices)
2 Small Potatoes
2 Small Turnips
Baby Carrots

Directions:

1. Cut off any fat, season with pepper and brown whole piece of turkey in skillet sprayed with Pam. Add onion and brown.
2. Spray crock pot with Pam and put carrots on the bottom, next add potatoes,turnips and onions.
3. Place turkey on top of vegetables.
4. Mix gravy with the wine and a 1/4 to 1/2 cup ofwater. Pour on top of the turkey and vegetables.
5. Cover and cook on low for 4-6 hours.

CROCK POT TURKEY BREAST

Ingredients:

3.5 lb turkey breast
2 cups chicken broth
1 onion
1 clove garlic
4 strips bacon
black pepper, to taste
1/2 cup honey

Directions:

1. Place turkey breast in crock pot. Add broth. Place onion in broth and press garlic in turkey.
2. Lay bacon over top and pepper to taste. Add honey and cook on low for approx. 8 hours.

CROCK POT MILWAUKEE SWEET TART SUPPER

Ingredients:

1 1/2 lb low-fat turkey kielbasa; cut into 3-inch pieces
3 can (10-oz. ea) Bavarian-style sauerkraut; rinsed and drained
3 large peeled Granny Smith apples; cored and cut crosswise into rings
1 medium onion, thinly sliced and separated into rings
1 can (14.5 oz.) chicken broth
1/2 teaspoon caraway seeds
8 medium peeled red potatoes; (about 3.5 lbs.), quartered
1/4 cup (1 oz.) shredded Swiss cheese

Directions:

1. Place half of sausage in an crock pot; top with sauerkraut, remaining sausage, apple slices, and onion rings.
2. Pour broth over mixture, and sprinkle with caraway seeds.
3. Cover with lid, and cook on high-heat setting for 4 hours or until apples and onions are tender.
4. Place potatoes in a saucepan; cover with water and bring to a boil. Cook 20 minutes or until tender; drain.
5. Arrange sausage mixture and potatoes on individual plates, and sprinkle cheese over sausage mixture.

CROCK POT NEOPOLITAN TOSTADA

Ingredients:
3/4 lb. ground turkey
1 eggplant; cubed
1 cup salsa
1 (6 oz.) can tomato paste
1/4 cup fresh parsley; chopped
1 Tablespoon chili powder
1 teaspoon ground cumin
1 teaspoon dried oregano
1 10 oz. pkg. frozen corn; thawed
4 pita rounds; halved and toasted
1/2 cup yogurt
2 cups lettuce; shredded
1/2 cup olives; sliced
1/2 cup cheddar cheese; shredded

Directions:
1. Combine turkey, eggplant, salsa, tomato paste, parsley, chili powder, cumin,oregano and corn in slow cooker.
2. Cover and cook on low 5 to 6 hours. Stir with a fork to break up large chunks of turkey.
3. Spoon about 3/4 cup cooked turkey mixture on each pita half. Top with yogurt, lettuce, olives and cheese, if desired.

CROCK POT 8 HOUR TURKEY STEW

Ingredients:
3 cups peeled, cubed potatoes
2 cups quartered mushrooms
1 1/2 cups chopped carrots
1 cup coarsely chopped onions
2 cloves garlic, minced
1 teaspoon each ground thyme and dried basil
1/2 teaspoon black pepper
2 lbs boneless, skinless turkey breast, cut into 1" cubes
2 Tablespoon all purpose flour
1/2 cup dry white wine
1/2 cup low-sodium reduced-fat chicken broth
1 1/2 Tablespoon tomato paste
1 teaspoon Worcestershire sauce
1/4 cup chopped fresh parsley

Directions:
1. Combine the first 8 ingredients in a 3-quart or larger crock pot. Pat turkey cubes dry and coat with flour. Arrange over top of vegetables.
2. Mix wine, broth, tomato paste and Worcestershire sauce in a small bowl. Pour over turkey.
3. Cover and cook on LOW setting for approximately 8 hours. During the last hour,stir once or twice, breaking apart any turkey cubes that have stuck together.
4. Stir in parsley justbefore serving.

Crock Pot Vegetables and Side Dishes

CROCK POT ARTICHOKES
Ingredients:
5 artichokes, remove stalks and tough leaves
1 1/2 teaspoons salt
8 peppercorns
2 stalks celery, cut up
1/2 lemon, sliced
2 cups boiling water
Directions:
1. Combine all ingredients in crockpot.
2. Cook on High 4 - 5 hours.

CROCK POT AZTEC
BLACK BEANS
Ingredients:
1 lb. dried black beans (or turtle beans)
16 oz. jar of salsa
Directions:
1. Rinse black beans. Cover with water, soak all night.
2. Drain beans and place in crock pot with salsa. Add enough water to just cover beans.
3. Cover and cook on low 8-10 hours.

CROCK POT ASPARAGUS CASSEROLE
Ingredients:
2 cans sliced asparagus, (10 oz each)
1 can cream of celery soup, (10 oz)
2 hard cooked eggs, thinly sliced
1 cup grated cheddar cheese
1/2 cup coarsely crushed saltines or Ritz crackers
1 teaspoon butter
Directions:
1. Place drained asparagus in lightly buttered crock pot.

2. Combine soup and cheese. Top asparagus with sliced eggs, soup mixture, then the cracker crumbs. Dot with butter.
3. Cover and cook on low for 4 to 6 hours.

CROCK POT BAKED POTATOES
Ingredients:
10 to 12 potatoes
Aluminum foil
Directions:
1. Prick potatoes with fork and wrap each in foil. Fill Crock Pot with potatoes.
2. Cover and cook on low 8 to 10 hours. (High 2 1/4 to 4.) Do not add water.

CROCK POT BAKED BEANS 1
Ingredients:
1 pound dried small white beans -- rinsed
4 1/2 cups water
1/3 cup molasses
1/4 cup brown sugar
1 onion -- chopped
1/4 pound salt pork -- cut into 1" cubes
1 Tablespoon dijon-style mustard
1/2 teaspoon salt
Directions:
1. In slow-cooker, combine all ingredients.
2. Cover and cook on LOW 13 to 14 hours, stirring occasionally, if possible.

CROCK POT BAKED BEANS 2
Ingredients:
1 lb. ground beef
3/4 lb. bacon fried and diced
1 onion lg chopped and browned
1 lge can pork and beans
16 oz. kidney beans, canned
16 oz. buttered lima beans, canned
1 cup catsup
3 Tablespoons white vinegar
1/4 cup liquid smoke

1 teaspoon salt
dash pepper
Directions:
1. Put all ingredients in crock pot
2. Cook 4-6 hrs on low.

CROCK POT BAKED BEANS 3

Ingredients:
2 cans canellini beans
2 cans black beans
2 cans red kidney beans
1 can chick peas
2 diced onions
2 Tablespoons prepared yellow mustard
1 cup molasses
1/2 cup brown sugar
3/4 cup maple syrup
Directions:
1. Rinse and drain beans and set aside.
2. On bottom of crockpot place diced onions, then pour on beans .
3. Drizzle on all other ingredients.
4. Cook on High for 6-8 hours stirring once about 3/4 of the way through.

CROCK POT BAKED BEANS 4

Ingredients:
24 to 32 oz. canned Pork and Beans, undrained
3/4 cup firmly packed brown sugar
1 cup ketchup
1 large onion, diced
1 teaspoon prepared mustard
2 to 3 slices bacon

Directions:
1. Combine all ingredients in crock pot.
2. Cover and cook on low about 6 hours.

CROCK POT BAKED BEANS 5

Ingredients:
2 large cans baked beans
1/4 cup molasses
1/4 cup ketchup
1/4 cup barbeque sauce
salt, pepper, garlic powder and diced onions to taste
Directions:
1. Combine all ingredients in crock pot.
2. Cook 6 hours on low.

CROCK POT BEANS

Ingredients:
1/2 lb. ground beef, browned
3/4 pound bacon (cooked and crumbled)
1 cup chopped onion, browned
2 20 oz. cans pork & beans
1 16 oz. kidney beans (drained)
1 16 oz. butter lima beans (drained)
1 cup Ketchup
1/2 cup brown sugar
3 Tablespoons white vinegar
1 teaspoon black pepper
1 teaspoon salt
Directions:
1. Combine the beef and bacon & onion to beans in the crock pot.
2. Cook on low 4-6 hours.

CROCK POT BLACK EYED PEAS

Ingredients:
1 16 oz bag of dried black-eyed peas
1 small ham hock
1 14 1/2 oz can of diced tomatoes with jalapenos
1 14 1/2 oz can of diced tomatoes with mild green chiles
2 10 1/2 oz cans of chicken broth
1 stalk of celery, chopped
salt and pepper to taste
Directions:
1. Pre-soak black-eyed peas according to the instructions on the bag.

2. Combine all ingredients and cook on low for 8-10 hours.

CROCK POT BLACK EYED PEAS AND OKRA

Ingredients:
2 (16 oz each) packages frozen Black Eyed peas
2 cups water
1 (15 oz) can Ranch Style Beans with Jalapenos undrained
1 cup chopped onion
1 cup chopped green pepper
1 cup chopped celery
1 (12 to 16 oz)package frozen sliced okra
1 can Ro-Tel tomatoes and Green chiles
Directions:
1. Dump all ingredients in Crock Pot.
2. Cook on low 8 to 10 hours.

CROCK POT BOSTON BAKED BEANS

Ingredients:
1 lb. small dry white beans
1 medium onion, chopped
4 slices bacon, chopped
1/4 cup light (mild) molasses
1/4 cup packed dark brown sugar
2 teaspoons dry mustard
1/4 teaspoon ground black pepper
1/8 teaspoon ground cloves
1 1/2 teaspoons salt
Directions:
1. Rinse beans with cold running water and discard any stones or shriveled beans.
2. In a large bowl, place beans and enough water to cover by 2 inches. Cover and let stand at room temperature overnight. Drain and rinse beans.
3. In 4 1/2 to 5 1/2 quart Crockpot, stir 3 1/2 cups water with beans and remaining ingredients except salt until blended.

4. Cover crock pot with lid and cook beans on low setting about 14 hours or until beans are tender and sauce is syrupy. Stir salt into bean mixture before serving.

CROCK POT BARLEY WITH MUSHROOMS & GREEN ONIONS

Ingredients:
1 cup barley
1 can (14 1/2 oz) roasted garlic chicken broth (about 2 cups)
3 green onions, thinly sliced (about 1/2 cup)
4 to 6 ounces fresh or canned mushrooms, sliced
salt or seasoned salt and pepper to taste
2 teaspoons butter or margarine
Directions:
1. Combine all ingredients in Crock Pot.
2. Cover and cook on low for 4 to 4 1/2 hours

CROCK POT BAVARIAN RED CABBAGE
Ingredients:
1 large head of red cabbage, washed and coarsely sliced
2 medium onions coarsely chopped
6 tart apples, cored & quartered
2 teaspoons salt
2 cups hot water
3 Tablespoons sugar
2/3 cup cider vinegar
6 Tablespoons bacon grease or butter
Directions:
1. Place all ingredients in the Crockpot in order listed.
2. Cover and cook on low 8 to 10 hours (High: 3 hours). Stir well before serving.

CROCK POT BROCCOLI

Ingredients:
2 packages (10 oz. each) frozen chopped broccoli, partially thawed
1 can (10-3/4 oz.) condensed cream of celery soup, undiluted
1-1/2 cups shredded sharp cheddar cheese, divided
1/4 cup chopped onion
1/2 teaspoon Worchestershire sauce
1/4 teaspoon pepper
1 cup crushed butter-flavored crackers (about 25)
2 Tablespoons butter or margarine

Directions:
1. In a large bowl, combine broccoli, soup, 1 cup cheese, onion, Worcestershire sauce and pepper.

2. Pour into a greased slow cooker. Sprinkle crackers on top; dot with butter.
3. Cover and cook on high for 2-1/2 to 3 hours. Sprinkle with remaining cheese. Cook 10 minutes longer or until the cheese is melted.

CROCK POT BROCCOLI SOUFFLE

Ingredients:
2 pkgs. frozen chopped broccoli (2 lbs.)
1 can cream of celery soup (undiluted)
1 cup real mayonnaise
3 Tablespoons grated onion
2 eggs, beaten
1 cup grated cheddar cheese
Ritz crackers
1 stick melted margarine

Directions:
1. Cook broccoli; drain and cool. Mix soup, mayonnaise, onion, egg, and cheese and add to cooled broccoli.
2. Put in a lightly greased 3 1/2-quart crockpot.

3. Mix 1 stack Ritz or buttery crackers (crushed) with margarine or butter. Put on top.
4. Cook on high for 2 to 3 hours

CROCK POT CARROT PUDDING

Ingredients:
4 large carrots, cooked and grated
1 small onion, grated
1/2 teaspoon salt
1/4 teaspoon nutmeg
1 Tablespoon sugar
1 cup milk
3 eggs, beaten

Directions:
1. Mix together carrots, onion, salt, nutmeg, sugar, milk, and eggs.
2. Pour into slow cooker and cook on high for 3-4 hours.

CROCK POT MARMALADE-GLAZED CARROTS

Ingredients:
1 package (32oz) fresh baby carrots
1/2 cup marmalade
1 Tablespoon water
2 Tablespoons brown sugar
1 Tablespoon butter
1/2 teaspoon cinnamon
1/4 teaspoon nutmeg
1 Tablespoons cornstarch
2 Tablespoons water
salt and pepper to taste

Directions:
1. Combine all ingredients in Crock Pot and cook on low for 7 to 9 hours, until carrots are tender.
2. About 15 minutes before serving, make a paste of the cornstarch and cold water; stir into carrots.

170

CROCK POT ORANGE GLAZED CARROTS

Ingredients:

3 cups Thinly sliced carrots
3 Tablespoons Butter or margarine
2 cups Water
3 Tablespoons Orange marmalade
1/4 teaspoon Salt
2 Tablespoons Chopped pecans

Directions:

1. Combine carrots, water, and salt in Crock Pot.
2. Cover and cook on high 2 to 3 hours or until the carrots are done. Drain well; stir in remaining ingredients.
3. Cover and cook on high 20-30 minutes.

Crock Pot Dessert Recipes

CROCK POT APPLE BETTY

Ingredients:

6 cups thinly sliced apples
1 cup granulated sugar
1 Tablespoon all purpose flour
1 teaspoon cinnamon
juice and zest of 1 lemon
1/2 cup melted butter
3 cups soft bread crumbs

Directions:

1. In a large bowl combine apples, sugar, flour, cinnamon and lemon zest.
2. In another bowl, combine butter and bread crumbs.
3. In prepared slow cooker, layer one third of bread crumb mixture, then one half of apple mixture. Repeat layers of bread crumbs and fruit, then finish with a final layer of bread crumbs on top.
4. Cover and cook on high for 4 hours until bubbly and brown.

CROCK POT APPLE BUTTER

Ingredients:

4 qts. unsweetened applesauce
7 cups granulated sugar
1-1/3 cups brown sugar
5-1/3 Tablespoons cider vinegar
5-1/3 Tablespoons lemon juice
2 teaspoons cinnamon
2 teaspoons allspice
1 teaspoon ground cloves

Directions:

1. Combine all ingredients in a slow cooker/Crock Pot.
2. Cover and cook 3 hours, stirring occasionally.
3. Remove lid and continue cooking until excess liquid cooks away (turn to low as necessary) 5-8 hours

4. Seal mixture in hot jars and process in a hot water bath for 10 minutes. Makes approximately 8-10 pints

CROCK POT APPLE-COCONUT CRISP

Ingredients:

4 large Granny Smith apples, peeled & coarsely sliced (about 4 cups)
1/2 cup sweetened flaked coconut
1 Tablespoon flour
1/3 cup brown sugar
1/2 cup butterscotch or caramel ice cream topping (fat-free is fine)
1/2 teaspoon cinnamon
1/3 cup flour
1/2 cup quick rolled oats
2 Tablespoons butter or margarine

Directions:

1. In a casserole 1 1/2-quart baking dish that fits in the slow cooker/Crock Pot, combine apples with coconut, 1 Tablespoon flour, 1/3 cup brown sugar, and cinnamon. Drizzle with the ice cream topping.
2. Combine remaining ingredients in a small bowl with a fork or pastry cutter and sprinkle over apple mixture.
3. Cover and cook on high for 2 1/2 to 3 hours, until apples are tender. Serve warm with vanilla ice cream or whipped topping.

CROCK POT APPLE CRANBERRY CRISP

Ingredients:
3 apples (like Gala)
1 cup cranberries
3/4 cup brown sugar
1/3 cup rolled oats (quick cooking)
1/4 teaspoon salt
1 teaspoon cinnamon
1/3 cup butter, softened

Directions:
1. Peel, core and slice apples. Place apple slices and cranberries in crock pot.
2. Mix remaining ingredients in separate bowl and sprinkle over top of apple and cranberries.
3. Place 4 or 5 paper towels over the top of the crockpot, place an object across the top of the crockpot and set lid on top. This allows the steam to escape.
4. Turn crockpot on high and cook for about 2 hours.

CROCK POT APPLE DATE PUDDING

Ingredients:
4-5 apples, peeled, cored and diced
3/4 cup sugar, or less, to taste
1/2 cup chopped dates
1/2 cup toasted, chopped pecans
2 Tablespoons flour
1 teaspoon baking powder
1/8 teaspoon salt
1/4 teaspoon nutmeg
2 Tablespoons melted butter
1 egg, beaten

Directions:
1. In the slow cooker, place apples, sugar, dates and pecans; stir.
2. In a separate bowl, mix together flour, baking powder, salt and nutmeg and stir into apple mixture.
3. Drizzle melted butter over batter and stir. Stir in egg. Set cooker on low and cook for 3 to 4 hours. Serve warm.

CROCK POT APPLE-NUT CHEESECAKE

Ingredients:
Crust:
1 cup (scant) graham cracker crumbs
1/2 teaspoon cinnamon
2 Tablespoons sugar
3 Tablespoons butter, melted
1/4 cup finely chopped pecans or walnuts
Filling:
16 ounces cream cheese
1/4 cup brown sugar
1/2 cup granulated white sugar
2 large eggs
3 Tablespoons heavy whipping cream
1 Tablespoon cornstarch
1 teaspoon vanilla
Topping:
1 large apple, thinly sliced (about 1 1/2 cups)
1 teaspoon cinnamon
1/4 cup sugar
1 Tablespoon finely chopped pecans or walnuts

Directions:
1. Combine crust ingredients; pat into a 7-inch springform pan.
2. Beat sugars into cream cheese until smooth and creamy. Beat in eggs, whipping cream, cornstarch, and vanilla. Beat for about 3 minutes on medium speed of a hand-held electric mixer. Pour mixture into the prepared crust.
3. Combine apple slices with sugar, cinnamon and nuts; place topping evenly over the top of cheesecake. Place the cheesecake on a rack (or "ring" of aluminum foil to keep it off the bottom of the pot) in the Crock Pot.
4. Cover and cook on high for 2 1/2 to 3 hours. Let stand in the covered pot (after turning it off) for about 1 to 2 hours, until cool enough to handle. Cool thoroughly before removing pan sides.
5. Chill before serving; store leftovers in the refrigerator.

173

CROCK POT APPLE PUDDING CAKE

Ingredients:
2 cups sugar
1 cup vegetable oil
2 eggs
2 teaspoons vanilla
2 cups flour
1 teaspoon baking soda
1 teaspoon nutmeg
2 cups unpeeled apple, finely chopped
1 cup chopped nuts (walnuts or pecans)

Directions:
1. Beat sugar, oil, eggs, and vanilla. Add apple with dry ingredients and mix well.
2. Spray a two pound tin can with cooking spray or grease and flour it well. Pour batter into can, filling no more than 2/3 full.
3. Place can in Crock Pot. Do not add water. Cover but leave cover ajar so steam can escape.
4. Cook on high 3 1/2 to 4 hours. Don't peek before the last hour of baking. Cake is done when top is set.
5. Let stand in can a few minutes before tipping pudding out on a plate. Serve half-rounds plain, with whipped topping, or a pudding sauce.

CROCK POT APRICOT NUT BREAD

Ingredients:
3/4 cup dried apricots
1 cup flour
2 teaspoons baking powder
1/4 teaspoon baking soda
1/2 teaspoon salt
1/2 cup sugar
3/4 cup milk
1 egg, slightly beaten
1 Tablespoon grated orange peel
1 Tablespoon vegetable oil
1/2 cup whole wheat flour
1 cup coarsely chopped walnuts

Directions:
1. Place the apricots on a chopping block. Sprinkle 1 T flour over them. Dip a knife into the flour and chop the apricots finely. Flour the knife often to keep the cut up fruit from sticking together.
2. Sift the remaining flour, baking powder, baking soda, salt and sugar into a large bowl.
3. Combine the milk, egg, orange peel, and oil. Stir the flour mixture and the whole wheat flour.
4. Fold in the cut up apricots, any flour left on the cutting block and the walnuts.
5. Pour into a well greased, floured baking unit*(see below). Cover and place on a rack in the slow cooker, but prop the lid open a fraction with a toothpick or a twist of foil to let excess steam escape.
6. Cook on High for 4 to 6 hours. Cool on a rack for 10 minutes. Serve warm or cold.

* Baking unit - some manufacturers are making units for slow cookers, but if you don't have one, a 2 pound coffee can works. Pyrex muffin cups also work and 1, 1 1/2 and 2 quart molds work. DO NOT LIFT THE LID WHILE BAKING THIS BREAD.

CROCK POT BAKED STUFFED APPLES

Ingredients:
6 medium tart red apples
1 cup light brown sugar
1/4 cup golden seedless raisins
1 Tablespoon grated orange peel
1/4 cup soft butter
2 cups very hot water
3 Tablespoons orange juice concentrate

Directions:
1. Wash, core and stem the apples, but don't peel them.

2. Stand them in a buttered mold and stuff them with 2/3 cup of the brown sugar, the raisins and the orange peel.
3. Fill the tops of the core cavities with butter and sprinkle the remaining sugar over the tops.
4. Place the mold in the slow cooker and pour the hot water into the cooker.
Sprinkle the orange juice concentrate over the apples.
5. Cover the cooker and cook on Low for 3 to 5 hours, or until the apples are tender.

CROCK POT CARAMEL APPLE EUPHORIA DESSERT

Ingredients:
2 medium cooking apples
1/2 cup apple juice
7 oz. caramel candy squares
1 teaspoon vanilla
1/8 teaspoon ground cardamom
1/2 teaspoon ground cinnamon
1/3 cup cream-style peanut butter
7 slices Angel-food cake; or 1 quart vanilla ice cream

Directions:
1. Peel, core, and cut each apple into 18 wedges; set aside.
2. Combine apple juice, unwrapped caramel candies, vanilla, cardamom and cinnamon.
3. Drop peanut butter 1 teaspoon at a time, over ingredients in crockpot. Stir.
4. Add apple wedges; cover and cook on LOW for 5 hours.
5. Stir thoroughly; cover and cook on LOW 1 additional hour.
6. Serve approximately 1/3 cup of warm mixture over a slice of angel food cake or ice cream.

www.ingramcontent.com/pod-product-compliance
Lightning Source LLC
Chambersburg PA
CBHW062043090426
42740CB00016B/3005